S0-AAC-523

Monetary Politics

Monetary Politics

The Federal Reserve and the Politics of Monetary Policy

JOHN T. WOOLLEY
Washington University

CAMBRIDGE UNIVERSITY PRESS
CAMBRIDGE
LONDON NEW YORK NEW ROCHELLE
MELBOURNE SYDNEY

Published by the Press Syndicate of the University of Cambridge
The Pitt Building, Trumpington Street, Cambridge CB2 1RP
32 East 57th Street, New York, NY 10022, USA
10 Stamford Road, Oakleigh, Melbourne 3166, Australia

First published 1984
First paperback edition 1985

Printed in the United States of America

Library of Congress Cataloging in Publication Data

Woolley, John T. (John Turner), 1950-

Monetary politics.

Bibliography: p.

Includes index.

1. Board of Governors of the Federal Reserve System
(U.S.) 2. Monetary policy – United States. I. Title.
HG2565.W66 1984 332.1'12'0973 83-21510
ISBN 0 521 25097 8 hard cover
ISBN 0 521 31247 7 paperback

for Jane

Contents

Preface

In this work, I examine the political relationships between the Federal Reserve System and the president, Congress, bankers, and economists, and inquire about the consequences of those relationships for the behavior of the Federal Reserve. Of the many previous works on the Federal Reserve with which I am familiar, none examines the Federal Reserve System's external political relationships so extensively. As it is, this work is limited in coverage both in time (approximately 1965–82) and in scope (only domestic monetary policy), and there is no attempt here to spell out a full policy model. In short, although the topic of this book could scarcely be called narrow, much remains to be studied. I am convinced that this kind of study is a necessary first step toward a more complete view of the Federal Reserve because the institution is so much influenced by its political environment. Indeed, on reflection, it is surprising that this field has not already been more thoroughly plowed. In any case, it is my hope that this analysis will contribute to a fuller understanding of this institution, which has such a large role in determining our economic well-being.

I have approached the Federal Reserve primarily at an institutional level. That is, the research was motivated primarily by a desire to understand an important institution that has heretofore been largely ignored by political scientists. With the institutional focus, it is easier to make links to the large literature dealing with other American political organizations and institutions. Thus, the study also relies throughout on analyses of interest groups and on studies of the presidency and Congress. I have also tried to introduce, where appropriate, themes relevant to the various political-economy traditions in political science.

This work first took form as a doctoral dissertation at the University of Wisconsin at Madison. Since then, it has been extensively revised and updated. In the years between starting the dissertation research and completing the manuscript for publication, I have incurred many debts related to this project.

At the outset, I searched for published analyses of the Federal Reserve that had an explicit and sustained political component. I found them mainly in works by Michael Reagan, Sanford Borins, Edward Kane, G. L. Bach, and Thomas Mayer. From their work, I learned a great deal, and this will be observable to others who also know those works. A more complete discussion of their writings and other especially useful works is found in the Bibliographical Note.

As a dissertation, the research was guided, first and foremost, by Leon N. Lindberg, chairman of my committee. Other committee members provided valuable and stimulating commentary from diverse points of view – Charles W. Anderson and Murray Edelman of the Political Science Department and Donald Hester of the Economics Department. These four not only were most encouraging but they also, as such a committee should, raised many challenging questions and suggested ways to broaden and improve the research. They performed the critic's most important task: to force one to be aware of and to justify one's analytic choices while facilitating the process of making those choices.

Other support associated with the University of Wisconsin must be acknowledged as well. The university itself provided a travel grant. J. Rogers Hollingsworth of the Department of History furthered my early research in many ways while I worked with him as an assistant at the Woodrow Wilson International Center for Scholars. Both a predissertation essay and new postdissertation material were included in volumes 434 and 459 of *The Annals of the American Academy of Political and Social Science,* edited by Hollingsworth.

The Brookings Institution provided invaluable assistance by awarding me a position as research fellow for 1977–8. Not only did this provide me with access to many officials on the basis of the institution's prestige alone, but I was able to work in an environment unusually conducive to this kind of research. I am particularly indebted to Ralph Bryant, senior fellow in economic studies. He was always encouraging, and was unfailingly patient with my requests for assistance. Further, Bryant allowed me to read drafts of his own book on monetary policy, *Money and Monetary Policy in Interdependent Nations,* from which I learned much. I am also grateful to Hugh Heclo for his interest, support, and friendship, and to Martha Derthick and Joel Aberbach for their encouragement. There was a lively and productive interaction among research fellows in economic and governmental studies. This group included Chris Deering, Diana Phillips, John Chubb, Kay Plantes, Warren Trepeta, Linda Cohen, Charlie Atkins, and Tom Thomas.

The research was supported in part by National Science Foundation Doctoral Dissertation Grant SOC77–20531. Without this source of funds, travel for essential interviewing and documentary research would have been impossible. Subsequently, similar work has been supported by faculty research grants from Washington University.

Much of the research was conducted at the excellent libraries at Brookings, the Library of Congress, the Research Library of the Federal Reserve, the Joint Bank-Fund Library, all in Washington, D.C., and the Lyndon Baines Johnson Library in Austin, Texas. Librarians in all of these institutions have been helpful, but I am particularly grateful to the documents librarians at the LBJ Library and the Library of Congress for helping me track down documents with the utmost efficiency.

Not least, the work was aided in countless ways by the officials who found time in their very busy schedules for interviews. I continue to be struck by the spirit of cooperation and generosity with which I was almost always met in the course of this research. Although relatively few of my conclusions hinge on interview data, the interviews provided many valuable insights and suggested issues for further examination. Political scientists should not underrate the value of interviews as a supplement to other research methods. The process of interviewing is discussed in detail in Appendix A.

I have also incurred many debts at Washington University. The atmosphere has proved to be very congenial, and I appreciate the ways my colleagues have encouraged the research. Several have read and offered valuable comments on one or more chapters – James Alt, Randall Calvert, Michael MacKuen, and Rick Wilson. Through the undergraduate research assistance program, I have benefited from the able assistance of David Butz, Paul Lombardo, and David Warfield. I also acknowledge the diligent and skilled typing of Valerie Karras, Tina Maines, and Joyce Rudolph.

In addition, I have profited from comments on portions of the work from Ralph Bryant, William Poole, Donald Hodgman, Robert Albritton, Donald Kettl, Jack Knott, Sidney Waldman, Thomas Mayer, the participants in the Brookings Project on Global Inflation and Unemployment (December 1978), and the participants in the Conference on the Role of Government in the Economy (Madison, Wisconsin, March 1981). The entire draft was read and closely criticized by Nathaniel Beck and by Raymond Lombra. I have particularly valued the friendly exchanges with Beck, one of the few political scientists who has been working in this area in the past few years. This work also benefited indirectly from stimulating exchanges with Barry Ames, Kenneth Cook, Lawrence German, Martha Harris, Lawrence Joseph, Edward Kane, Ira Kaminow, Joseph Pika, and John Sprague. It was a pleasure to work with Cambridge University Press, especially Frank Smith, my editor, and Helen Greenberg, the book's copyeditor; their diligence, patience, and care resulted in many clarifications and improvements in the work.

All of these persons have made the work much stronger than it otherwise would have been. Undoubtedly, each would feel justified in claiming that in some degree I have rejected his advice or ignored pertinent implications of his comments.

Finally, for priceless editorial advice, I thank Kate Woolley, my mother. By her many pages of suggested corrections, she proved that at least one brave soul read the entire dissertation, cover to cover, including the footnotes. By contrast, my wife Jane Rudolph refused to read the manuscript on grounds that living with me during the process of writing and revision was difficult enough. There is no amount of advice and criticism that I would have exchanged for her support, understanding, and love.

1

The Federal Reserve and the Politics of Monetary Policy: Introduction and Overview

Among powerful governmental institutions, the Federal Reserve is surely in the first rank. It is in the first rank because of the policy responsibilities it is assigned – determining monetary aspects of macroeconomic policy and regulating financial institutions. The Federal Reserve is important, and it is increasingly controversial. In the past two decades, there have been repeated new departures in monetary policy in response to economic crises. According to critics, policy has been conducted unsteadily. The Federal Reserve has been accused of destabilizing the economy. It has been criticized for seeming to say one thing and then doing another.

Nevertheless, political scientists have rarely studied the Federal Reserve systematically,[1] and economists have often had to undertake their own bootstrap political analyses of the institution. Perhaps political scientists have been misled because, despite the fact that the Federal Reserve's responsibilities are politically sensitive ones, it is supposedly independent of political influences. Plainly, the Federal Reserve is a key political institution. It defines, sets, and implements public policy in a central arena. It is engaged in conflict that is increasingly overt. Its actions have important consequences for other institutions that political scientists have studied extensively.

This work provides an introductory survey of some political aspects of the Federal Reserve System, particularly the System's relationships with other political actors. There is much work to be done in this area. However, it is clear that the same terms we use to understand other political institutions apply to the Federal Reserve. This work examines events of the past fifteen years, including many controversial episodes in the recent conduct of monetary policy. For instance, the analysis covers the conflict between the president and the Federal Reserve in 1965; the controversial policy of election year 1972; the congressional attempts to encourage monetary targeting in the mid-1970s; and the adoption of monetary targeting in late 1979.

This work is plainly an exploration. At the most basic level, I try to answer essential descriptive questions. I also advance a relatively broad interpretation of the Federal Reserve as a political institution. Like many other policy areas, monetary politics can be understood in large part by examining the objectives and resources of groups and organizations that contend with one another to try to define what policy should be. The Federal Reserve has two kinds of overarching objectives. The first is to achieve stable growth while guaranteeing financial stability; this involves the System inescapably in favoring certain societal interests over others. The second objective is to protect the System's long-run capacity for making an autonomous contribution to macroeconomic policy making. These two objectives are frequently inconsistent, and both draw the Federal Reserve into controversy. The result is monetary politics, the interaction of actors with partially conflicting objectives and unequal political resources. As we shall see, due to the nature of the issues being debated and the nature of the decision-making process, some political resources are more valuable than others. Influence in other policy areas may not translate into influence in monetary politics.

This chapter begins with a discussion of the political stakes of monetary policy. This is followed by the presentation of a simple framework for organizing and categorizing many of the conflicts and debates in which the Federal Reserve is embroiled. The chapter concludes with an analysis of the restricted nature of this policy arena. Later chapters examine an important subset of the groups and organizations that are attentive to the Federal Reserve. In those chapters, the kinds of issues raised in debates and the kinds of reforms proposed by various participants are examined in terms of the objectives and resources of each participant.

The Federal Reserve has a complicated institutional structure and two important decision-making forums. The Federal Reserve Board is located in Washington, D.C., and is composed of seven members appointed by the president for fourteen-year terms. The board has exclusive jurisdiction over many issues in bank regulation and sets the discount rate. The Federal Reserve System includes twelve district banks located in major cities throughout the country. The presidents of the district banks also serve as members of the Federal Open Market Committee (FOMC), which is the most important forum for monetary policy decisions. The FOMC makes decisions about how to try to influence interest rates, the money supply, and, ultimately, inflation and economic growth. Five of the district bank presidents, together with all seven of the board members, make up the voting membership of the FOMC. The president of the Federal Reserve Bank of New York is always a voting member of the FOMC and serves as its vice-chairman. The remaining voting seats reserved for presidents are rotated annually among the other eleven districts. The FOMC meets in Washington every four to six weeks, and members may confer by telephone at more frequent intervals. Their decisions are central to monetary policy, and it is the behavior of the FOMC that is of most interest in this book.

What is at stake?

Monetary policy and the economy

With the exception of some "rational expectations" theorists, there are very few economists who maintain that monetary policy does not have powerful effects on economic performance. In aggregate economic terms, a wide variety of theoretical approaches yield predictions of powerful effects of monetary policy on the economy. Recent economic events have confirmed this persuasively for the ordinary observer. In contrast, some rational expectations theorists have held that only policy surprises can affect economic performance. It is certainly correct that expectations matter, but many observers have found the strong case advanced by rational expectations theorists to be implausible. In any case, the policy ineffectiveness argument seems not to be persuasive to the Federal Reserve, and consequently it is not considered in the analysis to follow.

If monetary politics is not about whether monetary policy counts, what is it about? Typically, it is about maintaining large-scale economic balances – that is, keeping interest rates, exchange rates, bank credit, and so on in some appropriate relationship to inflation, employment, economic growth, and international payments flows. How much restrictive pressure should be put on the economy in order to reduce or slow inflation? Can we achieve a politically acceptable level of resource utilization without having to accept continuing or even accelerating inflation? How much should we – can we – cushion the economy from price shocks by following an accommodative monetary policy?

Economists of almost all philosophical and theoretical persuasions agree that inflation is ultimately a monetary phenomenon. Most economists also agree that economic growth is facilitated by an appropriately expansionary monetary policy. A sufficiently restrictive monetary policy can quite reliably produce a depression and even an economic collapse; too little money is dangerous, just as is too much. The trick, of course, is knowing what "just right" is and knowing how to achieve it. This is in large part a technical question. However, it is not a technical issue alone. It is not simply a technical issue because uncertainty about long-run constraints means that policy makers have to choose whether to err on the side of more or less restrictive policy. It is not simply a technical issue because there is a commonsense notion that pain caused by policy can be eased by reversing policy. It is not simply a technical issue because we often fight one problem at a time, and policy makers have to decide when to stop fighting one problem and shift their attention to another. And it is not simply a technical issue because the short-run nature of many political pressures prompts policy makers to subordinate consideration of long-run technical constraints.

Economists agree that inflation can occur in the short run due to supply shocks, such as an Organization of Petroleum Exporting Countries (OPEC) price increase or an agricultural shortage. Most would agree, too, that inflation can be caused in the short run by expansionary fiscal policy. If monetary policy does not accommodate these shocks, these kinds of inflationary episodes should result only in a one-time increase in the price level with eventual adjustment of output.[2] There should certainly not be a process of accelerating inflation. For this reason, it is said it is that inflation is ultimately a monetary phenomenon. Some economists make the stronger argument that inflation is *usually* caused by excessive growth in the money supply. This argument is controversial and often figures in debates over monetary policy.

If inflation is ultimately a monetary phenomenon, monetary policy is ultimately a political phenomenon. Choosing any theoretical position as a guide for the conduct of policy has important political implications for the government in power. Both accommodating inflation and fighting inflation hurt people in society, and people who are hurt can remove governments from office. There is a large and growing literature demonstrating that macroeconomic outcomes are related to government popularity and electoral success.[3] To my knowledge, none of these studies shows that popularity increases with inflation. However, they do show that popularity is hurt by declines in real income. Declines in real income could be the consequences either of inflation or of recessions caused by fighting inflation.

One can readily understand that inflation could be regarded by policy makers as an attractive second-best choice if the alternative involves damaging some economically important or politically powerful sector. Moreover, inflation-tolerating choices may be more likely if policy makers believe that they are confronting temporary shocks or disequilibria that will subside in the future. An inability to direct credit to particular sectors through distributive credit policy may place even more pressure on monetary authorities to accommodate inflation.

There are several commonly mentioned reasons for accommodating inflation in the short run. One involves government demand for credit. If government demands for loans in credit markets are increasing (e.g., because of deficits), then some private borrowers may be unable to borrow at prevailing interest rates because governments, which are relatively insensitive to interest costs of borrowing, will receive available funds at the margin. When such conflicts occur, monetary authorities may wish to provide sufficient funds to accommodate a substantial portion of the demands of borrowers who would otherwise be excluded. When the economy is near full employment, the result will predictably be inflation, and neither government nor the private sector will get the real value of the nominal amount of money borrowed. No one argues, of course, that one such episode is sufficient to produce a prolonged period of continuing inflation in a country.

Another important kind of accommodation is related to shocks, both real and monetary. A sudden restriction in the supply of an important commodity or a rapid movement in exchange rates may have distributive consequences that policy makers wish to avoid. A sudden or sustained exchange rate increase, for example, may handicap or threaten the existence of a favored export industry. Returning the rate to a lower level may involve tolerating a higher level of domestic price inflation than would otherwise seem desirable. A supply shock can cause a temporary burst of inflation independent of monetary policy. However, policy makers may choose to respond to the shock by an accommodative policy in order to shift the burden of adjustment. An accommodative monetary policy would reduce the transfer of real resources from one sector to another or from the domestic economy to a foreign economy. This kind of accommodation could help sustain high levels of domestic employment.

A third kind of distributive problem arises from attempts by social groups to regain lost ground following inflationary shocks or unanticipated monetary accommodation. It is to be expected that groups will attempt to recoup their past losses, and they may also attempt to avoid future losses if they expect similar inflation to occur in the future. Under such conditions, fighting inflation by monetary policy alone requires a willingness to accept whatever pattern of distributive consequences flows from existing patterns of economic vulnerability. Sustained pressure on the most vulnerable sectors may be very unpopular, even more unpopular than inflation itself. In this case, political problems arise because only one effective, but rather blunt, instrument is used to fight inflation – aggregate monetary policy. With such an approach, there is no assurance that the burdens of fighting inflation are borne equitably. Indeed, in such circumstances, considerations of equity can scarcely be entertained at all, or only with considerable difficulty. At the same time, there is the certain assurance that individuals, groups, and organizations will do all they can to reduce their own vulnerability and to shift the burden of adjustment to somebody else.

How does our society decide whether to accommodate inflation or not? Who decides what kinds of risks we should run in conducting policy? What kind of decision-making process governs in this critical area? Obviously, the interesting questions for both economists and political scientists are often about monetary *politics*, not monetary *theory*.

Technical debates among economists

Questions of how monetary policy affects the economy and how monetary policy should be conducted at a day-to-day level involve major disputes between economists and are often central in monetary politics. Here we enter the realm of the politics of expertise. Experts play a major role in this policy arena, as in many others, and it is important to have at least a nodding acquaintance with the issues that are central to their disputes. Moreover, it is important to focus on these debates because apparently technical debates often turn out to be nontechnical debates carried on by other means. One need not be an economist to grasp the essential features of these economic debates.[4]

One issue is pervasive in monetary politics and figures prominently in the analysis to follow. Economists have spilled a great deal of ink discussing whether monetary policy should or could be conducted with a "monetary aggregate" rather than an interest rate as the instrument of policy. A monetary aggregate is an analytic measure of the total volume of money or moneylike assets in the economy. For example, probably the most familiar monetary aggregate is M1, the sum total of all currency and checking deposits. This is usually conceived of as a measure of immediate buying power in the economy. Broader aggregates include other assets – savings accounts are included in M2. One may consider bank reserves to be a kind of very narrow aggregate. Bank reserves are the sum total of the fraction of deposits held by banks and not re-lent to borrowers. During the past decade, savings accounts have increasingly come to look like checking accounts, and new ways of managing money, such as money market mutual funds, have been invented. As a result, economists have debated whether monetary aggregates still adequately represent the economic functions they are supposed to stand for.

Policy instruments. It will be helpful to digress to discuss policy instruments. An instrument is a means of taking action that is or can be precisely and decisively controlled by the government. Thinking in terms of instruments is a useful way of clearly identifying discretionary policy actions and, thus, of distinguishing policy action (government behavior) from eventual outcomes; the latter result from both governmental and nongovernmental actions. Identifying the instrument is somewhat less of a problem in many policy areas than it is in the area of monetary policy. In most policy areas, the instrument is an expenditure or a regulation, exactly as we commonly think. And in most areas, the relationship between actions and intended results is reasonably clear. In monetary policy the instruments, in a very literal and narrow sense, are often not the same as those instruments commonly discussed, and the links to intended results are frequently rather obscure.

In a narrow, literal sense, monetary policy instruments include the setting of some administered interest rate such as *the discount rate;* or making direct loans to banks via the *discount window;* or selling and purchasing financial instruments by the central bank in *open market operations* – typically, various kinds of short-term government debt, such as *treasury bills.* In open market operations, the most important instrument in the United States, sales and purchases can be thought of as closely influencing interest rates (prices) and bank reserve aggregates (quantities). Both interest rates and bank reserve aggregates may themselves be discussed as instruments. Thus, one commonly reads newspaper articles noting that the Federal Reserve has "raised (or lowered) the federal funds rate" or "reduced bank reserves." How these prices and quantities relate to other objectives such as inflation or economic growth is still more complex, and interested readers would do well to consult an economics text for further enlightenment.

Market rates and bank reserves cannot both be completely determined by the government on a continuous basis. Nonetheless, it is possible that monetary policy authorities can achieve their desired outcome for either a particular interest rate or a particular monetary aggregate with reasonable precision given a sufficiently long time period. This period may be almost instantaneous, in the case of some short-term interest rates, or longer than a calendar quarter, in the case of some monetary aggregates. Success in controlling these prices or quantities depends on the ability of technicians to forecast what is happening in markets that completely determine these prices and quantities so that policy makers can offset undesired developments.

Interest rates versus aggregates. The central policy debate has focused on the following question: Is it more reasonable to pay attention to bank reserves or interest rates? In an article now widely cited, economist William Poole proposed that sometimes it should be interest rates, sometimes bank reserves, depending on whether authorities believe there is more stability in monetary events or in "real" economic events.[5] Despite widespread interest in Poole's formulation, the public debate throughout the 1970s continued to be divided between one group that argued strongly for paying attention almost exclusively to bank reserves (or some broader monetary aggregate) and another group that tended to favor interest rates or a complex combination of possible measures.

As I will discuss in more detail in Chapter 5, these two positions have important political implications. Those who advocate a focus on monetary aggregates typically stress that inflation is the most important objective of policy and that other objectives are secondary. They also tend to argue that other problems will be worked out satisfactorily if government resists the temptation to intervene. Those who focus on interest rates are much more likely to identify fighting inflation with the costs of high interest rates – and with fluctuating interest rates. That is, they are much more likely to acknowledge that distributive consequences deserve relatively strong consideration in policy making.

Realms of debate: non-issues

Despite the importance of technical issues in monetary politics, readers should not believe that monetary politics is exclusively or even primarily highly technical. There are, in fact, two realms of debate in monetary politics. One is highly technical, and the other, which I shall call "ordinary political discourse," is not. The distinction is important for many reasons, not least of which is that the debate in the technical realm most continuously and directly affects the conduct of monetary policy.

In the technical realm, the characteristic mode of discourse is economic analysis, and the questions have to do with effectively controlling the economic system. Technical discourse is governed by the standards of good economic analysis – precise language, logical consistency, mathematical rigor, empirical validation, and inclusive parsimonious theory. In technical discourse, normative issues are usually introduced only implicitly, often as assumptions that are treated as being noncontroversial. Such assumptions are political in that they embody judgments about the desirability of aspects of the status quo or favor some interests (e.g., the efficient) over others.

The realm of ordinary political discourse is often imprecise, unrigorous, empirically casual, and unself-conscious about the applicability of underlying theories. It is much more likely to be explicitly normative, explicitly concerned with distributive issues, and explicitly concerned with assigning responsibility for undesired distributive outcomes. In fact, ordinary political discourse is often preoccupied with assigning blame. Whose actions led us to our current dire straits? Government? Business? Labor? Congress? The Federal Reserve?

The two realms are somewhat separated institutionally. Technical discourse is preferred within the Federal Reserve. Actual behavior within the FOMC may not match the ideal, but the technical ideal governs. It dominates exchanges between the Federal Reserve and administration technicians at the Council of Economic Advisors (CEA) and the Treasury. The president and members of Congress operate much more within the realm of ordinary political discourse.

The implication of this division is important. What matters in the course of policy making is the ability to influence policy choice, not simply to react clumsily to past behavior. Since participation in the technical realm is often, but not always, a necessary condition for influencing policy choice, technical requirements tend to exclude and narrow the range of monetary politics. Of course, in this regard, the Federal Reserve and monetary policy are no different from other areas of complex policy.

In other ways, and again, like other governmental agencies, the Federal Reserve tends to afford some interests specialized access while relatively excluding others. As we shall see in Chapter 2, at its founding the Federal Reserve was conceived of as an institution to regulate and stabilize the banking system. It was intended to be close to bankers and financiers. We shall see in Chapter 3 that today, still, top Federal Reserve officials are individuals who have been tried and judged acceptable by mainstream business and financial figures. At its founding, the Federal Reserve was given a special structure to signal its autonomy from ordinary methods of political control. It was intended not to have to be responsive to those who suffer losses due to Federal Reserve decisions. And today, still, the process of making monetary policy continues to be closed to the nonexpert and to be executed in relative obscurity. These characteristics and processes, dating from the earliest days of the Federal Reserve, shape and constrain policy choice. I shall refer to their consequences as being the "non-issues" of monetary politics. In the concluding chapter, I shall reflect further on the implications of this institution's structure for economic management.

Relationships with external actors

Officials in the Federal Reserve can sometimes be heard to advance an apparently straightforward argument about the role of the Federal Reserve and its relationship with the rest of government. This argument, intended to prove that the System's policy is politically acceptable, is as follows:

> The Federal Reserve is independent within, not of, the government.
>
> Congress, in its wisdom, has made the Federal Reserve independent, and Congress can abolish or restructure the System if it is ever dissatisfied.
>
> If the Federal Reserve ever tried to ignore national objectives, its independence would be removed or limited.

> The Federal Reserve is still here and independent; therefore, its policy must be politically acceptable.

This argument was heard less and less often in the early 1980s as Congress's dissatisfaction with Federal Reserve policy became increasingly tangible. Nonetheless, it reveals the Federal Reserve's self-perception and the way it would like others to perceive it. It affirms the public, governmental nature of the Federal Reserve and its apolitical nature as an independent commission. It plays down the political resources the Federal Reserve might have at its command to defend its own policy preferences. It asserts that there are no inherent reasons why Congress might have difficulty controlling the Federal Reserve. It ignores the president entirely. It asserts that the absence of congressional action to change the System radically is evidence that the Federal Reserve is performing in a completely acceptable fashion.

In fact, in virtually every respect, this argument is misleading. Despite the public nature of the Federal Reserve Board, it is not neutral with respect to private interests. Rather than being passive before congressional power, the Federal Reserve has some formidable political resources of its own. Rather than being insignificant, the president appears to be much more effective than Congress in shaping monetary policy on an ongoing basis. Rather than reflecting the acceptability of Federal Reserve behavior, the absence of congressional action concerning monetary policy can just as accurately be perceived as a reflection of the weaknesses in Congress. I hope to persuade readers on each of these points in the following chapters.

Most discussions about the Federal Reserve as a political institution have dealt with its formal independence of the president. Since its inception in 1914, the Federal Reserve has always been organized as some variation of an independent agency. Independent agencies in the United States are quite common, and their form follows a kind of formula: They are subject to no direct, formal supervision or control by a cabinet secretary or the president.[6] They are headed by a multimember governing board (usually five members) whose members are nominated for staggered terms (usually five to seven years) by the president with the advice and consent of the Senate. Most boards must have a bipartisan composition, and since 1950 in most cases, the president has designated the chairman. Generally, the president may not remove a commissioner as easily as top-level officials in single-headed agencies.[7] This formula is intended to remove commission behavior from partisan politics and to elevate expertise as a governing principle. The Federal Reserve Board more or less conforms to the independence formula, and in this sense it is independent.[8] Whether this formula conveys any meaningful independence in policy action remains to be seen.

The Federal Reserve's relationships with other actors are marked by a tension between its nominal political independence and the kinds of tasks it is called upon to perform in the economic system. It is asked to be politically neutral while regulating an economic system that is not neutral in its results. It is expected to act on the basis of reflective scientific judgment in an environment that stresses political responsiveness. It is asked to make technically correct decisions despite conditions of economic uncertainty that make it difficult to avoid errors and despite a highly conflictual scientific debate as to what correct policy is.

The independence formula is supposed to insulate the System from at least some political influences. Critics, both liberal and conservative, have attacked this supposed independence. Some feel that Federal Reserve independence permits the System to sabotage presidential or congressional policy. Democratic control of policy, they argue, should be sustained even if it might produce a policy less than optimal by the standards of economic efficiency. Others feel that independence permits the System to follow an erratic and harmful policy course.

At the same time, there are many observers who support the independence of the central bank. Some of them hope to avoid having the course of monetary policy determined by pressure from other actors. They hope that the monetary authority will have sufficient political power to resist pressure. In particular, there are those who fear inflation and see the central bank as predisposed to fight it. They welcome independence as a hopeful indication of support for their preferences. Economists Assar Lindbeck and William Nordhaus have suggested that "depoliticizing" monetary policy may be a solution to the problems of economic instability they see resulting from democratic control of monetary policy.[9]

There are still others who argue that the interdependence of monetary and fiscal policy requires that there be full coordination and, thus, no independence. Nonetheless, they still might argue that all economic policy choices should be relatively depoliticized for the same reasons noted above.

Behavioral independence

Does the independence formula translate into independent behavior? It is useful to begin thinking about behavioral independence by distinguishing between two meanings of "independence." In one sense, a government agency may be said to *choose* a course of action independently if it does so without yielding to the pressures of others as to what that action should be. In another sense, a government agency may be said to be independent if its ability to achieve its objectives is not affected by the actions of others. The former kind of independence, an independence from political pressure in making decisions, is supposed to be promoted by the independence formula. The latter refers to functional interdependence. Typically, no actor controls all of the instruments relevant to achieving particular goals. Thus, any actor's ability to reach his or her objectives depends to some degree on the actions of others – even if the actor's own choice of action is completely free. There is no necessity for interdependent actors to cooperate in choosing their actions. It is clear that monetary policy is not independent in this second sense.[10] The effects of monetary policy actions are dependent in part upon fiscal policy, bank regulatory policy, and events in the private sector. It is political independence, the first kind of independence, that is my primary concern here.

Still, the fact of interdependence creates tensions between policy makers that will affect monetary policy, too. Policy makers who know that they are functionally interdependent have strong interests in assuring that their counterparts follow "correct" policies. Their success in such efforts depends on the extent to which there is political independence. Obviously, it is difficult to make definite statements about the dynamics of relationships that are largely conducted in private. However, it is possible to reach some reasonably firm conclusions. As a start, it is useful to have a criterion for identifying relationships involving some minimal level of independence in policy choice. For this purpose, I adopt the following: A central bank is independent if it can set policy instruments without prior approval from other actors and if, for some minimal time period (say, a calendar quarter), the instrument settings clearly differ from those preferred by other actors.[11] In the case of the Federal Reserve, there is no requirement for formal approval of policy action from any other officials. As a practical matter, then, my main concern will be with evidence of conflict between actions and preferences.

This is an explicitly political definition of independence. It means that at least occasionally, for some minimal period of time, the monetary authority is not fully dominated by other actors. It does not rule out the possibility of successful coercion of one actor by the other at times when no conflict is observed. I shall use this definition in subsequent chapters as a reference point in discussing the Federal Reserve's relationships with other actors.

Prior studies of the Federal Reserve's relationships with other governmental actors

Aside from the increasingly frequent journalistic account of the struggles between the Federal Reserve and the administration, there is a relatively meager scholarly literature describing in detail how these relationships have developed. A very useful historical account, concluding in the late 1950s, is A. Jerome Clifford's *The Independence of the Federal Reserve System*. Clifford details the swings in the Federal Reserve's position in government that are summarized in Chapter 2. He concludes that the Federal Reserve's independence can be desirable, useful, and of decisive importance in taking prudent economic policy action. Clifford sees the Federal Reserve's independence as both real and important, and as probably a good idea. He observes that sustaining that independence depends on the willingness of the Federal Reserve to explain its actions so that others can understand and accept it.[12] In other words, Clifford proposes that technical rigor and openness can dispel political suspicion. In both respects, Clifford's view is probably quite close to the commonsense, mainstream view of the Federal Reserve.

G. L. Bach has provided another historical overview of the Federal Reserve and a close examination of its policies from the 1950s through the end of the 1960s.[13] Bach's discussion is sensitive to political factors and remains an excellent introduction to this area of policy making. Of particular interest is his description of the details of coordination between the Federal Reserve and the president in the 1960s. Bach's overall conclusion is that the two institutions deserve "high marks" for coordination despite the perception of some observers that policies were pulling in separate directions. One observation is quite interesting, although cryptic: "The power and influence of the Federal Reserve in over-all macroeconomic policy making has usually been greatest when its distance ("independence") from the administration has been least, and least when the distance has been greatest."[14] By this, Bach apparently means that when the Federal Reserve is willing to enter into open discussion with the president and to provide information about its analyses, it has more influence over the president and thus over fiscal policy. If so, this obviously does not address the meaning of independence in quite the sense that I have proposed using it here; for Bach, independence implies isolation, not political autonomy. Bach's observation does remind us of something very important, however: Overt conflict – that is, overt exercise of central bank power – is evidence of a breakdown in negotiations. The power to take independent action may be the central bank's greatest bargaining chip. However, even if the central bank fails to take independent action, it may still be exercising influence.

In addition to these two works, probably the single most important and entertaining interpreter of the Federal Reserve's external relationships has been economist Edward Kane.[15] Kane's argument directly confronts the Clifford-Bach approach of taking the Federal Reserve's independence seriously. Kane calls his interpretation the "scapegoat" hypothesis. He argues that there is very little substance to the independence of the Federal Reserve, and that what little independence there is serves a useful function for other governmental institutions, especially Congress. Independence allows Congress to shift the blame for policy failures from itself to the Federal Reserve. Kane argues that this role is willingly assumed by the Federal Reserve, and that it accounts for the persistence of the agency's "independent" structure.[16] As I shall point out below, incentives for scapegoating are widespread, and there is nothing special about the Federal Reserve in this respect. Still, Kane's interpretation is often plausible and has the virtue of urging us to look behind appearances. But it is also difficult to verify in specific instances since it involves an assertion that people mean something other than what they say; at the same time, their actions are often ambiguous. I will return to this intriguing analysis in several subsequent chapters.

A framework for examining issues and relationships in monetary politics

Economists commonly examine policy in terms of three categories: policy makers' goals or objectives; policy makers' understanding of how policy actions affect the world (models); and policy makers' actions taken in light of their goals and models. Although this is a useful scheme, when used alone it is too simplified either for analyzing the debates in monetary politics or for understanding the activities that result in policy actions. Particularly important are *relationships,* which are excluded from the economist's decomposition.

Superiors and subordinates

An initial and also highly simplified way of thinking about the relationships and issues in this case is to think about the relationships between "superiors," or would-be goal setters, and "subordinates," or implementors. A superior, by definition, aspires to achieve particular policy goals; to do so, he or she relies on a subordinate to follow instructions. If all goes well, the relationship presents no problems. In the more likely event of failure, the superior can be thought of as analyzing the problem using the process indicated in Figure 1.1. The superior must ascertain whether failure resulted from lack of clarity in giving instructions, from incompetence or sabotage by subordinates (including the possibility that they are actually behaving as the subordinates for someone else), or from unforseeable events. Unforseeable events may call into question objectives that the superior had previously ignored, and a faithful and competent subordinate will and should respond to them. In such a case, failure is not really failure when the events are more closely examined. Unforseeable events may also indicate that the technical problems faced by the subordinate are made more difficult due to a higher probability of random events. In this case, failure does not imply incompetence; it simply means that the subordinate has a very tough job to do.

To summarize, a superior will have the greatest success in achieving policy goals when: (1) the superior can clearly specify his or her own policy goals; and (2) subordinates are trustworthy and competent. If both of these are true, then superiors know that failure must be due to the difficulty of doing the job, not to incompetence or sabotage. However, whenever superiors doubt the truth of (2), their lives become much more difficult, and so should those of their subordinates.

It is obvious that these two conditions frequently are not met in the real world. Superiors – that is, the president, Congress, or agency heads – often do not know exactly what they want, and

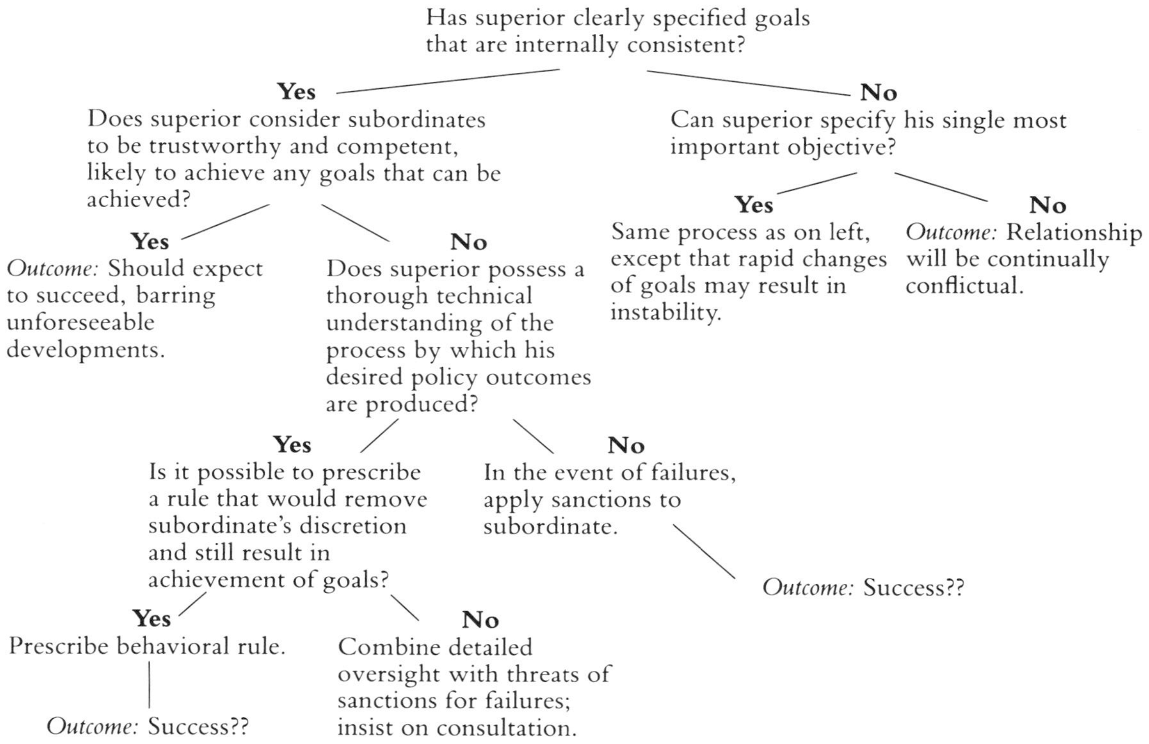

Has superior clearly specified goals that are internally consistent?

Yes

Does superior consider subordinates to be trustworthy and competent, likely to achieve any goals that can be achieved?

Yes

Outcome: Should expect to succeed, barring unforeseeable developments.

No

Does superior possess a thorough technical understanding of the process by which his desired policy outcomes are produced?

Yes

Is it possible to prescribe a rule that would remove subordinate's discretion and still result in achievement of goals?

Yes

Prescribe behavioral rule.

Outcome: Success??

No

Combine detailed oversight with threats of sanctions for failures; insist on consultation.

No

In the event of failures, apply sanctions to subordinate.

Outcome: Success??

No

Can superior specify his single most important objective?

Yes

Same process as on left, except that rapid changes of goals may result in instability.

No

Outcome: Relationship will be continually conflictual.

Figure 1.1

they cannot, or are reluctant to, reveal explicitly how they rank various outcomes. Subordinates have their own objectives that may not coincide with those of their superiors, and subordinates may not be entirely competent. In such cases, superiors have to consider how to achieve compliance on the part of their subordinates. As outlined in Figure 1.1, superiors basically have two options: They can specify a behavioral rule so that the subordinate's discretion is removed, or they can engage in some form of supervisory oversight. In the latter case, they can either apply a simple post hoc procedure of rewards and punishments for successes and failures, or they can engage in close and continuing technical supervision, combining the demand for consultation with the threat of future punishment for noncompliance.

Among the would-be superiors of the Federal Reserve, there is disagreement about the answers to every one of the questions posed in Figure 1.1. There are disagreements about whether Federal Reserve officials agree with the goals of the president or members of Congress. There are arguments about whether Federal Reserve officials are technically competent. There are disputes about whether Congress and the president have enough means available to punish or reward Federal Reserve behavior – and about whether they should have more. Not least, there are disputes about whether monetary policy should follow a behavioral rule. Each of these questions raises what I shall call the "issues" in monetary politics.

Figure 1.1 assumes that we can make several important and relatively basic analytic distinctions. First is the distinction between actors as to their degree of technical competence, and, among the competent, as to their degree of belief in the feasibility of behavioral rules. Second is the distinction between actors as to their degree of control over important political resources. These two together determine the strategy superiors will use to try to ensure their success. It does not really matter whether the superior perceives policy failure to be due to incompetence or betrayal. The range of solutions to choose from is the same: Punish, in the hope that the subordinate will learn or conform; supervise more closely; prescribe a rule to remove discretion; or replace the subordinate.[17] The solution a would-be superior selects is a function not of the problem but of what the superior can achieve given the resources at hand. Only actors with a high level of technical skill can aspire to engage in detailed technical oversight or can decide to prescribe a behavior rule. Only actors with a high level of political resources can realistically aspire to punish or reward policy performance.

Those with both a high level of political resources and a high level of technical skill can aspire to close and continuous surveillance and the meaningful threat of sanctions.

Other important assumptions must be made with this kind of analysis. First, the existence of the agency is not in question – that is, public sector performance of the function is not itself an issue. Although this seems to be true in the case of the Federal Reserve, both conservatives and liberals can be found who argue that critical problems cannot be solved unless the Federal Reserve is abolished.[18] A second assumption is that there is some agreement that the agency should be subordinate to an external actor. This is discussed in more detail below.

Another useful assumption is that subordinates want to keep their jobs and their discretion; they do not want to be punished or subjected to close supervisory oversight. Consequently, one expects subordinates to try to persuade superiors of their faithfulness and competence. Subordinates would be expected to account for policy failures by explaining how difficult the job is, and/or by pointing out that unforseeable events threatened valued but implicit goals and made their job harder, and/or by showing that superiors hold incompatible goals. Subordinates would be expected to resist any attempt to impose a rule removing their discretion, and to do so on the grounds that the technical situation is simply too complicated to make a rule practical. They would stress that they are not only educable but also completely up-to-date.

The problem faced by the superior is simple: How do you know if you are hearing the truth? The more complicated and uncertain the world appears to be, the more difficult it is for a superior confidently to answer that question. Is the job really difficult, or are subordinates trying to cover up their adherence to goals that conflict with those of the superior? The subordinate's argument for preserving discretion may be self-serving, but could it also be technically correct? It is very difficult to assemble definitive proof regarding such issues, so superiors who are not themselves technically sophisticated are dependent on additional layers of technical advice to answer these questions. Suspicious would-be superiors will surely respond to subordinates' arguments by dismissing them as purely political strategies, as smokescreens to hide incompetence or ill will.

Another problem occurs in political systems where one group of superiors may be held accountable to still other superiors (e.g., the electorate). Sometimes when there is an apparent policy failure, a superior may have an interest in believing that the subordinate's explanation is *not* the truth, independent of the facts of the matter. This belief permits the superior to shift blame to the subordinate. The subordinate's protests of innocence notwithstanding, the superior may take this kind of position in order to evade responsibility – for example, to avoid being blamed by voters. I shall consider in subsequent chapters an argument that the Federal Reserve has been used as a scapegoat in just this way.

Who is the superior?

This scheme is reasonably useful as long as subordinates and superiors are clearly identified. However, it is not entirely clear who is or should be the Federal Reserve's superior. Who *should* be giving orders to the Federal Reserve? Does the independence formula mean that no one should do so? Who *does* give orders? The president? Congress? Economists? Bankers? Asking who the superior is means asking whose preferences count.

There are various aspirants to the role. Congress has a firm legal claim to be the final authority on the Federal Reserve's existence. It is clear that the System is not formally answerable to the president, whereas it is formally answerable to the Congress. However, the president is charged by law with responsibility for macroeconomic policy, and the Federal Reserve is obviously important in this realm. Moreover, it is the president who appoints top officials in the Federal Reserve, and recent law states that monetary policy should be consistent with the president's economic program. Economists also claim some right to be considered as arbiters of Federal Reserve behavior. Economists claim to speak for the public interest, and they claim the right to evaluate the technical competence of the Federal Reserve. They also evaluate the appropriateness of potential descretion-removing rules of behavior. Bankers form the Federal Reserve's natural constituency and have been closely linked with the Federal Reserve since its founding. Bankers play a direct role in shaping economic performance and may thereby claim a special capacity to evaluate the appropriateness of Federal Reserve actions. Perhaps bankers are the most likely of all these groups to be the superior.

Merely from this glance at the possible superiors of the Federal Reserve, one can form some notion of how debates about monetary policy may shape up. One may suspect in advance that very few members of Congress will believe that they have the competence to evaluate the System's behavior on a technical level. Of those who do feel technically competent, even fewer will have the time or interest to engage in continuous technical supervision (nor will their staffs). Therefore, one might expect to find that members of Congress who perceive Federal Reserve failures will want to institute new and more effective forms of intermittent post hoc rewards and punishments. By contrast, presidents may feel that they have staff capabilities that allow them to engage in more continuous, detailed supervision of monetary policy. The president is, of course, the single most important actor in making fiscal policy, so the consequences of his actions are obviously important for the Federal Reserve. Presidents also know that they are in a position to try to alter Federal Reserve membership by their appointments. Thus, they may opt for a quiet but very close relationship with the Federal Reserve. Economists may focus almost exclusively on the technical questions. Lacking much independent political power, they may have to work closely with other actors who do have power in order to achieve results. However, they may have direct access to Federal Reserve policy makers on the grounds of expertise alone if they argue that they understand technical matters that are of interest to Federal Reserve officials. Bankers certainly have the command of technical, financial, and political resources that would be necessary for a nongovernmental group to influence policy. On the other hand, it is not clear that the financial industry is able to unite behind any clear short-term policy recommendation except in extreme economic conditions. However, if bankers are not able to function effectively as superiors in the short term, they may be able to help create an atmosphere at the Federal Reserve that is not open to other interest groups.

Strategies that succeed: the problem of multiple superiors

When many actors are trying to shape the behavior of a given organization, none of them may succeed in dominating its behavior. Thus, in terms of the definition of independence previously offered, behavior might be observed that differs from that preferred by a given actor, but it would not be clear whether that difference reflected the refusal of the organization to comply or was instead an organizational response to preferences expressed more effectively by others.

If the organization is responding to the preferences expressed by other actors, then apparently independent action reflects the relative weakness of the pressures applied by one actor and the relative strength of the pressures applied by another. Imagine that the Federal Reserve's behavior is a complex response to stimuli from Congress, the president, interest groups, and objective environmental conditions. It would be surprising if a change in stimuli from only one source – for example, one congressional committee – produced a dramatic change in the behavior of the ororganization. However, we might expect such an effect if we were dealing with some overwhelmingly dominant set of stimuli – for example, Congress and the president together.

Any organization or group attempting to influence the Federal Reserve must send a signal that is as clear as possible with respect to preferred policy action (i.e., at the level of policy instruments, if possible). Signals must be persistent and repeated. Messages that are internally contradictory, intermittent, or rapidly changing will be less important. Organizations should attempt to have the same signal coming from as many other organizations and groups as possible. Actors must also be prepared to impose sanctions, prescribe rules, or engage in detailed oversight in order to influence the Federal Reserve. This also means trying to affect the selection of Federal Reserve personnel so that some stimuli are more readily received than others.

Do we have reasons to suspect in advance that some potential sources of stimuli are more important than others? Yes. We expect the president to be more important than Congress simply because of the greater ease of organizing a consistent policy position in the executive branch. We also expect the president to be more important because of the expertise available to him and because of his domination in fiscal policy. We expect groups of economists to be important primarily when allied with either the president or members of Congress since economists, by themselves, have little political power. We expect bankers to be important when they assemble broad coalitions representing the financial industry. Otherwise, the internal fragmentation of the financial industry may preclude the presentation of a consistent, clear set of policy recommendations.

The political position of the Federal Reserve

Standard political science analysis alerts us to several factors that increase or decrease the probability that the Federal Reserve will be the object of political conflict. Similarly, it is possible to say a good deal about which interests are mobilized to try to influence monetary policy and which are not.

Under what conditions should we expect to see groups mobilized to try to influence policy? First, and most obvious, there must be an organized group whose interests are affected by policy. If policy impacts do not relate to the reasons for group organization, then there should be no mobilization. Second, impacts should be visible. Groups should be aware that their interests are affected. It is plausible to assume that where economic interests are concerned, tangible losses or benefits must exceed some minimal level in order to be perceived as important. Third, the relevant decision-making process must also be visible. That is, some distinct set of policy makers must be perceived as making policy. Finally, specific decisions must be perceived to be linked with subsequent visible impacts. The group must not only be able to tell who makes policy, it must be able to identify decisions likely to alter the nature of the impacts. In general, we expect that some groups will be more difficult to mobilize than others. Typically, we expect that large groups whose members are each affected by policy to a relatively modest degree (albeit with impressive aggregate quantities) will be less likely to organize effectively than small groups whose members each have a large stake in policy decisions.[19]

Impacts and groups

There is a fair amount of information available about the impacts of monetary policy, but it is far less detailed and precise than one might wish. Studies show that negative rather than positive tangible impacts are likely to be visible to currently organized interests, albeit *intermittently*. Restrictive policy seems to fall relatively heavily on housing and construction,[20] on small rather than large business (including agriculture),[21] and on small rather than large local government units.[22] Because wages tend to lag in adjusting to price changes in the United States, monetary policy can have a notable temporary effect on employment, output, and corporate earnings.[23]

The effects of changing levels of employment are not randomly distributed. For example, the size of the affected population is much larger than had previously been believed; income losses associated with cyclical rises in unemployment are heavier the poorer the family (for families with male heads) and significantly greater for blacks than whites.[24] It is not clear that unemployment impacts fall particularly (and predictably) on specific *organized* groups, although at the high levels experienced in the early 1980s, unemployment clearly hurt the unionized workers in declining "smokestack" industries.

The impacts of inflation are widely felt, too, although the distribution in terms of specific social groups is hard to specify.[25] For example, net debtors should gain and net creditors should lose from inflation that is not fully anticipated as long as there is no adjustment mechanism in their contract. For example, the expectation that bankers *oppose* inflation has been based in part on the fact that bankers are net creditors. Studies have shown, however, that nonfinancial businesses in the United States are about evenly divided between creditors and debtors.[26] Pre–1970s inflation has been shown to transfer income from profits to wages and salaries, and to transfer wealth from households to business and government and from upper-income to middle-income groups.[27]

Economic growth should reverse the pattern of unemployment – benefiting groups who would have been harmed by downturns. However, as all who are familiar with the term "sunbelt" now recognize, the benefits of growth are not equally distributed across geographic regions – nor are costs; consider, for example, pollution.

Business, large and small, agriculture, and construction, are well represented in Washington. Labor and state and local governments are also represented, well financed, and ably staffed. There is, however, almost no persuasive evidence that these groups have much sustained interest in *monetary policy* or, at least, that their resources are directed especially toward the Federal Reserve. Perhaps this is no surprise, given the formal independence of the Federal Reserve; that is, perhaps it proves that independence works. However, I think it more plausible that other factors, discussed subsequently, are more important for achieving this result.

A considerable literature can be used to show that changes in the overall levels of employment, inflation, and economic growth have important political consequences in electoral politics. It may be that the electoral arena is the primary arena for aggregating opinions about these very broadly felt conditions. Findings do show that changes in inflation, real disposable income, and, less clearly, unemployment affect presidential popularity.[28] Studies of voting in congressional elections have also shown mixed results, but influence has been consistently attributed to the growth of income and the rate of inflation.[29] Although this source of pressure may be important for Congress and the president, it should have no direct influence on the Federal Reserve, which, of course, is not directly exposed to electoral pressures.

The vulnerability of the Federal Reserve to interest groups

Obviously, many groups are affected by monetary policy, and most of them have some form of representation in Washington. Their impact on policy making should be enhanced because of factors making the behavior of the Federal Reserve easier to influence than that of many other agencies. The Federal Reserve is highly centralized in terms of decision making and implementation. Its behavior is measurable in relatively precise quantitative terms, and current indicators of policy actions are widely disseminated and easily obtained. Observers who know what they want from monetary policy can know rapidly whether or not they are getting it, and they can reasonably expect the link between policy decision and execution to be close and clear.

Despite these factors, the process of making monetary policy appears to be marked by the relative absence of interest group activity in directly shaping policy choice. In the recession of the early 1980s, several groups from industries strongly affected by high interest rates launched grass-roots mail campaigns aimed at the Federal Reserve. For example, construction industry groups mailed hundreds of chunks of two-by-fours to Federal Reserve Board Chairman Paul Volcker. This was a new phenomenon and reflected the much higher visibility monetary policy had achieved during the 1970s. But this kind of pressure is still relatively rare and very intermittent. This is largely because of the complex processes producing policy impacts, the nature of established channels of influence, and the nature of the decision process.[30]

The flow of policy impacts. The distributive consequences of policy flow not from specific decisions but from a series of decisions. Although it is often clear in retrospect that a decision to "begin tightening" was made at a particular FOMC meeting, tight money is the consequence of a long course of action, no specific element of which is clearly primary. Moreover, decisions are linked to eventual outcomes through a complicated process involving long lags, and the length of lags varies with respect to different effects. In purely analytic terms, linking policy actions with expected impacts is a fairly sophisticated business. Employment appears to respond more quickly than inflation. Some interest rates respond instantaneously, but others, such as those affecting the housing industry, adjust only after a considerable time. Thus, to the extent that interest groups mobilize in reaction to impacts rather than current policy actions, they might find themselves responding to actions taken weeks or even months earlier. Readers will also note that since the costs of restrictive monetary policy (unemployment) precede the benefits (lower inflation), monetary politics may be affected substantially because supporters and opponents of the policy are mobilized asynchronously.

Established channels of influence. Ordinarily, one would expect interest groups to try to gain access to those forums where decisions are made that regularly and directly affect them. However, since the most politically important impacts of monetary policy are felt intermittently, groups may find that they do not derive important benefits from regularly allocating resources to following closely the developments in this policy area. However, when groups do become concerned about monetary policy, they will find that established contacts and expertise often cannot be rapidly redeployed from one institutional setting to another even though these groups realize that they face a new problem with a different source. Thus, one would expect to find that groups affected intermittently respond to undesired impacts by acting through established channels of influence. In the case of monetary policy, this often means acting on and through Congress.

Nature of the decision-making process. Even those groups continuously affected by monetary policy – especially the financial industry – may find it difficult to pursue a direct-pressure strategy because of the nature of the monetary policy process. It is often not clear which decisions are critical in terms of changing policy, nor is it clear what the distributive consequences are of any particular decision. To some degree, the periodic setting of monetary targets has made some decisions more critical than others. However, targets are defined in terms of ranges, and the effects associated with different positions in the ranges may differ considerably. So, to an important and continuing degree, FOMC policy is established monthly in a paradigmatic incremental policy process, and policy may be adjusted between meetings by telephone conference. Policy is made in great secrecy. At best, nonofficial outsiders have only a general notion of the likely options before the FOMC at a given meeting.

Conclusion and overview

It is obvious that a great deal is at stake in monetary policy. Despite this fact, the arena is relatively restricted in terms of the number and variety of groups directly involved. By now, many of the issues are clear. And it is clear that to a significant degree, the issues have to do with how various superiors evaluate the Federal Reserve and how they try to assert the priority of their own view regarding the objectives and implementation of policy. The debates are lively and interesting, even if they are sometimes obscured by technical language; rarely are the debates fully resolved.

I have argued that actors choose their strategies for influencing the Federal Reserve based on the resources they control. We expect that some strategies will be more successful than others. However, arriving at the truth about relations between superiors and subordinates is very difficult. I will argue here for some conclusions about what the truth is, and I am reasonably confident that some of those conclusions are correct. However, it is inherently impossible, in many cases, to conceive of evidence that would provide conclusive proof one way or the other. So, there is an element of judgment here that may be more obvious than in some other kinds of studies of economic policy. It is not, I would argue, a difference either of degree or of kind.

Chapter 2 continues this introduction by presenting a historical overview of the Federal Reserve. The objective is to review a series of previous conflicts and to show what issues were at stake and how they were resolved. The following chapters examine four important relationships of the Federal Reserve: with economists, with bankers, with the president, and with Congress. Chapter 3 surveys top officials in the Federal Reserve, how they are chosen, what their backgrounds are, and how those backgrounds seem to affect their policy choices. This provides an opportunity to investigate one set of questions of interest in studying the non-issues of monetary politics: Is there reason to believe that some interests are systematically excluded from consideration in monetary policy?

Subsequent chapters are devoted, in turn, to each of the relationships previously mentioned. I shall argue that certain issues dominate each of these relationships. Bankers, I argue in Chapter 4, have a short-run economic interest in the consequences of regulatory and tax policy decisions perhaps equal to their interest in monetary policy decisions. In recent years, regulatory issues have appeared to be especially important, and seem to have had significant consequences for the conduct of monetary policy. Bankers also constitute an important and continuing element in the Federal Reserve environment, and thus may shape the non-issues of monetary policy. Bankers' preferences for relatively stable policy rules and relatively restrictive policy have been important in monetary policy. Bankers are the sole interest group with the combination of access and technical expertise required to successfully affect policy choice. On the whole, bankers support the Federal Reserve's independence because of its image as an inflation fighter. But their relationship with the Federal Reserve is scarcely one of seamless agreement and cooperation.

The importance of expertise in making monetary policy provides the basis for a close but often uncomfortable relationship between the Federal Reserve and economists. The System has been drawn repeatedly into bitter debates between warring camps of economists, and this has been detrimental to the System's independence. Particularly central is the debate between monetarists and other economists. This debate and the struggle for control of the Federal Reserve is the subject of Chapter 5. There I will argue that the monetarists were in no direct sense responsible for the 1979 decision of the Federal Reserve to begin monetary targeting.

Chapters 6 and 7 focus on the president and Congress. In these chapters, I argue that there are important differences in the resources available to each institution and in the capacity of the institution to define clear and consistent policy positions. Congress has tended to emphasize measures requiring closer reporting and better post hoc control over the Federal Reserve. The president finds it possible to work closely with the Federal Reserve on a continuing basis. As I will note, there are suggestions that Congress is becoming increasingly interested in playing a more substantive role with respect to the Federal Reserve.

Chapters 8 and 9 reflect on the significance of the analysis in the preceding five chapters. Chapter 8 examines the combined effects of external pressures on policy making in 1972, a year in which it is commonly alleged that partisan political consideration shaped monetary policy. This case study provides an enlightening and important example of the ways in which external pressures combined to shape Federal Reserve behavior. It is clear, in this case, that the Federal Reserve was very cautious about its relationship with the president and with Congress. It is also clear that it is a serious error to interpret policy making in 1972 as a simple case of partisan monetary policy.

Chapter 9, the final chapter, places the analysis of the Federal Reserve in the context of the current debate about political economy and the approaches to it.

2

A Capsule History of the Federal Reserve System

The discussion in most of this book assumes that there is general agreement about the need for a governmental agency to perform the functions of the Federal Reserve. However, this has not always been the case. There is a rich history of efforts to address the questions identified in Chapter 1 as central to monetary politics: Who should be the Federal Reserve's superior? Is the Federal Reserve's policy correct? This chapter provides a selective overview of the history of the System prior to the 1960s, including the development of the idea of the Federal Reserve and how it was countered.

The Federal Reserve System was designed in response to the inadequacies of the American financial structure in the late nineteenth century. These inadequacies repeatedly threatened the smooth functioning of the emerging mature capitalist order. Although the precise institutional structure of the Federal Reserve System was influenced by many short-term political factors, it is valuable in studying the contemporary System to recognize that the origins of the Federal Reserve lie in the failures of a maturing capitalist financial order and in the efforts of important groups to reform and stabilize that system.

Following those successful reform efforts, there were conflicts about the internal organization of the Federal Reserve System and important alterations in its relationship to the president. The formal structure of the System has now been unchanged for over forty years, but the issue of how the Federal Reserve should and does relate to external actors has hardly been resolved – nor has the debate about how policy should be conducted.

Throughout the period covered in this chapter, there has been very little explicit legislative guidance to the Federal Reserve regarding what goals it should pursue and what its relationship to the president should be. This lack of clarity has produced conflict on several occasions. However, as I pointed out in Chapter 1, clarity alone is not enough. High levels of expertise and careful, continuing monitoring are required for a superior to know whether or not the Federal Reserve is faithful and competent. Clarification of formal responsibilities helps to reduce normative ambiguity, but does not resolve the problems of the relationship between superior and subordinate.

Defining the role of government in financial matters

The history of banking and monetary regulation in the United States in the nineteenth century was marked by protracted and intense conflict. Many fundamental issues about the nature of the economy and the role of government were raised and resolved in those conflicts. However, the decision to establish the Federal Reserve did not involve a basic conflict about the financial system. Rather, that decision was marked more by the fact that certain basic conflicts had already been resolved.

An observer from the late twentieth century comparing the current political conflict about money, banking, and regulation of the economy with the conflicts of the nineteenth century is sure to be struck by the fact that most of what we now take for granted about money and banking was previously the object of bitter conflict. Where today is there any serious attack on the existence of banks as institutions? In the 1850s, banking was *prohibited* in five western states; banks had been excluded or severely restricted in three other states; and banks existed as state monopolies in two other states.[1] Today, what serious political movement is organized around the idea that paper money is unacceptable if not convertible into specie? In the late 1830s, a movement known as the Loco Focos enjoyed some influence and argued against *any* paper currency. Today, what movement is organized around the principle that it is unconstitutional for the federal government to establish a bank for regulating the economy? The Jacksonian attack on the Bank of the United States from 1829 to 1832 rested on such an argument.

The political battles about money in nineteenth-century America were battles about the distribution of power in society between regions and classes; they were battles between competing images of the good life. The exercise of discretionary control over the money supply was urged by some interests in the last quarter of the century as a counter to the redistributive effects of deflation.

These interests were, in fact, soundly defeated. Paradoxically, discretion in monetary matters was firmly entrenched about a quarter-century later – to serve the interests of the victors in the earlier battle.

Crisis and change in the U.S. monetary system

During the nineteenth century and the first years of the twentieth, a series of economic and political crises was resolved in ways that shaped the form and functions of the Federal Reserve today. Although the development of our banking system can be thought of as a logical – functional – response to the needs of a developing industrial economy, it was also much more than that. It was part of a series of political battles over the legitimacy of an industrial, corporate economic system.

In the second half of the 1800s, a series of financial crises occurred at the rate of one per decade. The onset of most of these crises was marked by suspension by the banks of conversion of paper money into specie. Each crisis provoked controversy and debate about the structure and regulation of banking and finance. Usually, some reforms were attempted by way of response. Congress showed a lively interest in the details of policy solutions. Repeatedly, the proposed standard for evaluating the existing arrangements was the degree to which these arrangments served the needs of business. Equally common, however, were suspicions that these proposed reforms were simply more clever ways to advance the interests of groups that already had great wealth and power. At the end of the 1800s, a hodgepodge of political protest movements emerged as reactions against industrialism, urbanism, and the gold standard favored by East Coast financiers. The political fortunes of the populists, pro-silverites, greenbackers, and agricultural interests rose with the periodic financial crises of the period. But after joining the ranks of seriously contending political powers in the early 1890s, these protest groups were decisively defeated in the middle of that decade.

The crises of the period can be clearly identified and enumerated. The first crisis, starting in 1861, began as a consequence of the stresses of Civil War finance. The most important result of this crisis was the establishment of a national system for chartering banks. Paper currency issued by these national banks gradually came to dominate the financial system. The second crisis, the crisis of 1873, was caused by government efforts to implement a hard money reform, replacing paper money with specie. The structure of bank reserves was too fragile to prevent a panic as banks scrambled for funds to cover the demand for bank reserves. The third crisis began in 1884 in response to international pressures for payment in gold for securities issued by U.S. firms and owned by Europeans. This crisis did not result in general suspension of specie convertibility, and stability was reestablished through cooperative action of the New York Clearing House Association.

The fourth crisis, the crisis of 1893, was in many ways decisive. The panic began with the failure of a prominent firm and was followed by the collapse of the stock market. There ensued the failure of other firms, two runs on the banks, the failure of the Erie Railroad, and still more bank suspensions. The remarkably clumsy response of President Cleveland, a Democrat, paved the way for the subsequent drubbings of the Democrats in the elections of 1894 and 1896 and, with the exception of the Wilson years, the domination of national politics by the Republicans until the 1930s. The election of 1896 marked the decisive defeat of the populist "silver inflationists," who were a potent threat to dominant eastern financial interests and whose strength had peaked early in the period of the crisis of 1893. It is no exaggeration to say that this crisis in finance capitalism ultimately resulted in the defeat of the opponents of the emerging concentrated industrial order. This crisis also provided momentum for discussions among bankers of needed reforms in the banking system. Those discussions were the direct precursors of the Federal Reserve. If the silverite cause was a challenge to the dominant interests in the 1890s, the monetary reforms proposed by farsighted bankers were quite the opposite.

Bank reform. The first solution proposed was the Baltimore Plan, advanced at the 1894 American Bankers Association meeting by two bankers (one from New York, the other from Baltimore) and the editor of the *New York Evening Post.* The plan, which was presented so as to deemphasize the "Wall Street" origins of the reform, suggested amendments to the National Banking Act to provide a less crisis-prone currency system. The centerpiece of the scheme was a new currency backed by bank assets (i.e., bank loans to business rather than gold or specie) and guaranteed jointly by the banks against emergencies through a central fund.[2] Although the plan was opposed by many larger banks and was thoroughly overshadowed in importance by bankers' concern for fending off the free-silver movement, the Baltimore Plan began a process of discussion and debate that continued at all subsequent association conventions until reforms were made years later.

The next major event in the discussion of bank reform was the Indianapolis Monetary Convention of 1897. This conference was organized by boards of trade in midwestern cities that had become particularly concerned about the need for monetary reform following the 1893 depression. The conference commissioned a report authored principally by University of Chicago economist J. Lawrence Laughlin. The substance of the report, quite similar to the Baltimore Plan, addressed the problem of maintaining flexibility in times of crisis. At that time, however, the need for reform was seen as a pressing concern only by a minority of the banking community, and many state chartered banks and smaller banks opposed the further national control implied by this proposal.[3]

The crisis of 1907. Despite some halfhearted attempts at reform legislation in the early 1900s, there was no significant reform pressure as long as the economy seemed to be healthy and expanding. This changed with the crisis of 1907. There was a sharp downturn; the net national product dropped 11 percent from 1907 to 1908. The most drastic part of the contraction followed a bank panic in October 1907 that culminated in widespread suspension of specie conversion and a feeling of national upheaval.[4]

Following the crisis, in 1908, Congress for the first time seriously took up the issue of bank reform. Several plans were debated including, most prominently, one drawn by Senator Nelson Aldrich and one other by Rep. Charles N. Fowler. These plans received little support and considerable criticism from banking and commercial groups.[5] The demand for some kind of reform was met instead by a compromise drafted by Rep. Edward B. Vreeland, known as the Aldrich-Vreeland Act, which essentially combined the two bills.[6] The Aldrich-Vreeland Act provisions were used only once, during the banking crisis of 1914 before the Federal Reserve was fully operational. The Aldrich-Vreeland Act was important primarily because it established a National Monetary Commission, with Aldrich as chairman and Vreeland as vice-chairman. The report of that group, presented early in 1912 and known as the Aldrich plan, provided the detailed recommendations upon which the Federal Reserve was later founded. The discussions of the group provided an opportunity to resolve many of the disputes that divided midwestern city banks and the large New York banks.[7]

The Federal Reserve: proximate sources

Like many innovations in public policy, the development of the precise outlines of the banking reform many perceived as necessary were shaped by relatively few key figures. The importance of a few figures in these reforms has seemed to some to be evidence of a conspiracy. According to one interpretation, the corporate-liberal view, if there was not a conspiracy then there was at least a coordinated effort by dominant financial groups to enlist government policy in the aid of their own position. Much of the literature discussing the founding of the Federal Reserve has been shaped by concern with this issue. This view has been fostered partly because the first major piece of reform legislation during this period, the Aldrich plan, was formulated in part at a secret meeting in 1910 at Jekyll Island, Georgia, an exclusive hunting retreat. In addition to Senator Aldrich, the group was composed primarily of New York bankers.[8] The secrecy was no doubt part of an effort – which was evident at other points in this reform process as well – to avoid charges that the reforms were intended to benefit Wall Street at the expense of the rest of the country.

The Aldrich plan

The Aldrich plan was a rallying point for pro-reform interests who provided the first organized support for the reforms that culminated in the Federal Reserve System. The plan called for the establishment of a national reserve association to hold part of member bank reserves, to determine the discount rates, to buy and sell financial instruments on the open market, and to issue currency.[9] Key questions were raised in the plan. In particular, there were technical questions about the kinds of assets that could be used to back emergency currency issues, and there were political questions about the structure of governance of the new reserve system. The first issue went to the heart of then popular theories of sound banking, the second to the question of the appropriate role for public officials in the organization.

Technical issues considered in the Aldrich plan included the issue of the kinds of assets to be eligible for discounting and to be counted as bank reserves. This decision would have important distributional consequences by giving official status to particular categories of assets and by creating a guaranteed demand for those assets. Another issue was whether notes (i.e., currency) issued by reserve associations should be counted as bank reserves in the same way as bank deposits with the reserve association.[10]

The issue that eventually doomed the Aldrich plan and dominated the debate on later proposals was that of control. What would be the role of banks? What would be the role of government? Who would control the regional banks? The Aldrich design involved a minor role for political influence. Under a complex formula, the board of directors of the National Reserve Association would reflect the fifteen districts (thirty members), the interests of banks holding stock in the reserve associations (nine members), and the government (seven members). Of these forty-six, only five were to be appointed by the president, and the governor would be selected from a list submitted by the bankers. Two deputy governors would be chosen by the other board members. In response to the American Bankers Association, Aldrich revised his plan so that the governor could not be removed by the president.[11] This scheme of geographically dispersed private control was intended to respond to the concerns of those who feared domination of the system by either Wall Street or Washington. President Taft's 1912 warning that there must be more government supervision and control served ample notice of the fact that the issue of control would be prominent in future debate – as, indeed, it was.[12] As for the Aldrich bill itself, it died in committee.[13]

Early support for the Aldrich plan came from the National Board of Trade and from a meeting of twenty-two prominent bankers called to consider the plan. The plan generated opposition from Democrats simply because it was associated with the name of Nelson Aldrich, a conservative New York Republican related by marriage to the Rockefellers. Supporters of the Aldrich Plan created the National Citizen's League for the Promotion of a Sound Banking System – in contemporary parlance, a single-issue interest group. It was funded largely by New York bankers but headquartered in Chicago, another effort to avoid arousing sensitivity about Wall Street. The administrative head of the league was J. Lawrence Laughlin, the University of Chicago economist who had drafted the report for the Indianapolis Monetary Commission. The league won endorsements for this proposal from the American Bankers Association and from a majority of state bankers associations.[14]

The Aldrich plan held out attractive prospects for national banks. In particular, the national banks would have been permitted to extend their operations to areas currently denied to them under the National Banking Act. This would have eliminated any competitive advantage the state chartered banks had. Kolko argues that this was a major factor attracting big bank support for the scheme.[15]

The Glass bill

The Democrats won the presidency and the Senate in the election of 1912, and Senator Aldrich retired. The focus of debate about bank reform shifted to the House Banking Committee and its chairman, Carter Glass. By a remarkable coincidence, Glass hired to assist him in drafting legislation an economist who had been a graduate student of J. Lawrence Laughlin – one H. Parker Willis. Willis had worked with Laughlin in writing the Indianapolis Monetary Commission report and was familiar with the previous plans and discussions. It is not surprising, then, that the Glass bill drafted in early 1912 closely resembled previous plans.

According to the Glass plan, there would be at least fifteen regional banks, controlled largely by bankers. However, at the national level, the Glass plan had some structural differences from the Aldrich plan. Although there would be a thirty-six-member national board with only six presidential appointees, there would also be a nine-member executive board including all six presidential appointees. The other three members were to be elected by the regional banks. This executive board would have the power to require regional reserve banks to rediscount the paper of other regional banks. This power was considered to be a significant concession to the advocates of central control.[16]

Demands by important bankers for more banker control over the proposed agency were countered by President Wilson's insistence on greater governmental controls. Glass agreed with the bankers, but Wilson's insistence on this point made compromise necessary.[17] As it developed, a large and important portion of the banking community finally decided to support the compromise formula arrived at by Glass and Wilson. The compromise placed all central authority in a seven-member board appointed by the president. The membership included, ex officio, the secretary of the Treasury and the comptroller of the currency. Two members of the board were to have backgrounds in finance. In order to prevent possible Wall Street domination and to guarantee some western representation, no more than one member of the board was to be from any given reserve district. To minimize political control, board members would be appointed to ten-year terms with staggered two-year appointments. Normally, then, it would not be expected that any given president would have an opportunity to appoint an entire board during his tenure. In exchange for these concessions, the bankers received compensation. First, there were several technical changes in the legislation that they desired. Second, there was to be a special Federal Advisory Council composed entirely of bankers, which would meet with the board at least four times a year.

The developing debate

A number of general characteristics of the debate should be noted. There was an overwhelming consensus in Congress that reform along the general lines proposed by Aldrich and Glass was necessary. Bankers were unequally attentive to the developing dispute, and there were important disputes between different groups of bankers. Some, especially major East Coast bankers, were in favor of a central bank, but one that was entirely banker dominated. Some, especially midwestern country (rural) bankers, were in favor of only regional currency associations to respond to problems caused by periodic and sometimes localized currency shortages.[18] It seems clear from most accounts that officials of large banks were interested and involved in the deliberations. Not all were enthusiastic supporters of the reform taking shape, primarily because of the large government role in the proposed system. Kolko argues that to some degree, the dissatisfaction of bankers was overstated during the debates of 1913 for the purpose of extracting a more favorable compromise.[19] In any case, many important figures in the private financial world seem to have believed by the end of 1913 that the Glass bill was a reasonably satisfactory piece of legislation.

Bankers had an additional incentive to support this compromise. In 1912 and early 1913, a subcommittee of the House Banking Committee chaired by Rep. Arsène P. Pujo (D., La.) was holding hearings on the "money trust." The committee was investigating the control of major banking organizations and their interlocking interests with other large corporations. Their findings about the Morgan interests alone disturbed reformers:

> This inventory . . . showed a single network of interests commanding more than three times the assessed value of all the real and personal property in New England; or more than twice the value of all the property in the thirteen Southern states; or more than all the property in the twenty-two states west of the Mississippi.[20]

The Pujo subcommittee hearings helped keep the issue of bank reform alive, and in mid-1913 some members of Congress began pressing for further investigations. Indeed, Glass seems to have successfully mobilized some banker support for his position by warning that the eventual alternative to the Glass bill would be more radical legislation being promoted by agrarian and populist interests.[21]

It is clear that important issues concerning the functioning of the System were resolved in Congress, and to some scholars this is important evidence against the corporate-liberal argument that the Federal Reserve was basically designed by bankers to serve their interests.[22] However, the basic design remained intact from Aldrich plan to Federal Reserve Act. The bill passed in late December 1913, with substantial majorities in both houses, but with almost straight party-line votes (Democrats in the majority).

The conception of the role of the Federal Reserve

Goals

The original Federal Reserve Act specified only that the System should "furnish an elastic currency, . . . afford means of rediscounting paper," and accommodate the monetary and credit needs of commerce, agriculture, and industry. According to Timberlake, members of Congress supporting the Federal Reserve Act thought they were creating a group of autonomous regional reserve banks, not a central bank. These regional banks were to promote the elasticity of the currency and thereby prevent crises. Some believed that the new institution would function like a public utility, with the object of keeping interest rates low and stable. Too, the System was to serve its members as a clearinghouse.[23]

Superiors and subordinates: private versus public power

Congress was ambiguous as to how much power was to be located in Federal Reserve Board as opposed to the regional banks, an issue that was finally settled only after years of conflict. As for the Board's relationship with other actors, the designers of the Federal Reserve System seem to have had ideas about power relationships that strike present-day observers as inconsistent, if not naive. In debates on the measure, several reformers argued that the Federal Reserve was an extension of democratic control over the banking system. Others hoped that the System would be independent of politics but bound by rules (see the following discussion) such as the principles of scientific management. Still others hoped that the Federal Reserve would behave in the detached nature of a "supreme court of finance."[24] "Congressmen," Timberlake observes, "seemed to want an objective, scientific, disinterested, nonpolitical organization." Indeed, he continues, with a note of derision, "the only eligible appointees would have been a group of vestal virgins."[25]

In part, this optimism flowed from a belief that organizational structure could solve problems of political power. The case of bank regulation posed a characteristically American dilemma, one that still figures in debates about the Federal Reserve: How shall private power be contolled without further augmenting public power? The solution chosen was the independence formula described in Chapter 1.[26] Reformers preferred a decentralized Federal Reserve System in order to reduce the threat of Wall Street domination and to avoid the threat of government domination. The "independent" governing board was intended to be a public coordinator of private regional banks but to remain separate from any larger system of public power. The System was conceived in the spirit of other Progressive reforms that stressed faith in expertise, faith in the effectiveness of tinkering with the machinery of government, and distrust of politicians.[27]

By stabilizing the currency, the Federal Reserve was intended to provide a kind of public good for the economy. It was clear that the private banking system was not capable of preventing emergencies, and efforts to do so on a local basis by New York bankers were of dubious legal status. Even clearinghouse associations had been attacked as illegal monopolies. But the Federal Reserve System was intended to do more than just provide an emergency currency. It was also to provide *all* currency according to the principles of sound banking. Clearly, this is a public function. It seems surprising, from our vantage point, that private governance of such an activity should have been advocated seriously in 1913.

Rules

The founders of the Federal Reserve System assumed that the gold system and the real bills doctrine provided objective and appropriate criteria for regulating the money supply.[28] According to the real bills doctrine, regional banks would discount only "self-liquidating" short-term commercial loans – that is, short-term loans to business for the purpose of creating products for sale (thus, "real bills"). This process was believed to be secure and self-limiting, since the reserve banks would create exactly the amount of money required for commerce and no more. The belief of the founders in these two rules must have been important in their willingness to provide considerable autonomy to the district reserve banks; such objective criteria for behavior would sharply reduce the opportunities for corruption or misbehavior.

The role of the System as a central bank with discretion expanded rapidly when the country de facto left the gold standard in World War I. Even though the gold standard was briefly reestablished in the 1920s, it never again played the constraining role that the System's designers had assumed. However, even had the gold standard been preserved, present-day analysis indicates that confusion in the then dominant banking theories (real bills doctrine) would eventually have forced a realization that the Federal Reserve already amounted to a central bank with discretion.[29] However, if the effective elimination of the gold standard confronted the System with the reality of its continuing discretion, there was still no clear statement from Congress as to the standards that should govern policy.

Resolving the question of the location of power over monetary policy

The Federal Reserve Act did not state clearly whether final authority for policy rested with the Federal Reserve Board in Washington or with the district banks. The lack of clear external policy guidance made this problem even more pressing. As the discretion exercised by the Federal Reserve became more obvious, so it became more important to resolve the issue of where internal authority was located. There was a period of conflict between the district banks and the board during which the district banks, especially the New York bank, initially dominated.[30] The dominance of the board, however, was fairly secure by the end of the 1930s.

In the early years of the System, the heads of the district banks, then called "governors," attempted to establish their own organization to determine policy independently of the board. The board succeeded in quashing the Governors' Conference in 1916, although it was reestablished in 1922 as a body for primarily technical consultations.[31] Some had viewed this as an attempt by commercial bankers to gain in practice what they had lost in Washington in 1913 – the right to effectively run their own central bank. Seen from that perspective, the board stood for public control.

The issue of the Federal Reserve Board's authority over the district banks surfaced again after World War I. The district banks were making open market purchases of Treasury assets in order to obtain interest-earning assets that would boost their sometimes nonexistent profits. In response to Treasury complaints that these uncoordinated market sales and purchases disrupted the government securities market, five eastern reserve banks formed a committee in 1922 to execute joint purchases and sales. The committee was headquartered in the Federal Reserve Bank of New York. Decisions on open market sales and purchases were obviously important policy issues, so the operation of this committee concerned the board. In the spring of 1923, in an effort to reassert board control, the board transformed this bank committee into a System committee of the same composition, known as the Open Market Investment Committee. However, this did not successfully resolve the question of whether the ultimate responnsibility for policy lay with the board or the banks.[32]

During the 1920s, the Board asserted it's right to review decisions of the Open Market Investment Committee and to disapprove them if it preferred. This controversial assertion of authority was resisted in open disputes in 1927 and 1929. In 1930, the board reorganized the System again, constituting an Open Market Policy Conference composed of the governors of all twelve district banks, to replace the Open Market Investment Committee. Banks remained free to withdraw from the conference or to choose not to abide by conference recommendations, but they were expected to explain any noncooperation to the Federal Reserve Board.[33]

The reforms of the 1930s

The reforms of the Banking Act of 1933 made the Federal Open Market Committee (FOMC) a statutory body – still composed of the twelve Federal Reserve Bank governors – and lengthened the term for appointments to the board to twelve years.[34] However, in many respects, the Banking Act of 1935 was more crucial. This act renamed the Federal Reserve Board the "Board of Governors of the Federal Reserve System" and designated the heads of district banks as "presidents." The appointments of district bank presidents and first vice-presidents were made subject to board approval. Simultaneously, the composition of the FOMC was transformed to include the seven board members and only five of twelve bank presidents, serving in rotation. Reserve banks could no longer engage in their own transactions without explicit permission of the FOMC. This substantially consolidated the internal domination of the System by the board.

The Banking Act of 1935 again lengthened the terms of appointment for governors – to fourteen years – and established the System's independence of the normal budget process. Proposals that the board be bipartisan were rejected, and interest representation was maintained; in this respect, the board is atypical, but not entirely alone among regulatory commissions.[35] The secretary of the Treasury and the comptroller of the currency were removed from the Board as ex officio members. An annual report to Congress was required. Also in 1935, Congrss rejected proposals for more specific language concerning the objectives of the Federal Reserve.[36] The Federal Reserve was left with considerable authority and little meaningful policy guidance.

It is of interest to note the political circumstances in which this transformation was effected. Roosevelt planned in late 1934 to propose to Congress a work relief program costing at least $4 billion. Marriner Eccles, his proposed appointee to fill the recently vacant post of board chairman, urged Roosevelt to press for reforms in the Federal Reserve, not only to clarify that control of monetary policy was in public rather than private hands but also to ensure that private interests did not have the power to prevent Roosevelt from financing his program. The reforms in the 1935 act elicited considerable opposition from bankers, and efforts were made to delay Eccles's confirmation in order to win compromises on the legislation. Eccles's nomination was eventually confirmed just prior to Senate consideration of the Banking Reform bill. Major protagonists in the Senate conflict included, in the opposition, familiar figures from 1913: Senator (formerly Rep.) Carter Glass and H. Parker Willis. Eccles has summarized the arguments of the opposition in terms that sound quite familiar to observers of debates in the 1970s and 1980s:

> The common thread in the testimony of all of them was somewhat like this: Title II [reforming the Federal Reserve]

> was not needed. The existing Federal Reserve System was working quite well – this despite the fact that it had failed to prevent the banking collapse of the thirties. Any powers the government needed to launch various policies within the System were already on hand. If there were any changes to be made in the System, the matter should be turned over for further study to a group of experts. There was no emergency that required quick action. Enactment of Title II would destroy the regional setup of the System. It would subject the whole System to political domination by the President of the United States.[37]

The combination of a strong Democratic Congress, Roosevelt's energetic support for reform, and careful political maneuvering by key participants resulted in a compromise generally to Eccles's liking. The administration had to be satisfied with a less governmental System than it would have liked. For example, the administration would have preferred to retain the secretary of the Treasury and the comptroller of the currency as ex officio members on the board. More important, in the administration version, the FOMC would have been composed entirely of board members, who would have been advised by five of the district bank presidents.[38]

Subsequent developments

Reforms in the 1930s consolidated the formal independence of the Federal Reserve. If the independence formula works, it should have increased the System's behavioral independence, too. However, the behavioral independence of the System did not noticeably increase. Instead, System policy was very passive. The Federal Reserve helped to stabilize the market for government securities – as the Treasury desired.[39] During World War II, the Federal Reserve's policy was governed by the requirements of war finance. This was not a controversial issue.[40]

After the war, indeed, several years after the actual conclusion of hostilities, a conflict emerged about monetary policy. Those on one side stressed the need to contain inflation, and they argued that this could be done only if the Federal Reserve was not committed to maintaining a stable, low yield (high price) for Treasury securities. On the other side were those who maintained that, in effect, there was a tacit commitment on the part of the Treasury not to let yields rise (prices fall), and that if prices fell, refunding of debt by the Treasury would become more difficult because investors would lose confidence in government debt. The conflict became more pressing with the onset of the Korean conflict in mid-1950. Government spending (and borrowing) was expected to grow rapidly, and given high levels of capacity utilization, this might be expected to produce inflation if the Federal Reserve persisted in following the agreed-upon policy of keeping interest rates low.

Conflict between the Federal Reserve's policy on interest rates and the Treasury's preference for interest rates became evident in the fall of 1950. In early 1951 this conflict broke into the open, and President Truman himself became directly involved in discussions to resolve it, including a meeting with the entire FOMC. Disagreements continued following those meetings, however, and the Federal Reserve attempted to reiterate its view that continued support for a particular pattern of interest rates was not desirable. There was some congressional support for the Federal Reserve position, particularly from Senator Paul Douglas.

President Truman then announced the formation of a committee to consider ways to resolve the problem; the committee was to include officials from outside the main two organizations, the Treasury and the Federal Reserve. Shortly therafter, perhaps spurred by a desire to avoid opening this issue to a larger audience, the Treasury and the Federal Reserve announced an "accord with respect to debt-management and monetary policies." Lengthy hearings were held in Congress the following year (1952) to determine the exact meaning of the accord. As Clifford explains, the hearings revealed only a consensus that there would be close consultation on matters of interest rates and that interest rate movements would be less restricted than in the past.[41]

The Federal Reserve moved cautiously to gain experience in the operation of the new market arrangements. In early 1953, the FOMC voted to adopt new procedures involving both a commitment to correct "disorderly markets" and a decision to restrict operations to short-term treasury bills. There is general agreement that clear exercise of Federal Reserve independence came only in 1953, after the election of a new administration sympathetic to the Federal Reserve's concerns about inflation. Even then, there was little evidence of vigorous use of Federal Reserve independence, and, indeed, the System seems to have decided to provide support for Treasury refunding operations without urging from the Treasury.[42]

Again, the accord left the System without clear operating

guidelines. Previously, its task had been to support the price of public debt. Now the Federal Reserve was again in the position of having to define for itself rules to govern operations. Friedman and Schwartz argue that policy came to be dominated by a concern for counteracting cyclical variations in money and credit, "leaning against the wind."[43]

The terms of the Employment Act of 1946 (maintaining full employment and price stability) were not directed to the Federal Reserve, although the System indicated in congressional hearings in 1952 that it could accept the act's goals "providing it is explicitly within the framework of a stable price level."[44] Finally in 1977, the Federal Reserve Act was amended to enjoin the System to "maintain long run growth of the monetary and credit aggregates commensurate with the economy's long run potential to increase production so as to promote effectively the goals of maximum employment, stable prices, and moderate long-term interest rates."[45] As overall guidance to the conduct of policy, the language of the legislation and the debate preceding it were not as clear-cut as this excerpt might suggest. This is discussed further in Chapter 7.

Lack of clear-cut policy guidance has not meant, of course, that Federal Reserve discretion has not been used. It has meant, on the contrary, that principles guiding policy have been derived from sources other than law – from the accepted principles of sound banking, from economics, from personal reflection.

Conclusion

Major innovations in our financial system have almost always followed crises. War led to greater control at the national level and produced sudden increases in the national debt, providing both the need and the opportunity for central bank management of the monetary system. Currency crises provoked debate over both banking and the nature of the currency. Until the end of the 1800s, such debate often incorporated radical challenges to the gold standard and, in effect, to the distribution of debt and wealth in the society.

The Federal Reserve was not conceived in pristine isolation as part of a scheme to create a great free and equal society. It initially emerged as a pragmatic response to a failure in a capitalist financial structure. The Federal Reserve System was the product of a political order that had repulsed the basic challenges to the underlying economic order. It became a prominent item on the agenda of reform only after more fundamental monetary reforms had been considered and rejected. Still, the Federal Reserve was a compromise. Forward-looking members of the banking establishment saw that some device had to be found to permit banks collectively to insulate themselves from any particular source of panic in the economic system. Progressive politicians sought a formula for preserving some degree of democracy against the growing concentration of economic power.

Although the Federal Reserve was conceived as a crucial element in stabilizing and shoring up the maturing capitalist order, some argue that it has become a source of inflation and weakness in the economic system that produced it. In short, even though fundamental questions of political economy are no longer at stake, it is argued that routine decisions could pose a threat to stability. Some argue that the source of the threat is within the Federal Reserve itself, in the mistaken theories and practices that guide its behavior. Others see the threat as emerging from the external political world. Still others believe that the Federal Reserve is no threat at all, but that it is performing its conservative duties in a remarkably thorough fashion. It is not possible to resolve decisively the debate about the Federal Reserve's contribution to instability. If that were possible, it would have happened long ago. It is possible to throw further light on the nature of contemporary relations between the Federal Reserve and the external political world. And it is to that task that we now turn.

3

Recruitment and Selection of Federal Reserve Personnel

In Chapter 1, I suggested that the relationships of the Federal Reserve and interested outsiders – would-be superiors – could be thought of in terms of issues and non-issues of monetary politics. Questions actively under debate are the issues. When policy creates important consequences that are not currently a central object of discussion or debate, these potentially controversial consequences are non-issues. There is, of course, a relationship between issues and non-issues. Structuring debate so as to keep issues on or off the agenda is probably the most important maneuver of all political conflict. This chapter is about processes of recruitment and selection to the top posts in the Federal Reserve, processes that can keep certain kinds of issues off of the agenda entirely.

For some, to call attention to these processes and to suggest that they have political consequences is to be gratuitously contentious. They find it difficult to imagine things working differently. However, one of the more interesting questions about monetary politics is the reason why conflict is usually restricted to a relatively narrow range of issues – usually technical issues. One can agree that the issues under debate have important implications by almost any standards and still be struck by the narrowness of the conflict and the terms of debate. The analysis in this chapter, viewed together with the history in Chapter 2, provides part of the answer to this question.

Students of politics have converged on the problem of recruitment and selection of officials from various theoretical positions, but usually, in the final analysis, for the same reason. The basic reason is the belief that who does the job may be just as important as the job description. One commonly expects that the values people bring to public sector posts reflect their social class background, their education, their previous employment, and their political party identification. There are large literatures on each of these areas and substantial disagreement on the findings. Some researchers find that class, employment, and ethnic identification prior to assuming public sector posts are relatively unimportant in accounting for behavior. Others argue that recruitment processes serve to underwrite systemic inequalities in profound ways. From this perspective, recruitment processes reinforce dominant values by guaranteeing that individuals holding dissident views are excluded from positions of authority no matter what their class or employment background. Still others are interested in the question because they suspect that partisan or interest group identifications facilitate the corruption of public policy for private or partisan ends rather than legitimate public ends.

In this chapter, I present data on the backgrounds and recruitment of members of the Board of Governors, presidents of district Federal Reserve Banks, and top monetary policy staff at the board. I will investigate the degree to which the Federal Reserve is linked to particular groups and parties via recruitment. I will argue that the process of selecting and evaluating candidates guarantees that appointees are responsible, moderate, and known to relevant technical groups. I will also point out that in terms of educational background, Federal Reserve personnel closely resemble top officials in both the public and private sectors. Finally, I will briefly explore the links between behavior and background.

Recruitment processes

In a purely formal sense, one becomes a member of the Federal Reserve Board by being appointed by the president and confirmed by the Senate. One becomes a district bank president by being nominated by the district bank board of directors and approved by the Board of Governors. Top monetary policy staff, like other top bureaucrats, are selected from among a number of candidates; usually, candidates are already employed in the Federal Reserve.

Widely accepted generalizations are made about the political nature of each of these selection processes. First, appointments to the Federal Reserve Board are important presidential appointments, and since tenure in office is quite long, it is generally believed that presidents exercise special care in selecting nominees whom they find ideologically compatible. Second, since the board, and especially the chairman, exercises a virtual veto over selection of district bank presidents, it is believed that district bank presidents are individuals who reflect the preferences of the board – or perhaps of the chairman. In the eyes of some Federal Reserve officials, the presidents are essentially employees of the board.[1] Third, almost all recruitment to top staff positions at the board is internal, which means that there are strong tendencies toward a substantially narrower outlook among top board staff than among the relevant external groups of technical experts. Here, I shall examine each of these generalizations, with the bulk of the analysis focused primarily on board members, who constitute a majority of the FOMC.

Choosing nominees for the board

What role do private sector elites play in the choice of board nominees? What kinds of characteristics make some potential nominees more attractive than others? Usually, it is impossible to offer much convincing evidence in response to such questions. Officials either conduct their most explicit discussions so that no permanent record is kept, or they make sure that the permanent record is shielded from public scrutiny for many years. The only public record is usually in journalistic accounts of uncertain reliability. Fortunately, much of the detailed documentary record of the Johnson administration is now public. That record, plus information gathered in interviews, provides many answers to the two questions just posed. Additionally, and fortunately, the record indicates that much of the journalistic account is accurate, if limited in detail.

The Johnson years are a particularly useful period to examine because it was a period in which reasonably liberal values influenced much of domestic policy – values one presumes to be unpopular in a central bank. Not since the Johnson years has there been a Democratic president with the political support and the congressional majorities that might be consistent with a policy course that ignored the preferences of financial and business elites. There are occasional hints that Johnson did just that in making certain decisions. However, to a striking degree, the Johnson appointees to the Federal Reserve, including the most liberal, met the test of private sector elite approval.

Bernstein wrote in the mid-1950s that "partisan political considerations unfortunately have dominated the appointment of commissioners" to independent regulatory commissions.[2] More recently, Heclo has argued that political patronage has played a decreasing role in the selection of officials for many top government positions.[3] Heclo observes that membership in relevant issue networks has become an increasingly important criterion for appointment. At an abstract level, technical criteria are in competition with purely partisan criteria; the dominance of technical criteria facilitates the exclusion of many controversial issues from broad debate. Because technical criteria have long been the dominant criteria for appointment to the Federal Reserve Board, one might expect that issue networks would also be particularly important for the Federal Reserve as well.

By all indications, in appointments to the Federal Reserve Board, partisan considerations have rarely been dominant. This has been a source of some pride to several former governors interviewed during this research. George Mitchell, a Kennedy appointee to the board, had close ties to Adlai Stevenson II and to Chicago Mayor Richard Daley that, he believes, probably made his appointment marginally more attractive to Kennedy.[4] William Sherrill had been touted to President Johnson based partly on his prior political support:

> He is your man – LBJ all the way – active in your campaign. Totally loyal without a doubt. . . . His is the new Johnson look – young, brilliant, articulate, but loyal to the hilt.[5]

But it does not appear that Sherrill's Federal Reserve appointment was primarily a political payoff. Prior to Andrew Brimmer's appointment, he had advertised himself to Walter Heller as a "100 percent Johnson man" who told "Kennedy men" that the achievements of the Johnson administration "are the direct product of the leadership and skill of President Johnson."[6] Partisan allegiance was clearly a very important factor in most Johnson administration appointments.[7] However, these two cases appear to be atypical among board appointees. And unlike the appointments to many commissions, there is little evidence of successful congressional influence on the presidential choice of board nominees.

Rather, candidates have been judged by their experience, technical expertise, and acceptability to particular constituencies. Three broad constituencies have been closely consulted about most Federal Reserve appointments, and the field of serious candidates excludes those that prominent mainstream bankers, businessmen, or economists find not to be acceptable.

Each administration has its own trusted, and reasonably distinguished, set of economists serving on the Council of Economic Advisors (CEA) and at the Treasury. In many cases, it is clear that Federal Reserve appointees have been known personally to key administration economists or to private economists close to the administration prior to appointment.[8] These economists provide a means of gaining quick and confidential access to other economists and to the financial sector for obtaining evaluations of candidates.

Established officials from business and finance are asked to vouch for the ability, reliability, and good judgment of a serious candidate. In no respect should the candidate be perceived as extreme. In 1965, economist Seymour Harris, who had been promised an appointment to the Federal Reserve Board by John Kennedy, was not appointed by Johnson when a position became available. Among the many factors considered in Johnson's decision was the information relayed to him from Commerce Secretary John T. Connor (through presidential aide Jack Valenti) that the unanimous reaction of the business community to a Harris appointment was that it would be "a disaster."[9]

Recruitment processes vary with the administration, but the mechanisms of consultation and investigation change relatively little. Much of the consultation is by telephone. Sometimes, reliable messengers circulate lists of potential nominees to key groups for their advice. The FBI investigates in detail the backgrounds of a few serious candidates. Within the administration, a group or individual usually identifies potential appointees well in advance of the date of appointment. In the second Nixon administration and the Ford administration, the recruitment process came to be concentrated substantially in Arthur Burns's hands at the Federal Reserve Board. During the Carter administration, Vice-President Mondale directed administration efforts to identify candidates for the Federal Reserve.

In the Johnson administration, board candidates of all backgrounds were expected to pass muster with representatives from the financial community. Andrew Brimmer, a black, was an economist in the Commerce Department and had a background in academia. He recalls learning first that he was a potential candidate from a banker friend who had been asked to review the acceptability of a list of potential candidates. Brimmer also received confirmation from economists he knew.[10] Virtually every other candidate could have heard it from a banker friend, too. Sherman Maisel, an academic and something of a liberal, had many financial sector contacts, too. Immediately prior to his Federal Reserve appointment, Maisel had come to the attention of Johnson administration recruiters as an unsuccessful candidate for a position at the Federal Home Loan Bank Board. At that time, he was able to generate supporting letters within a matter of hours from six savings and loan association officials, from the president of TransAmerica (one of the largest nonbank financial corporations in the world), and from a former partner in Bache and Company, a Wall Street investment firm.[11]

Johnson administration documents show considerable concern about how appointments might affect the confidence of the financial community. In making the decision to appoint Andrew Brimmer, the president probably came as close as any president has to selecting someone clearly less preferred by financiers than another candidate. Board Chairman William McChesney Martin argued that Brimmer lacked "stature" and was not yet "universally recognized as indisputably qualified." Appointing yet a fourth economist (following Mitchell, Maisel, and Dewey Daane, who was appointed in November 1963), Martin argued, would not preserve the balance of interests specified in the law, and this "would damage confidence and gravely impair the ability of the Federal Reserve to carry out functions of vital importance to the economy and the government alike."[12]

Martin supported the appointment of another candidate, Atherton Bean, a respected Minneapolis businessman and former chairman of the Federal Reserve Bank of Minneapolis. Martin told the White House that Bean's appointment "would assure continued confidence in [the Federal Reserve's] work both at home and abroad."[13] Walter Heller also advised President Johnson that Bean's appointment would probably produce "a little more willing cooperation from the business and banking community on your financial guidelines and price guidelines." Heller also relayed warnings from highly placed members of the financial community that they objected to Brimmer's appointment and that such an act might provoke Martin's resignation.[14]

Ultimately, of course, Brimmer was appointed – after Johnson had received word that Martin would neither resign nor publicly fight the appointment, and after Martin had informed Brimmer that he would be treated as a "junior" appointee.[15] It is clear that Johnson wanted to make a symbolic gesture by appointing a black person to this important post.[16] At the same time, there is little doubt that Johnson welcomed the opportunity to punish Martin for the board's decision a few weeks earlier to raise the discount rate over White House objections.[17]

William Sherrill's appointment was justified, among other reasons, on the basis of his "current stature in bank supervision and his ability to communicate effectively with representatives of the regulated industry."[18] Subsequently, Sherrill's appointment was widely applauded by bankers.[19] One candidate competing with Sherrill for Federal Reserve Board membership was judged to be unacceptable despite the fact that he made a favorable impression on CEA member Arthur Okun, seemed to understand current problems and offered imaginative solutions, communicated well with economists, and supported the administration's views. The reasons for excluding this candidate were that he was not known to members of the financial community and that those who did know him regarded him as rigid and uncompromising in his views.[20]

No one is seriously considered for the Federal Reserve whose views are very far from center, which obviously excludes anyone who harbors doubts about the basic structures of the economic system.[21] Within these bounds there is room for some disagreement on issues of monetary politics, but many monetarists who are perceived to be "rigid" or "impractical" may be ruled out. Candidates must have the support, or at least the respect, of some constituency, and they must not be vigorously opposed by any of the major groups. They must be known quantities. They must not be thought to be erratic, whimsical, radical, or unwilling to compromise. Preferably, they should have demonstrated success in business, finance, or economics.

The president scarcely has a free hand in making Federal Reserve appointments. Financial and business elites as well as economists are clearly important in defining acceptable candidates. The decision is not precisely dictated by these groups, although there seem to be no cases in which their objections – in contrast to their preferences – have been ignored. Thus, Andrew Brimmer was regarded as acceptable but lacking in experience, and as less preferable than another candidate. It is also traditional to assure that appointees do not gravely offend Senators in whose state they reside.[22] But beyond avoiding giving offense, presidents are constrained in Federal Reserve appointments by the need to try to make affirmative gestures that will reassure business and finance.

This is particularly critical for the appointment of the chairman. For example, in the Kennedy administration: "Kennedy was still thinking [in late 1961] of replacing Martin, but as the date for reappointment or new appointment came up, Martin's standing in the domestic and international financial community kept rising . . . and by the time the date arrived, Kennedy had decided to reappoint Martin."[23] The impact on banking and business confidence of William McChesney Martin's reappointment as chairman was carefully considered again in 1967 by the Johnson administration.[24] At the time of that announcement, "the banking community reacted with a figurative sigh of relief."[25]

Carter's appointment of G. William Miller was preceded by lengthy discussions in the financial press of Arthur Burns's value as a source of "confidence."[26] In 1979, *Business Week* trumpeted that Carter's choice of Paul Volcker as chairman was forced by the state of foreign exchange markets: "Shattered confidence in the Carter Administration left the President no choice but to select a man who would be instantly hailed as the savior of the dollar, *even though that meant bringing in a Fed chairman far more conservative than Carter would have preferred*."[27]

In the evidence from Johnson administration appointments, one can see that private sector officials in high business and financial positions do exercise general control over the process of selecting Federal Reserve officials. This is surely a critical step in assuring that unacceptable issues are kept off the agenda. If elites exercise a veto over appointments, they should be able to guarantee that their values prevail. Still, there remain two other questions worth examining: Does the recruitment process produce officials who themselves have elite characteristics? Do observable background differences have any significant link to behavior?

Occupational backgrounds of successful candidates

Consider first the question of the background characteristics of successful candidates. I have classified officials in terms of their occupation during the longest period of their career and their occupation immediately prior to their Federal Reserve appointment. I distinguish five kinds of backgrounds: First, I classify as "private financial" all officials with prior employment in commercial banking, mortgage banking, savings and loan associations, or the stock exchanges.[28] "Public financial" includes all public sector employment in financially related posts at all levels of government including, for example, the Treasury, the Federal Deposit Insurance Corporation (FDIC), the Export-Import Bank, the International Monetary Fund (IMF), and state and local budgetary and financial positions. A third category is the Federal Reserve, excluded from the "public financial" category where it might otherwise belong.

Table 3.1. *Previous occupational histories: members of the Board of Governors, 1955–82 (N=31)*

	Longest job (%)	Immediately prior job (%)
Public financial	15	36
Federal Reserve	21	16
Academic	26	16
Private finance	26	16
Other private	13	16
Total	101	100

Sources: Federal Reserve Bulletin, Who's Who in America.

The "academic" category includes academic teaching and research pointments, administrative positions such as deanships, and appointments in quasi-academic research organizations such as the National Bureau of Economic Research and the Brookings Institution. Finally, "other private" includes business, accounting, law, and any other category of private for-profit employment. No other categories were required.

Board of Governors

Table 3.1 summarizes the information on all members of the Federal Reserve Board between 1955 and 1982. The first column shows membership distribution according to the category of longest employment, and the second column shows the membership distribution according to the category of employment immediately prior to appointment. Neither of these, of course, provides a direct measure of social class background in the classic sense of *parents'* social class background. However, the data in the first column give some interesting suggestions about the most significant factors in an individual's career.

In the period 1955–82, 26 percent of board members had spent their prior career in private finance as defined here – close to the percentage one would find if there were always two financial representatives on the board (i.e., $2/7$ = 0.29). In the period 1965–75, however, there was at most one member with a primarily banking background on the board. The "other private" category accounts for another 13 percent of board members. In other words, some 39 percent of board members have had backgrounds primarily in the private for-profit sector. Business and financial elites may define the parameters of acceptability for appointment, but this does not result in a board that is dominated by members primarily with financial and business backgrounds. Nor should we expect that it would be for two reasons. First, expertise in private business and finance may not be as valuable as other kinds of expertise when it comes to the macroeconomic function. Second, pay for board members is very modest – much less than most talented candidates could expect to earn in the private sector. In fact, even one former academic has estimated that he suffered a two-thirds cut in income when he joined the board.[29] Still, it is striking to observe that 45 percent of all board members appear to have *never* held primary, full-time employment in the private for-profit sector since completing their formal educations (data not reported in Table 3.1).

In comparison to appointees to other regulatory commissions, board members are only infrequently recruited directly from the related industry.[30] Another striking contrast between top Federal Reserve personnel and those at other regulatory commissions is in the relatively minor role of lawyers at the Federal Reserve. Forty-five percent of governors have been economists – that is, they received an academic degree in economics and were at some time employed in a job with "economist" in the job title. By contrast, lawyers dominate most regulatory commissions; "economists, engineers, political scientists, and members of other professions are few and far between."[31] In contrast to incumbents in top posts in other agencies (including the Treasury), the Federal Reserve Board has had twice as many holders of doctoral degrees.[32] This kind of distribution is exactly what one would expect to find in an agency that relies heavily on expertise in the conduct of policy and as a source of legitimacy.

Twenty-one percent of board members spent the longest period of their career in the Federal Reserve System itself. For nearly 40 percent, the Federal Reserve System provided their first job. Including board members who had previously been members of district bank boards of directors, fully 60 percent of board members have had some official association with the Federal Reserve prior to their appointment. This is not to say that the Federal Reserve is a self-perpetuating system – although some critics are worried about this. Rather, this finding supports Heclo's idea that being a participant in, and known to, relevant expert networks is a controlling condition for appointment. Indeed, if we look at the remaining members who had no previous direct links to the Federal Reserve, we find that every one either had a significant period

Table 3.2. *Educational backgrounds of Federal Reserve officials compared to other elites*

Category	Elite universities (%)[a]	Prestigious institutions (%)[b]
All federal executives	27	42
Board of Governors	43	55
District bank presidents	19	36
Industry elites	—	55
Financial elites	—	50

[a]Harvard, Yale, Princeton, or Stanford.
[b]See note 35.

of employment in responsible private financial positions (seven in all) or held responsible public sector financial positions (five more).[33] In order to gain elite approval, candidates must be responsible members of appropriate networks that are defined largely in terms of financial experience and knowledge.

A common index of elite status is education, particularly in highly selective, prestigious institutions. A study of all U.S. federal executives appointed between 1933 and 1964 found that 27 percent of those who had done graduate work had studied at one of four elite universities – Harvard, Princeton, Yale, and Stanford.[34] By comparison, during the period studied here, 43 percent of the members of the board with graduate degrees received their degrees from one of those institutions (see Table 3.2). A more recent study found that about 42 percent of top government officials have been educated at "prestigious" institutions – a somewhat lower percentage than elites in the private sector.[35] By contrast, 55 percent of Federal Reserve Board members attended one of these prestigious institutions, a figure identical to the rate for leading corporate executives.

District bank presidents

No details are publicly known of the deliberations that precede selection of district bank presidents. Reports from the Burns era seem to suggest that occasionally, when Burns felt very strongly, he made sure that particular individuals were not appointed as presidents. However, in that period and in other periods before and after, it seems clear that district bank boards of directors have

Table 3.3. *Major prior employment of district bank presidents serving 1955–82 (N = 44)*

Occupation	Longest job (%)	Immediately prior job (%)
Public financial	5	9
Federal Reserve System	55	61
Academic	7	2
Private finance	25	16
Other private	9	11
Total	101	100

Sources: Who's Who in America; American Men and Women of Science, Economics.

often played a substantial role in selecting presidents. In at least one case, the Federal Reserve Board chairman went to some lengths to let people know he was keeping "hands off."[36] Both circumstantial and documentary evidence suggests that district bank presidents have often been able to guide the selection of their successors. Since in many Federal Reserve Banks the directors nominate the senior vice-president to succeed the president, the president has an obvious means of influencing the succession through his selection of a vice president.[37] This pattern occurs less frequently at some of the larger district banks, which pay higher salaries and recruit primarily from the local financial and business communities – for example, New York, Boston, and Chicago.[38]

Whether the board of directors or the Board of Governors determines the selection, it is clear that elite criteria dominate the process, as in the selection of board members. Two-thirds of the district bank boards of directors are drawn (by law) from the district banking community and from district commerce (usually major businesses). The board, which is itself elite approved, supervises the balance of appointments.

Data on the backgrounds of officials prior to their appointment as district bank president reveal a different pattern from that of members of the Board of Governors. In particular, a much higher proportion are drawn from within the Federal Reserve itself. (See Table 3.3) For 55 percent of presidents, the longest prior employment was in the System, compared to only 21 percent for governors. Eighty percent of the district bank presidents had some official association with the Federal Reserve prior to their appointment, as opposed to only 60 percent of board members.

Like the members of the Board of Governors, each of the remaining presidents held a responsible position in private or public sector financial networks prior to appointment, with one exception – the dean of a major business school.[39] Interestingly, 36 percent of presidents during this period have had careers primarily in the private for-profit sector – a percentage almost identical with that of the Board of Governors. Frequency of employment in private finance has also been essentially the same among presidents and governors. Only 34 percent of the presidents had *no* prior full-time employment in the private for-profit sector (versus 45 percent of the board).

In terms of educational background, the presidents resemble national elite groups less than do members of the board, as one might expect given the regional emphasis in these appointments. Only 19 percent have advanced degrees from Harvard, Yale, Princeton, or Stanford (see Table 3.2), and only 36 percent attended prestigious universities. In short, district Federal Reserve Bank presidents possess elite characteristics somewhat less frequently than do board members, but there is no indication that they are any less acceptable to members of a national elite.

Board staff

Almost all staff members involved with monetary policy are professional economists. The staff constitutes one of the major links between the Federal Reserve and the economics profession. There is continuous input by academic economists into the Federal Reserve via the staff, and the staff helps to shape the technical character of FOMC discussions. Since academic economists are an important source of critical commentary about the Federal Reserve, it is important for System prestige that the staff be regarded with respect by academic economists in general.

During the 1960s, the Federal Reserve staff tried deliberately to eliminate the idea that had developed in the 1940s and 1950s that the System did not value academic economic research. They tried to recruit new staff from top academic programs and used System budgetary flexibility to offer salaries and working conditions that were very attractive by most academic and government standards.[40] To some degree, the effort seems to have been successful. Among the very highest staffers in the System during the years 1969–81, about half (53 percent) had received their Ph.D. from universities with economics graduate programs ranked in the top ten or eleven.[41] This is, however, a notably lower percentage than holds for all economists active in American Economic Association meetings from 1959 to 1969. Among that group, 70 percent held Ph.D.s from the top ten economics departments.[42] At the same time, Tobin has remarked on the fact that the "professional stature" of the board staff increased substantially during the period 1961–71.[43]

Background and behavior

What consequences, if any, do the differences observed in occupational background have for policy behavior? Given the restrictions elites impose on recruitment, there is little reason to believe that occupational differences would have any important consequences. Rather, one would expect very similar policy preferences to be the result. And there is some evidence suggesting that this is true. For example, in FOMC votes on the monetary policy directive in a seventeen-year period, only 34 percent of votes involved any dissent at all, and of these split decisions, 60 percent involved only a single dissenting vote. That is, 86 percent of the time, FOMC decisions were unanimous or all but unanimous. Although it is true that formal FOMC votes may overstate the degree of agreement, it is hard to avoid the conclusion that FOMC consensus is extremely high and is largely the consequence of recruitment processes.[44]

However, in the only prior work to address this question with respect to the Federal Reserve, Canterbery argued that backgrounds do make a difference.[45] He hypothesized that members with backgrounds in law or banking should be less likely than economists to dissent in favor of easier policy in voting on the "domestic policy directive" in the FOMC. Canterbery argued that bankers and lawyers are more likely to favor higher interest rates and a lower price level no matter what the position of the business cycle, but this would be true especially when economic uncertainty is high. On the other hand, economists would be more likely to take positions that vary with the business cycle but would tend toward an "easier" policy when uncertainty is high. On average, then, one should observe economists casting dissenting votes in favor of easier policies much more frequently than do lawyers or bankers.

Because formal voting on domestic monetary policy decisions

Table 3.4. *Proportion of all FOMC dissents favoring easier policy, 1965–81*

Background of dissenter	Dissents favoring ease (%)	*N*
Public financial	89	9
Federal Reserve	32	59
Academic	25	40
Private financial	25	44
Other private	57	7
All private	29	51
Public + Federal Reserve System + academic	34	108
Total	24	159

in the FOMC is usually highly consensual, only a relatively small number of dissenting votes are available to examine in total; some members never dissent. However, following Canterbery, I have examined each dissenting vote cast in the period 1965–81 and classified it as to whether the dissenter favored a more restrictive or less restrictive policy. We can derive a quick and only slightly inaccurate test of the Canterbery hypothesis by examining the relationship between dissents and the occupational categories previously defined. Most FOMC members with formal training in economics and with employment as economists fall in the background categories public financial, Federal Reserve, or academic. Similarly, most members with backgrounds in banking and law fall in the categories private financial and other private. Any differences should emerge in the differences between these categories of members. What we see in Table 3.4 is that the direction of dissent appears to be unrelated to occupational category in the hypothesized direction, and the results do not suggest an obvious counter-hypothesis.

Although Canterbery's hypothesis appears not to hold, there are at least three others of interest. First, if presidents select board members whose views reflect the president's ideology, then there might be a relationship between the party of the president appointing the dissenter and the direction of dissent. So, one would expect that appointees of Democratic presidents would tend to dissent more frequently in favor of easier policy than would Re-

Table 3.5. *Party of appointment and dissenting votes, members of the Board of Governors, 1965–81*

Number of dissents favoring	Dissenter appointed by: Democrats	Dissenter appointed by: Republicans
Firmer policy	4	24
Easier policy	25	18

Notes: Chi square = 11.7 (with continuity correction; significant at less than the 0.01 level).
D.f. = 1.
Q = gamma = −0.79.
N = 71

publican appointees. This hypothesis has the virtue of appearing to apply generally in an analogous case to Supreme Court appointees.

Second, since bank presidents are in some sense subordinates of the board, there should be a similar pattern of dissent between board members and bank presidents. If board members' views dominate at the bank level, then the relative division between dissenters favoring more or less restrictive policy should be the same for board members and bank presidents.

There is a competing expectation here. Bank presidents work in a very different milieu than board members, one that is much more completely dominated by business and financial concerns on a day-to-day basis. Therefore, to the degree that the board's milieu is more liberal than that at the district banks, one would expect to see board members dissent more frequently in favor of less restrictive policy than would bank presidents.

There appears to be support for the first and third hypotheses. First, for board members, dissents favoring less restrictive policy are much more likely to be made by Democratic than Republican appointees. (See Table 3.5.) There is no controlling background variable at an individual level that can account for this difference. At the same time, data in Table 3.6 show that fully 90 percent of dissents by district bank presidents are in favor of a more restrictive policy. Again, no controlling background variable can account for this difference. In short, among district bank presidents

Table 3.6. *Direction of dissenting votes by district bank presidents and members of the Board of Governors, 1965–81*

Number of dissents favoring	Dissenters who are: Board members	Presidents
Firmer policy	28	79
Easier policy	43	9

Notes: chi square = 45.3 (significant at less than the 0.01 level). D.f. = 1
Q = gamma = −0.86.
N = 159.

who dissent, there is virtually no variation in terms of direction; they overwhelmingly favor a more restrictive policy. These findings suggest that despite an elite-dominated recruitment process, both the context of current employment and the party of appointment influence voting on issues in monetary politics, even if only in a modest way. This finding is, of course, consistent with my earlier observation that there remains room for disagreement within the bounds of elite consensus. Substantively, it means that there is a liberal–conservative division in monetary politics even if the differences are not great.

Movement out of the System

Do Federal Reserve officials frequently move out of the System and into positions in the private financial sector? Many reformers fear that this possibility will tempt officials to shape their decisions while in office so as to position themselves for more lucrative post-official employment. Also, knowledge and friendships gained while in public office may be turned to profitable advantage in the private sector. At least one study has claimed that movement *out* of the System into banking provides the basis for a close link between private finance and the New York Federal Reserve Bank.[46] A statement by a former governor confirms that this is an important phenomenon:

> I have interviewed the money market dealers and banks. They have very large staffs made up in part of former Federal Reserve people. They are paid to figure out what the Fed is up to and they are very good at it. They are usually right on the money in perceiving our actions and intentions.[47]

The Federal Reserve Act prohibits members of the board from being employed at member banks for a period of two years after leaving office, except if they served the full term for which they were appointed.[48] This, of course, permits them to take other kinds of positions in the financial community. In any case, there is little evidence of movement from the Board into the financial sector. Of twenty-two former governors during the period 1955–82, only two eventually held full-time employment in the financial sector, although others have served on the governing boards of financial organizations.[49] Others have been financial consultants. Other members took positions in private industry, law, universities, policy research, or interest groups.[50] Compared to other industry regulators, Federal Reserve Board members are among those least likely to be employed subsequently by the industry they regulate.[51]

District bank presidents and staff are generally less well known, and consequently more difficult to trace after they leave the System. Somewhere between 20 and 40 percent eventually hold a full-time job in the financial sector. This seems to be less common for district bank presidents but increasingly common for staff – particularly staff of district banks.[52] There are many examples of prominent private financial officials who have had at least some experience in the Federal Reserve System; Table 3.7 notes a few of them. This list is purely illustrative and is composed entirely of names of persons cited as experts in articles in *Business Week* or the *Wall Street Journal*. Anyone who attempts a similar task would quickly note that many oft-quoted financial experts have no previous links to the Federal Reserve. Some individuals listed in Table 3.7 did not hold highly responsible positions in the Federal Reserve, and there are suggestions that some staffers left because of policy differences with their superiors. Nonetheless, this is a reasonably impressive list of financial analysts, and it is striking that they are all Federal Reserve alumni. It seems to be generally acknowledged that former Federal Reserve staffers are attractive to the financial industry because it is hoped that they know something about Federal Reserve policy processes.

One interesting example from Table 3.7 is Guy Noyes, a senior

Table 3.7. *Examples of former Federal Reserve staff subsequently in prominent financial sector posts*

Name	Affiliation[a]
Richard A. Debs	President, Morgan Stanley International (FRB, New York, 1960–76)
Tilford C. Gaines	V.P., Manufacturer's Hanover Trust (FRB, New York)
William N. Griggs	Senior V.P., J. Henry Schroder Bank and Trust Co. (FRB, Dallas)
David M. Jones	Economist, Aubrey Lanston (FRB, New York, 1963–8)
Jerry L. Jordan	Senior V.P., Pittsburgh National Bank (1976–81) (FRB, St. Louis, 1967–75)
Helen Junz	V.P., Townsend-Greenspan & Co. (Board staff, 1962–77)
Henry Kaufman	Partner, Salomon Brothers (FRB, New York, 1957–61)
Lawrence A. Kudlow	Economist, Bear Stearns & Co. (1979–1981) (FRB, New York, 1973–5)
Guy Noyes	Senior V.P., Morgan Guaranty (Board staff, 1948–65)
John D. Paulus	Chief economist, Morgan, Stanley Co. (Board staff, 1972–8)
Robert Roosa	Partner, Brown Brothers Harriman & Co. (FRB, New York, 1946–60)
Robert W. Stone	Senior V.P., Irving Trust (FRB, New York, 1963–5)
Thomas D. Thomson	Senior V.P., Crockett National Bank (Board staff, 1965–75)
Richard Youngdahl	President, Aubrey Lanston (Board staff, 1943–54)

[a]Information includes positions held during 1979–82.

vice-president of Morgan Guaranty (the country's fifth largest bank). He was a Federal Reserve economist for seventeen years, last as director of the Division of Research and Statistics. A prominent case not included in Table 3.7 is that of Charls Walker, currently head of Charls Walker and Associates, one of Washington's major lobbying operations. Walker was an economist at Federal Reserve district banks for nine years before joining (in turn) the Treasury, the American Bankers Association, and the Treasury (again).

Conclusion

As of the early 1980s, no appointees to top positions in the Federal Reserve were drawn from labor, although among the 130-plus directors of district banks and their branches, a handful were union officials. Two blacks had been appointed to the Board of Governors. In 1978 a woman was appointed to the board, and in 1981 another was made president of a district bank. In short, with a few recent departures, the Federal Reserve continues a long history of administration by white, male, upper-middle-class technicians. In this chapter, data have been examined supporting the following conclusions:

Federal Reserve officials usually hold responsible positions prior to their appointment. They are usually not among the top private sector elites, but they are commonly members of established networks dealing with financial matters. Their appointments are approved by other members of those networks.

Some elite characteristics, especially education at prestigious institutions, are observed among Federal Reserve officials more frequently than among other top officials in the public sector, and at rates comparable to those of top private sector officials.

With the exception of some staff members, there is little evidence that former Federal Reserve officials usually achieve high positions in private finance after resignation or retirement, although officials who do not retire usually assume other elite posts not in finance.

There is no predicted relationship between previous employment and education and the voting behavior of Federal Reserve officials on decisions concerning domestic monetary policy.

There is a modest relationship between the appointing political party and the voting behavior of board members.

The voting behavior of district bank presidents is consistently conservative, and this appears to be related to the fact that, compared to board members, presidents have closer continuing links to private finance and business.

The constraints of elite approval for appointees would appear to present no obvious problem for Republican presidents. Within these bounds, Democratic presidents have usually been able to find candidates reflecting their general philosophy. Elite consensus is not monolithic. But the differences would not be regarded as significant by someone who believes, as do many radicals, that party differences make little policy difference. Interestingly, only with regard to partisan difference can one see systematic differences in behavior between board members.

4

Bankers and the Federal Reserve

Common sense indicates to many that bankers probably rank quite high among would-be superiors of the Federal Reserve. They control money, organization, information, and expertise. This view is reinforced by several analysts who have suggested that bankers are indeed a very important reference group for the Federal Reserve. This perspective is held by analysts from different ends of the ideological spectrum, who see two kinds of problems that result. The first problem, one that interests principally liberal analysts, is that the System's relationship with bankers may restrict and bias the policy process further in the direction of elite values. Thus, with respect to goals for general policy targets such as inflation and employment, this relationship might reduce further the likelihood that the Federal Reserve would regard employment as the most important objective.

The second set of problems, which have been of more concern for relatively conservative analysts, has to do with the ability of bankers to shape policy at a technical level. In this case, analysts fear that bankers' short-term policy preferences make it less likely that policy makers will achieve control over the money supply – which is viewed as essential to effective anti-inflation policy. Not surprisingly, the conservatives have exactly the opposite fear of the liberals. The conservatives fear that bankers' influence will produce more inflation, not more unemployment. The liberals' concern is primarily in the realm of non-issues in monetary politics. The conservatives' concern is squarely in the middle of a debate that has been lively, if not of great interest to most Americans.

The question of capture

Both of these concerns can be thought of as raising again the old issue of regulatory capture. Capture of regulatory agencies by their regulated constituents is a familiar, if not entirely accurate, staple of the scholarly literature.[1] The Federal Reserve was originally intended to be closely linked to banks. Under the independence formula, however, the System was not supposed to become the banks' captive, and periodic reforms have been intended to confirm the System's independence of both private finance and partisan politics. Still, contemporary liberal critics have regularly assailed the System's closeness to bankers.[2]

Bankers, as we have seen, initially *were* the Federal Reserve at the district level. They have long been guaranteed a formal voice in national-level decision making through the Federal Advisory Council and through the requirement of financial representation on the Board of Governors. In fact, bankers were being guaranteed access to the Federal Reserve at a time when the legality of labor unions and union strike activities was not yet firmly established.[3] Perhaps the privileged access granted to bankers at that time may have persisted in a period when it would be appropriate to have a truly neutral site for the conduct of monetary policy.

Prior to 1980, the System's most obvious direct constituency was *member commerical* bankers. As of December 1978 there were 5,564 member banks, representing 38 percent of all commercial banks. However, they were disproportionately the big banks; member banks controlled about 70 percent of all bank deposits. The Depository Institutions Deregulation and Monetary Control Act (DIDMCA) of 1980 subjected all depository institutions to the Federal Reserve's reserve requirements. Although member banks are still distinguished from nonmember banks and retain minor privileges, the effect of the DIDMCA may have been to so enlarge the population of regulatees that capture is no longer a viable possibility.[4] An alternative view, and one that is quite plausible, is that the combined effects of a long legacy of links to large commercial banks plus continued special regulatory responsibility for those same banks provide adequate grounds for suspecting capture.

Another qualification of the capture theory is that since 1970 the financial industry can no longer be discussed adequately without making many kinds of distinctions. For example, there are vast differences within the banking community between the giant multinational banks with billions of dollars in assets and deposits and the thousands of relatively small banks with assets and deposits of less than 100 million dollars. More important is the emergence of new competitors to banks – money market mutual funds, securities dealers who operate in many respects like banks (e.g., Shearson-

American Express, Merrill Lynch), and even department store chains that seem to be on the verge of selling notes that are for most purposes indistinguishable from time deposits in banks (e.g., Sears).[5]

Given these innovations in policy and in the financial industry, many may find it dubious to propose that banks control the Federal Reserve. Nonetheless, it is clear that banks and the Federal Reserve have had a special relationship. One prominent contemporary analyst suggests that bankers influence the Federal Reserve more than any other industry group.[6] Given the long history of concern, let us look more closely at this relationship and how it has developed in recent years.

Bankers' interests

What do bankers want that the Federal Reserve could produce? And how important is aggregate monetary policy to those objectives? It is quite clear that monetary policy can mean a great deal to any institution involved in financial matters. It is also clear that regulatory and tax decisions can be equally important.

Studies are ambiguous about the relationship between the interests – that is, profits – of specific categories of financial institutions and types of monetary policy action. This is not entirely surprising, given the complexity of such a problem. It seems reasonably clear that the banking industry is a countercyclical industry, which poses for bankers a political problem of some importance. High interest rates resulting from a tight monetary policy can produce substantial bank profits at a time when the rest of the economy is in, or entering, a recession. On the other hand, one study has shown that commercial banks benefit from expansionary policy, suggesting that good business is good business for banks, too.[7] Among the factors presumably being held equal in the study is inflation, which, of course, could result from expansionary policy and could harm bank profits.

The generally accepted theoretical analysis is that banks are highly averse to unexpected inflation. In general, "net monetary debtors" – that is, firms and individuals with monetary liabilities exceeding monetary assets – are expected to gain during periods of unanticipated inflation.[8] Banks, typically net *creditors*, are expected to lose from inflation, and thus systematically to oppose it. Judging from bankers' rhetoric, this expectation is amply confirmed in practice.

This would seem to suggest a very general opposition to anything resembling easy money policies, and might be advanced as an explanation for the Federal Reserve's willingness to boost interest rates in recent years. On the other hand, high interest rates have also been the lifeblood of a new major competitor to the banks – money market mutual funds. Surely banks have not welcomed this development.

Other research suggests that banks and other major participants in securities markets put primary value on market stability and policy predictability.[9] Thus, bankers may care relatively little about the ease or tightness of monetary policy so long as they are not caught by surprise by sudden shifts in policy. This opinion has been conveyed directly to the board by Federal Advisory Council members. Wall Street's cries of protest when policy does seem unpredictable have been well documented in the financial press.[10] These concerns have been heightened in recent years because changes in banking practices have increased the vulnerability of bankers to rapid interest rate movements. Banks have begun to practice "liability management," which means aggressively making loans and then funding the loans with money borrowed ("bought") in short-term (or relatively short-term) money markets. As a result, many banks have become more vulnerable to vigorous anti-inflationary monetary policy than they are to inflation itself, because sharp upward movements in interest rates force banks to buy money at rates higher than they have loaned it.[11] Vulnerability of this sort seems, in fact, to be highest for the big multinational banks some observers suspect of being the Federal Reserve's closest friends.[12] Thus, perhaps the Federal Reserve did not respond more forcefully to the inflation of the 1970s out of a desire to protect the large banks.

Here enter some of the issues previously mentioned. The bankers' concern for stability and policy predictability lead them to support two kinds of policies that are roundly criticized by prominent monetarist economists.[13] One is the interest rate targeting approach to monetary management, and the second is "lagged reserve accounting." Some critics have suggested that the primary reason for these devices is that they reduce the risks bankers face in credit markets. Interest rate targeting appeals to the desire of bankers – and many others as well – for predictability in financial relationships. Interest rate targeting can, of course, be justified in terms of the standard Keynesian analysis as the method for achieving a demand for money consistent with a given (target) level of national income. As critics are quick to point out, this approach works only if the Federal Reserve moves interest rates fast enough and far enough as the economy moves. This, the critics note, has not been the case on several occasions. Why not? Partly, they say, because of the Federal Reserve's concern for providing the stability financial markets want.

Another explanation for interest rate targeting is that it is something the Federal Reserve has been doing in one way or another since before the accord. It is a well-established bureaucratic routine, by now part of a conventional way of operating. In the early 1950s, it was argued that restricting open market operations to very short-term interest rates was a way of avoiding the inflationary dangers associated with trying to stabilize long-term markets. Stabilizing long-term rates had been the reason for the conflict with the Treasury in the early 1950s. However, critics still suspect that the acceptance of the economic theory and the bureaucratic routines have been reinforced, and in many ways shaped, by the desires of the Federal Reserve's banker constituency.

The second practice monetarists have criticized, lagged reserve accounting, was instituted in 1968. After 1968, banks did not have to have reserves on hand as of the accounting date, but rather could wait for two weeks to accumulate them. That is, the banks had to meet the official reserve requirement two weeks after their "reservable deposits" were toted up. According to the critics, this meant that banks could do business in the knowledge that they would always be able to obtain funds necessary for reserves, frequently at bargain rates, from the Federal Reserve. Banks knew this because the lagged reserve practice allowed banks to present the Federal Reserve with a dilemma: Either supply the amount of reserves needed to validate the business done two weeks ago or experience much more interest rate volatility. Interest rate volatility, of course, is what the Federal Reserve was believed to want to avoid. The Federal Reserve, it has been argued, took the easy way out – that is, it validated business previously transacted. Critics claimed that this meant the Federal Reserve had surrendered control over the money supply to the banks. And because monetary control has been seen as necessary for mastering inflation, this practice appeared to confirm the malign influence of the banks and their foolish shortsightedness. Short-run policy was in their interest but threatened their long-run viability.

Regulatory preferences of bankers

Bankers have consistently looked to their regulators to protect them from their competitors. This has meant that as much as possible, nonbanks should not be able to do banking business (take deposits for demand accounts, make commercial loans), and any advantages given to competitors should be matched for banks. In particular, bankers have expected their regulators to take a tolerant view of innovations that the industry undertakes. Some evidence suggests that the banking industry has innovated in order to avoid the problems caused by the combined effects of high interest rates and interest rate ceilings on bank deposits. Innovations help by "opening up 'escape hatches' through which alert market participants can flee some of the effects of financial stringency on their operations for a while."[14] However, innovation has damaged monetary control and provoked more efforts at regulation by the Federal Reserve.[15] Again, if diminished monetary control weakens inflation control, then bankers' preferences on regulation may be in conflict with their long-run preferences on monetary policy.

There is, of course, no reason why the preferences of bankers about the Federal Reserve's policy need be consistent, even if this is taken to refer only to commercial bankers. Bankers can prefer a short-term policy that maximizes the stability of markets and a long-term policy that assures little or no inflation. They can prefer a regulatory stance that permits them to undertake whatever innovations are necessary to protect their competitive position. The short-term prescription conflicts with the long-term one; the regulatory prescription makes it more difficult to know how to achieve either of the other two. The implication is that in a sense, bankers may be confused about what they really want. And if the Federal Reserve is their captive, it may be confused, too. But this is exactly the kind of problem Federal Reserve independence is supposed to avoid. If the Federal Reserve is particularly close to bankers, it is in order to take care of their long-term needs, not their short-term wants.

Bankers' political resources

Nonetheless, the suspicion of capture lingers. Do bankers control mechanisms and resources adequate for translating their preferences into policy – assuming their preferences can be defined clearly enough to justify the effort at translation? Bankers have been characterized as having many political resources, some arising from organizational and financial sources and others from the fact that the Federal Reserve needs the political support of bankers. I will examine, first, direct mechanisms that bankers may use to influence the Federal Reserve: control of recruitment and direct contacts. Then I will examine less direct ways of influencing the System: their joint need for political allies and the information bankers control.

Control of recruitment

Data in the previous chapter indicate clearly that bankers play an important role in the selection of Federal Reserve officials. But neither the board nor the FOMC is composed primarily of bankers, however that term might be defined, nor do most top officials retire into the banking industry. The recruitment process does guarantee a broad similarity in outlook, in values, and in terms of analysis, but it is very doubtful that the influence of bankers through the recruitment process is sufficient to guarantee them detailed control of policy.

Direct pressure

Bankers command a substantial lobbying organization in Washington involving many former government employees. Most of the lobbying effort appears to be oriented toward the Banking Committees in Congress and the taxwriting process, not the Federal Reserve. The American Bankers' Association (ABA), the largest and most inclusive association representing bankers, has a large staff of registered lobbyists, many with prior experience on Capitol Hill, at the Treasury or at the Federal Reserve.[16] The ABA's elaborate lobbying structure is backed up by a grass-roots lobbying organization built around "contact bankers" from each congressional district.[17] Of course, in addition to the ABA, there are more than ten other national organizations representing different segments of the industry. These financial interest groups have also been represented by experienced Washington hands.[18] Many large banks have their own corporate lobbyists in Washington, often with substantial "insider" experience.[19]

There is disagreement about the effectiveness of the bank lobby in dealing with Congress. In some cases, it has been characterized as strong, forceful, and successful, able to achieve its goals. In others, it has been perceived as divided, defensive, and relatively ineffective.[20] In 1980, bankers appeared to have won a considerable victory over the savings and loan associations, their traditional competitors, with the passage of the DIDMCA.[21] However, since then the thrift institutions have been quite successful in arguing for a slower pace of deregulation and for new financial instruments (e.g., the all-savers certificate) to help their industry.[22] Still, bankers have usually been successful in resisting undesired reforms that directly affect their interests.[23]

Bankers do little direct lobbying of the Federal Reserve Board about monetary policy. This is reflected in the ABA's decision not to allocate research staff primarily to following monetary policy. The ABA monitors monetary policy only in a general way. A primary source of information in recent years has been quarterly oversight hearings by the Banking Committees of Congress – scarcely an up-to-the-minute source.[24] This is equally true of the Association of Reserve City Bankers, which does not monitor monetary policy at all through its Washington office.[25] The view of some bank lobbyists is that bankers do not need to lobby the Federal Reserve in order to make their general preferences known. They argue that anyone who pays close attention to the media knows that bankers generally prefer less inflation and a lower rate of growth of the money supply. The implication of this view is that direct contacts would do nothing more to influence Federal Reserve decisions.

There is more contact on regulatory issues, although the line of separation from monetary policy is admittedly a fine one. Each year, delegations from the state banking associations come to Washington to visit their regulators and other relevant officials in the city. These meetings and the continuing involvement in questions of bank regulation reinforce an awareness of and sensitivity to bankers' concerns.[26] However, bankers are not invited to lobby Federal Reserve Board members personally about specific pending regulatory decisions. Board members are proud of maintaining a formal aloofness from this sort of lobbying by bankers.[27]

Formal contacts. The only regular, formalized opportunity for Federal Reserve Board members to meet with bankers is in the Federal Advisory Council (FAC). Bankers in the FAC usually have their own in-house economists who are capable of briefing them adequately on current monetary policy and its implications for their institutions.[28] Thus, there is little doubt that the FAC provides an opportunity for bankers to clearly express their preferences to the board. The meetings are arranged so that a series of agenda items, involving both regulatory and monetary matters, is considered in the course of a lengthy session, usually attended by several board members. Bankers are asked to express their views on a number of issues identified as being of interest to the board. A reading of the minutes of FAC meetings shows that the interactions are typically dominated by the board and its questions rather than by the bankers.

More so than his predecessor, William McChesney Martin, Arthur Burns believed that bankers provided a useful source of information that should be exploited.

> Burns was very interested in how practical decision-makers reacted to policy. He pushed harder [in the FAC] than either Martin or Eccles to ask pointed questions about banking and how they were responding. . . . Burns and [Governor] Mitchell particularly learned how to use this mechanism, and it was clear that the bankers often found their questioning uncomfortable.[29]

By 1970, most observers agreed that the impact of the FAC on policy was quite low, continuing a lengthy decline in influence stretching for more than 20 years. At times active and vocal in early policy debates, by the end of the 1940s the FAC was operating quietly. Recently, it has surfaced when it has been convenient to the Federal Reserve Board that it do so – as in 1974, urging caution in bank lending practices. Otherwise, the FAC has been virtually invisible and relatively unimportant.[30]

The FAC has also been used as an informal means of notifying the banking community of the board's concerns about bank behavior and of potential risks involved in current banking practices. For example, in 1972 board members complained about the practice of extending loan commitments without exercising sufficient caution about problems that might be encountered in future periods of tight money.[31] It does not appear, in retrospect, that this complaint had much impact on banking practice.

There is considerably more formal contact at the district Federal Reserve Bank level. This especially involves the presidents, but Federal Reserve Board members often visit the district banks for meetings with the boards of directors. The boards of the district banks are typically dominated by commercial bankers. Of course, by statute the Class A directors *are* bankers. Extensive documentation shows that the Class B directors, elected by member banks to represent consumers of bank services, are dominated by officials of very large manufacturing firms.[32] In 1976, one-quarter of Class B directors were former directors of commercial banks. Referring to both Class B and Class C directors, the House Banking Committee staff concluded that "one in five of the seats intended to be populated by non-bankers and public members ends up being filled by former bankers only recently removed from the narrow confines of the industry."[33]

Informal contacts. On many occasions, Federal Reserve Board members are thrust into social interactions with bankers.[34] On frequent trips for speaking to bankers and other financial groups, board members inevitably fraternize with bankers over dinner, at cocktail parties, and at receptions. It is not uncommon to find references in the *Federal Open Market Committee Minutes* to recent meetings with groups of bankers or businessmen, or both.[35]

Given the varied kinds of contacts between Federal Reserve officials and bankers, and given the relative absence of contacts between Federal Reserve officials and representatives of other major organized interests, it is accurate to speak of the System as being a banker's milieu. By contrast, as AFL-CIO economist Markley Roberts observes with only slight hyperbole, "Fed officials don't lunch – or even consult – with consumer or worker representatives."[36] At a more general level, a former governor agrees: "the Fed interacts far less frequently with debtor groups or the less wealthy than with the Establishment, which prefers a more restrictive monetary policy."[37] This does not exclude the possibility of indirect influences through Congress or the president. But any advantages of this sort favoring bankers must be taken seriously.

Indirect pressure

Potential as a political ally. There is some evidence from past congressional battles that bankers are willing to use their resources to support the Federal Reserve's independence because they value its role as an anti-inflation spokesman (see Chapter 7). If one assumes, correctly, I believe, that the Federal Reserve values its independence, and if one suspects that Congress might find it convenient occasionally to threaten to reduce that independence, then perhaps the Federal Reserve should quite reasonably be on the lookout for potential allies to resist congressional threats. Under such circumstances, can the Federal Reserve ignore the preferences of bankers if it may need them in the future as political allies? At the same time, in order to perform its role in the economy, the Federal Reserve needs to be able to maintain flexibility, not to be too reliant on bankers' political support, not to be too bound by bankers' preferences. In that case, perhaps, one should not be surprised to find evidence of conflict between bankers and the Federal Reserve – nor should that be taken as indicating a division on basic questions.

Kane argues that, prior to the DIDMCA, the dual banking system gave bankers greater leverage over the Federal Reserve. Under the dual banking system, bankers have the option of being regulated by federal regulators – for example, the Federal Reserve – or state regulators. Regulators have traditionally set the reserve requirements for banks, but the DIDMCA gave complete control of this to the Federal Reserve. Prior to the DIDMCA, there had been a history of declining membership in the Federal Reserve as a proportion of all commercial banks. To the extent that the Federal Reserve needed political allies, this trend may have strengthened the hand of the remaining member banks. Moreover, the decline in membership was viewed as a danger to the Federal Reserve's prestige (and perhaps to its number of employees) as a bank regulator. Thus, the option for banks to switch to state regulation provided an additional form of influence over Federal Reserve regulatory policy in a way that may have obstructed monetary control. Certainly, the Federal Reserve claimed that declining membership was a threat to its monetary control. The DIDMCA reduced Federal Reserve vulnerability to this kind of threat, and thus may have reduced bank influence at the Federal Reserve. On the other hand, it may also have simply focused the attention of more bankers more clearly on the Federal Reserve.

A source of valued information. Contacts with bankers concerning monetary policy occur primarily at the initiative of Federal Reserve officials and are conceived of as a means of gaining information rather than soliciting advice. The Federal Reserve values the feedback from market participants about the consequences of policy.[38] However, Federal Reserve questions inevitably convey valuable information to bank economists about their concerns.[39] In these exchanges, however, bankers get *information*, not *control* over policy. As a result of this information, they may be better able to evade the consequences of policy changes, which would, as the rational expectations theorists argue, make policy less effective. It is also reasonable to suspect that access to this information is not shared out equally in the financial community.

The Washington representative of the Association of Reserve City Bankers thought it obvious that the Federal Reserve Board should be in touch with members of his organization – at the board's initiative. If the board wanted some input from members, he said, "they just pick up the phone and call five or six of them."

> From a monetary policy standpoint, our only input is on the request of the Fed, and that, as I said, would be from some of the [association] members themselves [not from the Washington office]. They know these people from way back, and they just call them if they want to know something. They would call maybe a half dozen. . . . I think that's the only thing we have to do with monetary policy.[40]

One former member of the Board of Governors, a businessman, observed that he had personal friends highly placed in several banks, and that he occasionally used these contacts when he wished to obtain or convey information. This is almost certainly true of others as well given the general existence of personal ties to the financial sector. These practices are of political interest primarily because they reinforce the Federal Reserve's special awareness of and sensitivity to the financial community.

What have the bankers received?

Is there any evidence to suggest that Federal Reserve officials pay close attention to bankers' preferences? There is, of course, ample evidence that the Federal Reserve is a conservative place – as most bankers probably desire. And certainly, the high profile of bankers at the Federal Reserve contributes to a sensitivity to bankers' concerns unequaled for any other interest group. Federal Reserve rhetoric has been opposed to inflation, and the importance of modest rates of growth in the money supply has been clearly and repeatedly stressed. But has this orientation relied especially on the political action of bankers, or is the recruitment process at the Federal Reserve, together with the sheer economic power of banks, sufficient to produce this kind of result? On the other hand, could bankers possibly be better off than they would be with a Federal

Reserve that reflects their values without having to be pressured to do so?

There is some interesting evidence that bankers are perceived at the Federal Reserve Board as being ignorant about monetary policy and politically inept. It would surely not be surprising to discover that officials trading heavily on an image of neutral technical expertise professed offense at those with such obvious self-interest. In at least one public statement, bankers have been criticized by a Federal Reserve official for their lack of attention to and understanding of evolving Federal Reserve policy. Governor John Sheehan characterized an ABA statement on monetary policy as reflecting a "disturbing lack of study and presentation anywhere near to being adequate to the subject."[41] A former board staffer told me with some fervor:

> Bankers don't know anything about monetary policy. They don't have the foggiest notion about how it works. . . . One way to lose in Congress is to get banking into it. They are stupid, clumsy, and arrogant. . . . There are very few issues where you would want the bankers to know anything.

Another former high Federal Reserve staffer, obviously disdainful of bankers' economic expertise, assured me that "no member of the Board would *ever* ask a banker [for advice] about monetary policy."

Still, evidence suggests that bankers themselves *are*, relatively speaking, happy with Federal Reserve monetary policy, even if they do no more than reinforce a direction the Federal Reserve is already inclined to take. The annual statements of the ABA for the Joint Economic Committee (JEC) clearly show that bankers basically like what the Federal Reserve has been doing.[42] Bankers have not liked everything the System did, but in comparison with another very different group, organized labor, bankers have sounded like a Federal Reserve cheering section.

The bankers' comments to the JEC have usually contained three elements. First, inflation is identified as the most pressing economic problem. Second, government economic policy in the recent past is characterized as being insufficiently restrained, or fears are expressed that restraint is about to give way. Third, the errors of or problems associated with monetary policy are seen as mitigated or partly explained by the constraints of fiscal policy blundering. For example, in the 1967 statement, the decline of the housing industry associated with tight money was excused as being the consequence of an inadequately restrained fiscal policy.[43] In

1974 and 1975, ABA statements suggested that deficit spending was likely to be associated with overly easy monetary policy.[44]

The AFL-CIO commentary has also repeated certain themes, but they contrast strongly to those of the ABA. First, employment is always discussed as the central problem. Usually, the levels of unemployment in government projections are criticized as being unacceptably high. Second, government economic policy is seen as overly restrictive or as about to become so. Third, there is a call for an examination of the structure of the Federal Reserve, and selective credit controls are recommended. Frequently, concern is expressed about the health of the housing industry.

Both groups have varied their rhetoric depending on the actual economic situations. Bankers have been more relaxed when monetary policy has been obviously quite restrictive; labor has been more relaxed when the economy has been growing rapidly. Overall, these contrasts support the liberal view of the role of bankers and suggest that we can discount some of the conservatives' concern that bankers cannot distinguish their short- from their long-term interests. But perhaps this can be judged more clearly from an examination of the specific issues that concern bankers.

Interest rate targeting

With respect to interest rate targeting, the case for banker domination looks much weaker since 1979. In October 1979, the Federal Reserve announced that it was changing its operating procedures to begin targeting bank reserves, not interest rates. Since that time, interest rates have varied dramatically (see also Chapter 5). It is also clear that many large banks, which have been thought of as the Federal Reserve's core constituency, have been hurt by this interest rate variability – both directly through losses on outstanding loans and indirectly through the loss of deposits to money market funds.[45]

Whatever else may be the case, it is clear that the innovations of October 1979 were not a response to banker pressure, and it appears that bankers' responses have not been the primary factor in subsequent developments of this technique. There is a substantial consensus that the October 1979 changes were inspired by the realization that the money supply could be controlled only if interest rates were allowed to rise very far, very fast. The only politically attractive way of letting that happen was to renounce the control of interest rates as an objective. This was politically attractive since it could be said that the resulting interest rates were market determined rather than set by the Federal Reserve.

Lagged reserve accounting

In 1982 the Federal Reserve Board voted to do away with lagged reserve accounting in February 1984. The banking industry generally opposed the proposal, but its objections were overridden. This action was a double blow to the banking industry because it is expected to result in a further increase in volatility of short-term interest rates.[46] It appears that on this issue the Federal Reserve Board was forced to take an action because of its prior commitment to monetary targeting that many members would have preferred not to take. The Federal Reserve staff, monetarist economists, and the Treasury all favored the action. All agreed that this change had the potential for somewhat more accurate monetary control. Under the circumstances, the board felt that it was necessary to take the step in order to show its seriousness about monetary targeting, thereby reducing its credibility problems.

Regulatory issues

If the banks have been losing on the monetary issues, have they been winning some compensation on the regulatory issues? Sometimes they have, but it helps their cause if the bureaucratic interests of the Federal Reserve coincide with the interests of the bankers.

Bank holding company regulation. Banks have long been attracted to the holding company form because it has been a way to circumvent various prohibitions: against branch banking in some states, against interstate banking, and against bank involvement in nonbank financial activities or in nonfinancial activities. In 1968, for example, First National City Bank of New York launched a wave of holding company formations when it discovered that it could open a nationwide chain of loan offices by forming a one-bank holding company (CitiCorp) that owned both the bank (Citibank) and the finance offices. In opposition to the bankers, the Federal Reserve had always fought for government (especially Federal Reserve) regulation of bank holding companies, and moved in the late 1960s to argue (as it had in the 1950s) that one-bank holding companies needed to be regulated. Further, a number of regulatory decisions about bank holding companies by the Federal Reserve Board in the early 1970s were very unwelcome to the banking industry.

Payment of interest on savings accounts. Payment of interest on savings accounts has been regulated since 1933, when ceilings were placed on the interest rate to be paid by banks. The actual regulation was referred to by the Federal Reserve as "Regulation Q." Post–1945 ceilings were below the rates paid by banks' competitors. In 1966, this gap was required by act of Congress; it was understood at the time to be a temporary response to a crisis in the housing market.[47] It provided the basis for a sustained conflict between the banking and savings and loan industries. Regulation Q has never been favored by the banks, but the official Federal Reserve position has fluctuated. The DIDMCA calls for eliminating the ceilings and the differential over a period of years. Nonetheless, within the Depository Institutions Deregulation Committee, the chairman of the Federal Reserve has not been pressing for the more rapid removal of interest rate ceilings favored by many bankers.[48]

Interstate banking. This issue splits the banking industry between small local banks and big multinational banks that have a potential for operating as nationwide banks. Given the substantial political resources of the small banks and the savings and loan associations, one might expect that the Federal Reserve, being a prudent organization, would move cautiously through this minefield. And indeed it has. Although the Federal Reserve seems to back interstate banking, it has been hesitant to move rapidly in that direction. A number of relatively recent actions have served to hasten the day of interstate banking, but they were often not due to the efforts of the Federal Reserve Board. For example, the DIDMCA removed some of the distinctions between state and national banks by allowing the Federal Reserve to regulate all depository institutions. This, some have suggested, might reduce the resistance to chain banking since fewer regulatory changes would be required.

More important are the combined effects of financial innovation and the financial weakness of the savings and loan industry. The challenge to the banking industry from the money market funds and the securities industry has propelled the nation toward a defacto nationwide banking system independently of regulatory action. One would expect the Federal Reserve to take steps to permit its clients to meet the competition. The need to rescue failing savings and loans has led regulators to propose permitting banks and other savings and loans to make acquisitions across state lines that would otherwise have been refused. As savings and loans come to resemble banks in terms of the functions they perform, this kind of action also establishes a de facto national banking system.

Challenge from the money market funds. One of the most important challenges to the banks has been from the money market funds. The cause can be traced primarily to the Regulation Q ceilings that, before 1983, prevented banks from competing successfully for funds in a high interest rate environment. For several years, the Federal Reserve was relatively lenient toward bank innovations that would let banks offer accounts that paid higher interest rates but were not passbook savings accounts. More seriously, for some time, the Federal Reserve has advocated subjecting the money market funds to reserve requirements (administered by the Federal Reserve, of course) to put them on the same competitive basis as the banks.[49] However, any hopes for this proposal were dashed when it turned out that the money market funds could mobilize political support as effectively as the banks and the savings and loans combined.[50] Finally, when some consensus emerged in favor of letting the banks offer their own money funds, the Federal Reserve opposed it on the grounds that the additional interest payments involved could be crippling to the industry.[51] The plan won congressional approval despite Federal Reserve objections as part of a package that received broad endorsement from both the banking and savings and loan industries.[52] All in all, this regulatory history is, to say the least, not precisely consistent with the capture theories.

Conclusion

Despite the recent evidence that the Federal Reserve has taken a number of steps that bankers opposed, there remains the interesting possibility that both liberal and conservative analysts' fears about the relationship of the Federal Reserve and bankers are well founded. As for the liberals, they can claim, quite correctly, that compared to other private sector groups, bankers enjoy unusually good access to the Federal Reserve. They can also correctly note that bankers applaud restrictive policy, which the Federal Reserve seems to prefer, if not always to follow. At the same time, the conservatives can argue that the Federal Reserve appeared to follow the bankers' bidding for many years in ways that were ultimately harmful, and summoned the strength to oppose them only when a genuine crisis was threatening. Although its motives may not be entirely clear, the Federal Reserve did fail to take the actions that would have proved to the conservatives that it is indifferent to the short-run, parochial interests of bankers.

In a less narrow sense than the simple capture hypothesis, it is suggested by many analysts that the purpose of the Federal Reserve is not to do what bankers want, but to do what they need. It is in this sense that the conservatives' criticism is particularly interesting, since they assert that the Federal Reserve has not been able to perform this vital function.

It is important to keep in mind that, as with other actors to be examined in subsequent chapters, the Federal Reserve's relationship with bankers is not a constant, undifferentiated one. Bankers usually are not able to define a policy preference that is precise and clear and that can receive widespread support in the industry. Moreover, the capacity of bankers to do this at any time has surely declined in recent years as the financial industry has been transformed. We should expect the greatest degree of cohesion and mobilization of bankers and the greatest clarity of expressed preferences whenever inflation is beyond the range of recent "normal" experience, especially when it is accompanied by rapid monetary growth. Under more normal circumstances, other more parochial concerns will divert and divide. The Federal Reserve will receive correspondingly more ambiguous messages from bankers, and the field of influence may then be dominated by a relatively small group of powerful multinational banks that can speak with a clear, coherent voice. At such times, we should also expect other actors, for example the president, to play an important role in influencing policy.

Perhaps this idea can be expressed in a more general way. When the confidence of the financial sector is in question, then it is the task of the Federal Reserve first and foremost to secure that confidence, by drastic means if necessary, but never so drastic as to cause a genuine economic collapse.[53] Securing confidence means considering in a focused way the long-term interests of finance and vigorously fighting inflation. If, however, confidence is seriously in question only intermittently – say, late in economic upswings or during an unexpected bank failure – then in the intervening periods the Federal Reserve might be open to other kinds of considerations in policy making. When confidence is not threatened, public officials are more free to pursue less fundamental objectives, including attending to the desires (as opposed to the needs) of particular constituencies. From 1979 to 1982, an almost unrelenting sense of crisis dominated monetary policy. It propelled the Federal Reserve into important reforms in late 1979, and those reforms involved overruling bankers on several related issues.

So, recent history should inform the conservatives that bankers' short-term preferences need not always prevent the Federal Reserve from taking important reform steps. However, a longer view indicates that this will not always be the case. Since the importance of bankers' short-run preferences for Federal Reserve behavior is likely to vary through time, the conservatives' analysis may be partially correct. This same line of argument suggests that in some sense, the fears of liberals are also justified. Eventually, it *will* be financial confidence above all else that sets the parameters of Federal Reserve behavior. But this does not mean that at other times the Federal Reserve will be unable to consider other factors. Although important actors such as the Federal Reserve clearly recognize a responsibility to stabilize financial confidence in crisis periods, this does not guarantee that policy between crises may not actually help to cause a future crisis.

Even if bankers do not shape Federal Reserve decisions in an ongoing, detailed way, and even if many Federal Reserve officials have disdain for bankers' economic expertise, the Federal Reserve is still a central *bank*. It is socially and politically close to banks and banking. This is important because the Federal Reserve is not simply a passive reflection of pressures from its environment. When considering the actions initiated by the Federal Reserve, can we seriously believe that these actions will not reflect the System's history, its constituency, and the values of its carefully selected officials?

5

Economists and the Federal Reserve

Could *economists* be the Federal Reserve's superiors? Should we imagine economists as effete intellectuals in ivory towers, or as bosses of the Federal Reserve? Many readers will find the former image more likely. I hope to persuade them, however, that there is something to the second image – at least for some groups of economists. The Federal Reserve depends on expertise, and economists are the relevant experts. It is worth at least entertaining the possibility that economists are very important at this institution.

Economists have been closely involved with the Federal Reserve from its founding. The Federal Reserve may be the first instance of the institutionalized application of economic expertise in the service of the government. The contemporary role of economists in monetary policy making is striking as well. We have seen in Chapter 3 that in terms of sheer numbers, economists are prominent at the board. An important prerequisite for participating actively in debates on monetary policy questions is an ability to frame arguments in the appropriate technical language – which is usually the language of economics. This shapes monetary politics both at the level of non-issues and at the level of issues.

Non-issues

Because debate is strongly influenced by mainstream economists who are relatively narrowly specialized in monetary economics, there is a strong tendency for policy debate also to be restricted to narrow technical issues. Distributive issues, for example, have not been a primary concern and can be perceived at all only with some effort. This is not to say that members of the FOMC or their economist advisors are indifferent to distributive questions. There is evidence that some FOMC members are concerned about the consequences of their policies on competition between financial institutions, on unemployment, and on losses and gains among wealth holders. Still, no one reading the *FOMC Minutes* could imagine for a moment that the meetings are dominated by debate over distributional issues – especially income inequality – despite the fact that monetary policy clearly has important distributive implications.

In part, this is explained by the fact that in terms of members' background, training, and employment milieu, such problems appear to be much less important than the issues of macroeconomic stabilization that dominate debate. This may also reflect a perception that distributive questions are more appropriately dealt with by other branches of government – although it is not immediately obvious why that should be the case. The downplaying of these issues is also a consequence of the prominent role of economic theory and language in shaping the agenda for debate in monetary policy. The technical language of monetary policy tends to be associated with what Kuhn would call the "puzzle-solving" of "normal science," which assumes that there is already substantial agreement on an overarching paradigm.[1] In the case of mainstream economics, the overarching paradigm takes as a given the distribution of income. In the case of more technical debate among monetary economists, the discussion is focused on questions such as the appropriate specification of money demand functions, the appropriate definition of monetary aggregates, the nature of the money multiplier, the stability of the velocity of circulation, the selection of optimal policy indicators or instruments, or the nature of the portfolio adjustment process. Questions having to do with income distribution, other inequalities, the appropriate direction of future industrial development, and so forth are put aside. All of the technical issues may have other consequences, but the debate usually does not reflect those consequences in any explicit way. The fact that these consequences are not made more explicit has the effect of restricting participation in a debate that need not be inherently restricted. There is no reason why a nontechnical monetary policy debate could not take place in Congress and the media. That would be possible, however, only if informed officials took it upon themselves to emphasize the really important issues – which are also issues that can be comprehended by persons without technical training.

Like any science, economics is dominated by certain relatively well-defined paradigms indicating which issues are puzzles to be solved and what counts as an acceptable solution. Various commentators have argued that mainstream economics incorporates valuational terms in its theory, often unself-consciously,[2] and that the definition of the predominant puzzles in the discipline precludes serious consideration of many otherwise important problems. The result is an inherent conservatism vis-à-vis the societal status quo.[3] The logic of the analysis itself regularly places "scientific" opinion on one side of political issues clearly involving important distributional questions, for example, free trade, minimum wages, and usury laws.[4]

By placing efficiency and individual utility maximization at the center of their analyses, it is argued, mainstream economists logically conclude that private-enterprise market systems are preferable ways to organize economic activity. As a result, economists are encouraged to accept and to justify the inequalities and power differentials that are part of private-enterprise market systems. As scientists, then, economists argue for and support dominant economic interests on basic issues about the structure of economic power.[5]

At the same time, economists help to define and to defend the "social welfare" (i.e., efficiency), and they have an analytical framework that permits them to challenge interests whose demands on government can be categorized as being "only" self-serving. In doing this, economists help identify for the state the appropriate actions it should take to regulate and sustain the economy. The terms political scientists ordinarily use to analyze interest groups are not adequate to describe the relationship of economists to monetary policy making and the Federal Reserve. Although the behavior of some subgroups of economists cannot be distinguished from that of interest groups,[6] we cannot understand economists as just another pressure group. Economists are an important source of policy knowledge and advice. They provide justifications, both large and small, for the economic system and the policies used to regulate it. In their role as advisors to other policy makers, economists also judge the competence of Federal Reserve officials and their faithfulness in following the objectives sought by various would-be superiors.

Monetarists and the issues in monetary politics

Economists have contributed important analyses that tend to call into question the validity of Federal Reserve independence. This conclusion has emerged from studies on the relative potency of monetary and fiscal policy. Research on policy making with a "consolidated budget constraint" (i.e., long-range budget balance) has produced some consensus that in principle it is impossible to anticipate the impacts of either fiscal or monetary policy without knowing about the targets and instruments being used by both.[7] The institutional implication is that a logical prerequisite for macroeconomic policy is fully coordinated control of both kinds of instruments. These arguments do not, of course, specify exactly *how* the instruments should be coordinated, and therefore do not necessarily call into question the existence of some sort of political autonomy for technical experts making macroeconomic policy. But any system permitting independence on the part of the monetary authority would seem to be ruled out.

Many of the most prominent debates on monetary politics have been debates between warring camps of economists – not between groups familiarly identifiable as Republicans or Democrats, bankers or labor. The issues in these debates are viewed by the participants as the most central issues of monetary politics. Since the early 1960s, there have been vigorous debates between monetarist economists and mainstream neo-Keynesians.[8]

The issues in this debate were confronted in Chapter 1. The most clearly identifiable position is that of the monetarists. There are many varieties of monetarists, and there is disagreement among them on many specific points. Three distinct varieties of monetarism have been identified: that associated with Milton Friedman, that associated with Karl Brunner and Allen Meltzer, and the rational expectations variant.[9] Nonetheless, it is reasonably clear that there is a set of policy recommendations upon which almost all monetarists agree and around which they unite. These include the following:[10]

1. The reserve base or a similar measure should be the indicator of monetary policy.
2. The money stock is the proper (intermediate) target of monetary policy.
3. Monetary policy should be guided by a monetary growth rule.
4. Since the private sector is inherently stable, it will perform adequately if government policy does not create disruption. Thus, policy should not be destracted from the stable growth rule by unemployment crises or the

failure of specific institutions, or by other transitory private sector instabilities.

5. Inflation should be regarded as a greater concern (relative to unemployment) than most economists tend to believe.
6. Government intervention should be limited and reduced.

The defining characteristic of the monetarists is their insistence that monetary policy should be guided by a simply rule: Achieve a steady, stable, low rate of growth in the money supply. Monetarists urge that policy not deviate from this monetary rule. Typically, this conclusion has been reached by means of an argument that the processes linking monetary policy action and macroeconomic outcomes are extremely complex and not fully understood, and that the time lag between action and outcome is long and variable. Consequently, policy should not attempt to fine-tune macroeconomic quantities such as prices and employment, because it cannot reliably be done.

Operationally, there have been divergent prescriptions. Some analysis has led to a preference for targeting M1, currency plus demand deposits, either on theoretical grounds or because the statistical link with the Gross National Product (GNP) or prices has been close over a given sample period. It may be more common now for monetarists to prefer to try to control the monetary base (bank reserves plus currency), which, unlike any of the other monetary aggregates, is more precisely controllable by the central bank. For all practical purposes, controlling the monetary base means controlling bank reserves, since currency is typically provided to meet the current demand. It does *not* mean targeting short-term interest rates or quantities such as free reserves that can be misinterpreted as restrictive despite the fact that more and more bank reserves are actually being provided by authorities.

At another level, monetarists commonly believe that there is no lasting tradeoff between unemployment and inflation; this is often called the "natural rate of unemployment hypothesis." This means that efforts to lower unemployment by stimulative monetary policy can achieve only temporary reductions in unemployment with the long-run effect of higher inflation. The natural rate hypothesis is roughly equivalent to saying that, given a current mix of labor skills, unemployment is a function of the institutional factors that prevent laborers from offering a "market-clearing" wage and from voluntary decisions to select leisure over work. Examples of such obstacles include minimum wage legislation and union wage bargaining. Some monetarists would agree that some kind of government policy might be successful in reducing unemployment, but they are quite clear that monetary policy is not appropriate for this purpose. From this kind of analytic perspective, it follows quite logically that monetarists are usually particularly concerned with lowering inflation and are little inclined to see unemployment as a macroeconomic problem.

In terms of the academic debate, monetarists have clearly won substantial victories, although there is still very deep disagreement with their core proposal that policy should focus exclusively on achieving steady growth in the monetary aggregates. There was a day when major macroeconomic models showed almost no powerful effects of monetary policy, and monetary policy was discussed almost exclusively in terms of control of interest rates. That day is long past. Monetary economists of all schools agree that there are dangers associated with close control of short-term interest rates. And most economists agree that money matters very much for macroeconomic performance. But beyond that, the opponents of the monetarists differ in many ways and at many levels of analysis.

For example, one line of argument from opponents of the monetarists for many years, now associated with "optimal control theory," is that the monetary aggregates are only one of many useful sources of information for policy makers about the economy. Many potential instruments may be stably linked with such ultimate targets as economic growth and inflation, and policy makers should not hesitate to pay attention to these variables. There is valuable information about the course of events from many sources: interest rates in many markets; credit flows of all sorts; and particular parts of the monetary aggregates. Nonmonetarists have also argued for the importance of paying attention to reports from bankers about the nature of their loan demand, to the tone and feel of markets, and so forth.

These kinds of arguments are, not surprisingly, typically associated with a view more favorable to government stabilization and less sure of the inherent stability of private markets. However useful it may be to target monetary aggregates, the argument goes, there is no reason at the outset to believe that a constant rate of growth of the money supply is appropriate at all times for the indefinite future. Moreover, say the opponents, what is money?

In a rapidly changing financial system, "money" is a concept with no constant empirical referent, and thus with no stable links to the things we really care about – growth, employment, and prices. At a given time, different measures of money give very different indications of the degree of stimulus to the economy. To which measures should policy makers pay most attention?[11]

Some opponents would contradict the monetarists by arguing that monetary policy can do things to increase employment – at least in the United States. Other opponents argue that it is incorrect to claim simply that inflation is a monetary phenomenon. On the contrary, a great deal of inflation can occur independently of monetary policy, thus forcing policy makers to choose whether they want to accept that inflation or to get rid of it by creating unemployment. Others argue that the money supply really is not something that can be controlled as the monetarists propose. The money supply does move with the condition of the economy, but it is the economy that determines the money supply, not the other way around.

It can readily be seen that there are also disagreements about what economic consequences are important. Many nonmonetarists, for example, stress the need for a policy to guarantee market stability, orderliness, and a high level of investor confidence, and to avoid inflicting losses on major financial sector participants through volatile interest rates. They might claim that whether one favors more or less unemployment or inflation, economic stability is impossible without a smoothly functioning financial market. Monetarists, on the other hand, are less concerned about markets. They are more likely to assume that money markets can adjust without solicitous central bank oversight. From the monetarist perspective, all that is needed is for policymakers to stop creating uncertainty by misguided attempts at fine tuning, and markets will do everything else that is needed. Their motto is, policy instability creates instability in the economy.

Whatever their successes in reshaping the academic debate, monetarists have not succeeded in getting most economists to agree with the strongest points in their program. This is clear from the results of a survey of economists.[12] The relevant questions and the published responses are presented in Table 5.1. Divisions among various subsamples of economists are reported in Table 5.2. The entries in Table 5.1 indicate that economists as a whole substantially agree with one element in the monetarist program – stressing the money supply as a target. However, the other element, the

Table 5.1. *Agreement among economists with two propositions related to the monetarist position*

Propositions	Generally agree (%)	Agree with provisions (%)	Generally disagree (%)	Sum (%)
1. The money supply is a more important target than interest rates for monetary policy	48	23	29	100
2. The Fed should be instructed to increase the money supply at a fixed rate	14	25	61	100

Source: J. R. Kearl, Clayne L. Pope, Gordon C. Whiting, and Larry T. Wimmer, "A Confusion of Economists?" *American Economic Association Papers and Proceedings, American Economic Review* 69 (May 1979):30.

monetary rule, is overwhelmingly rejected. It is striking that the greatest disagreement with the monetarists is found among the economists in leading graduate programs (see Table 5.2). Other academic and business economists are more in agreement with the monetarist position. It seems accurate to regard general agreement with proposition 2 as characterizing "true monetarists." Using this criterion, a generous estimate of the proportion of monetarists among all economists is less than 20 percent, and is even less among economists teaching in leading graduate programs.

These debates clearly have tended to take shape along liberal-conservative lines. Monetarists are usually conservative, although it is less true to say that neo-Keynesians are usually liberal.[13] To a large degree, it is correct to see these debates as ideological and political. But it is not correct to see them as satisfactory substitutes for a broader debate. They are too technically dense; the agenda is too much set by technicians.

Monetarists are not simply a group of economists participating in an obscure debate about monetary theory. They are also a particular manifestation of a more general neo-liberal (or, as the current analysts might have it, libertarian) political position. This broad ideological position is characterized particularly by mistrust of government, by the belief that exercise of government discretion

Table 5.2. *Breakdown of responses to questions about monetarist propositions by subsample of economists*

	Proposition	
Subsample group	1	2
Top academics[a]	1.6 (0.82)[b] (N = 24)	1.3 (0.70) (N = 24)
Other academics	2.3 (0.85) (N = 73)	1.7 (0.76) (N = 77)
Government	2.2 (0.82) (N = 46)	1.4 (0.69) (N = 46)
Business	2.4 (0.84) (N = 56)	1.5 (0.69) (N = 55)

Key: The main entry is the average score of respondents based on the following scores: disagree = 1; agree with provisions = 2; agree = 3.
[a]See note 12.
[b]Standard deviation.

(often as a consequence of misguided democracy) produces more harm than good, by a desire to reduce government spending, and by a desire to increase reliance on the free market. Monetarists should be understood as pressing specific elements in a neo-liberal political program. These elements, of course, have to do with monetary policy.

Mainstream economists and control of the Federal Reserve

There have been two kinds of efforts to link academic economics and the Federal Reserve. The first has arisen from within the institution and reflects the desire of top Federal Reserve officials to possess the best possible technical information. This is a laudable goal for any governmental agency; public policy should be informed by the best possible advice. It is also something that reinforces the power of the agency since, if all goes well, no outsider can possibly advance an argument that cannot be rebutted squarely or, at the very least, discredited by a thousand technical quibbles. The second effort was external. There have been two waves of attack on the System from academia. The first wave came from the "new economics" of the 1960s, the second from the monetarists.

The efforts from within the Federal Reserve to improve relationships with economists coincided almost perfectly with the efforts by the neo-Keynesian new economists to export their doctrines to the Federal Reserve. Contributing to the demand for better economics within the System were the economists appointed to the Federal Reserve Board by Presidents Kennedy and Johnson: George Mitchell, Dewey Daane, Sherman Maisel, and Andrew Brimmer. These were aided in their good works by the staff director, Daniel Brill. Crusading new economists at the Council of Economic Advisors (CEA) – James Tobin, Walter Heller, Gardner Ackley, Arthur Okun, James Deusenberry – were also enthusiastic in their efforts to "spread the gospel" to the Federal Reserve. The tone of the period can best be captured in the optimistic writings of participants such as Heller and Okun.[14]

At the Federal Reserve Board, George Mitchell established the Economic Consultants Group (ECG) in 1963, chaired by G. L. Bach of Stanford, in order to increase direct contact between board members and outside economists. The ECG still meets several times a year with the board for confidential discussion. The invited academics – the composition of the group varies – present studies of interest to board members. In 1966 the board staff began a joint collaboration with Massachusetts Institute of Technology (MIT) economists on a new quarterly econometric model (the MPS model) of the United States that has become a benchmark for research on the impact of monetary policy on the economy.[15]

The CEA economists felt a close kinship to the staff economists working at the Federal Reserve, many of whom had been educated at the institutions where the leading new economists taught. The CEA economists used the Federal Reserve staff as a source of information about important decisions and hoped that the staff, in turn, would help educate board members. In discussing the issue of reappointing William McChesney Martin as chairman, Gardner Ackley noted that Martin's apparent conversion to the new economics was a point in his favor. Ackley wrote to President Johnson:

> George [Mitchell] stressed something which Brimmer had also told me (and I failed to report on my conversation with him) – namely, that Bill [Martin] was increasingly becoming a fol-

> lower of the "New Economics." George feels that Bill is very much inclined to go along with the majority of his Board and his staff. Now that the "New Economics" is firmly in the saddle in both places, Bill can be counted on to cooperate.[16]

In considering the Brimmer appointment in early 1966, Heller wrote Johnson that the CEA would help "*along with the Fed. staff* in keeping him on a Johnsonian expansionist track."[17]

The Federal Reserve seems to have had substantial success in upgrading the quality of its staff and ensuring its prestige among academics. One indicator noted in Chapter 4 shows that in terms of educational background, the staff compares reasonably well with active members of the economics profession. Tobin has praised the increased stature of the staff. Lombra and Moran have concluded that by the early 1970s Federal Reserve forecasting was the equal of any private forecast.[18] Henry Wallich, a board member and former Yale economist, has characterized the staff as "outstanding." Wallich says that in its particular areas, the staff has strengths "greatly exceeding the density of coverage of major topics that is possible even in the economics departments of leading universities."[19] The editor of one of the leading journals for monetary economics reports that 8 percent of the articles have been contributed by Federal Reserve staff, who constitute a much smaller proportion of all monetary economists.[20] In short, efforts to link the Federal Reserve to academia have been a success.

At the same time that the neo-Keynesians were achieving dominance in the academic world and attempting to colonize key government agencies, their primary academic opponents, the monetarists, were beginning their own effort to shape policy debate and action. In the 1960s, the monetarists were not as successful as the Keynesians in gaining media attention and high government posts, but their criticisms of the Federal Reserve and monetary policy were being noted both in academia and in the Federal Reserve itself.[21] The monetarists had discovered even then that there was a market for their arguments among members of Congress who were shopping for criticisms of the Federal Reserve.[22] Although the successful political organization of the monetarists did not occur until the early 1970s, it is clear that the monetarist critique, together with the increased role of economists in the System, affected policy and procedure in the 1960s.[23]

In 1966, the FOMC began to consider staff econometric forecasts of the economy when making its decisions. The "Blue Book" was introduced linking policy choices to future (forecast) financial conditions. Maisel suggests that the staff had been eager to begin forecasting exercises, and that he and other Federal Reserve Board economists supported them.[24] The FOMC altered its operating procedures in June 1966 to include in the policy directive what came to be known as "the proviso." After this reform, the policy directive stated that certain "money market conditions" would be sought *provided* the trend of bank reserves remained within acceptable limits. These vague verbal formulas were accompanied by statements of quantitative expectations for the open market desk in New York.[25] In this development in particular, Federal Reserve governors who were economists seem to have been influenced by outside criticisms of System operating procedures, especially after failures of the System to achieve its policy objectives using the operating procedures then being followed.[26]

The embarrassing forecasting failures in 1968 and other indications that current operating procedures were falling short of expectations led again to internal controversy. This time, reevaluation was assigned to a System committee headed by a Maisel.[27] This committee could not be characterized as monetarist, but it was certainly sympathetic to some of the arguments monetarist economists were then advancing. Although the committee's report was not formally adopted by the FOMC, its analyses did support the decisions in the early 1970 meetings, coincident with Arthur Burns's assumption of the chairmanship, to place more stress on monetary aggregates.[28] This eventually led to the two-stage policy-making process the committee followed throughout most of the 1970s. In this process, the FOMC made quarterly revisions of year-long monetary targets and monthly decisions on how to use policy instruments (principally the federal funds rate) to reach longer-range targets.[29]

The monetarist counterthrust

By the early 1970s, the monetarist critique had developed substantially in prestige and prominence. For some years, there had been active interest in monetarist propositions at the Federal Reserve Bank of St. Louis. The St. Louis bank had become, in effect, a government-funded organizational center for monetarist economists. Its monthly *Review* repeatedly was at the center of the debate between monetarists and their opponents. The Nixon CEA had a distinctly monetarist cast and commented on monetary policy from that vantage point. Many business and bank economists had embraced some variant of monetarist analysis.[30] The Federal Reserve Board and its economists were increasingly visible participants in a public debate about the role of monetary aggregates in monetary policy.[31] The monetarists had achieved remarkable success in setting the agenda for debate, and they did so by using techniques of political organization quite familiar to students of public interest groups.

Ten or so leading monetarists – the composition changes – began regular semiannual meetings in 1973, calling themselves the Shadow Open Market Committee (SOMC). They "shadow" the activities of the Federal Reserve's main policy-making body, the FOMC. Although recent press reports about the SOMC have been rather brief, early reports indicated that it consisted mostly of academic economists.[32] SOMC meetings are well organized, full-day affairs. Papers are presented, policy options are discussed, and a press release is issued commenting on Federal Reserve policy and recommending an alternative course.

Particularly important in the organization of the monetarists have been Friedman, Brunner, and Meltzer. The most obvious is Milton Friedman. As far as most observers are concerned, Friedman alone has been monetarism's leading light. He is known for winning the Nobel Prize for economics and for his frequent columns in *Newsweek*.[33] More vigorous, if less well known, are Karl Brunner and Allan Meltzer, who have organized and chaired both the SOMC and the Shadow European Economic Policy Committee.[34] Brunner is closely associated with the activities of the Federal Reserve Bank of St. Louis through former students. In the United States, Brunner has founded two professional journals that have greatly expanded the opportunities for airing monetarist arguments.[35] Together, Brunner and Meltzer have edited the *Carnegie-Rochester Conference Series on Public Policy*; it is not an exclusively monetarist outlet, but it gives heavy play to monetarist arguments.[36]

Like most economists, monetarists account for the behavior of policy makers by reference to a model of rational decision makers who seek to optimize the attainment of various goals. Monetarists following this logic would assume that the Federal Reserve is composed of rational actors, but they would also observe that the System fails to adopt the appropriate (monetarist) policy-making procedures. Why would rational actors behave in such a fashion? The monetarists appear to infer that the Federal Reserve must be politically constrained from following the correct policy path. They apparently conceive of the Federal Reserve as engaging in an optimizing process that includes yielding to external political threats. This is, of course, an assumption that many analysts of Federal Reserve behavior have found to be productive.

Such an analysis implies a political strategy of altering the political constraints on the Federal Reserve, and this appears to be the kind of strategy the monetarists have adopted. In order to influence their "ultimate target," the Federal Reserve, the monetarists concentrate on three "intermediate targets:" the president (and the Treasury), Congress, and the press. This strategy is complex. The monetarists have been quite successful in getting substantial press coverage, much of which has been intended to place the Federal Reserve on the defensive. As for Congress, monetarists have had success particularly through the efforts of one key staffer, Robert Weintraub (this is discussed further in Chapter 7). As for the president, recent Republican presidents have been receptive to monetarist advisors, but not until the election of Reagan could one say that there was any evidence of clear enthusiasm for monetarism. Under Reagan, several prominent monetarists were appointed to high administration positions.

Economists' conflicts and Federal Reserve behavior

How much impact have economists really had on Federal Reserve behavior? Have the analytic problems of economists really been important in FOMC deliberations, or have clever Federal Reserve politicians merely used economists and their arguments to justify the policies they pursue for some other reasons . . . or both? This is the kind of question pundits love to pose because, as with all good pundits' questions, it is often hard to obtain the evidence that could constitute a definitive answer.

Consider the following evidence offered in support of the notion that economists have mattered a great deal. First, insiders and close observers have almost always attributed a great deal of influence to the economic staff. For example, Whittlesey in 1963, Borins in 1969, Maisel in 1973, and Wallich in 1982 all note the influence of staff economists in policy making.[37] The staff plays a critical role for the FOMC in distinguishing between transitory and permanent factors underlying target misses. The staff tells the FOMC what the consequences of policy will be and can bring particular problems to the attention of members. All of this suggests that the influence of economists is considerable.

Second, there have been several policy changes that appear to have been made in response to a changed consensus of mainstream economists. There was the switch of the FOMC to an emphasis on monetary aggregate targets in 1970. At least two separate studies have shown that, despite continuing constraints on the range of interest rate movement permitted, the FOMC really did use monetary targets in implementing policy in the 1970s.[38] The October 1979 switch from interest rates to bank reserves as the instrument of policy and the widening of tolerance bands for interest rate fluctuations were the kinds of changes many economists recommended. This appeared to be a radical departure in monetary policy practice, and certainly would not have been possible without the years of economic research and debate that came before.

If, in these reforms, the Federal Reserve was responding to economists, it was not welcoming the monetarists. The MPS model used in econometric forecasting at the board has been criticized for its Keynesian structure, and Wallich suggests that the model's "powerful role in FOMC deliberations . . . may well be excessive."[39] There has been hostility to the monetarists on the part of the staff, and in the early 1970s some board members publicly made their own lack of faith in monetarism clearly understood.[40] As Wallich says, "Burns was no monetarist, and neither were the rest of us."[41]

As for the notion that economists do not have influence, there are some strong indications that staff advice is ignored, and that the logical consistency of economic analysis gives way in actual practice of FOMC decision making to casual ad hoc-ery. The FOMC, as one member has put it, has responded to the monetarist-Keynesian battle by "ducking in between," so that the two sides end up shooting at each other rather than at the Federal Reserve.[42] An examination of decision making in the early 1970s found that the FOMC did not choose among the consistent alternatives presented by the staff, but instead combined inconsistent specifications from competing alternatives.[43] This occurred, for example, in 1971 when five of seven board members were economists, as were seven of twelve district bank presidents.

In short, neither the high levels of staff expertise nor the accumulated experience of FOMC members resulted in a policy process that was particularly bound by analytical consistency. The evidence needed to show whether such practices have continued in more recent periods is not publicly available. It is clear, however, that the FOMC has still not made a firm commitment to a particular theoretical position, nor to a particular operating procedure, nor to particular targets. Anthony Solomon, president of the Federal Reserve Bank of New York, expressed this in 1982 in words that have a very familiar ring to anyone who has spent much time studying monetary politics:

> My own instinct is that there is no single approach to monetary policy that is best for all times and places. As conditions change, the approach will probably have to change, too. . . . In adapting to this changing world, policy-makers will continue to benefit importantly from the results of economic research on these matters.[44]

Solomon's approach is what one would expect of a subordinate, as discussed in Chapter 1. Many outside economists would agree that it is the correct approach as well.

The policy changes of 1979

There are serious doubts that changes in operating procedures adopted by the Federal Reserve in 1979 can properly be attributed to outside economists in any immediate sense, and some have doubted that it really was much of a change at all. Certainly, it would be incorrect to suggest that the 1979 change was due to monetarist influence. There has been scant evidence that board staff have been interested in directly involving monetarists any more after the changes than before.

Monetarists have advanced an explanation of what happened in 1979 and, after some months of equivocation, they pronounced a strongly negative verdict on the nature of the change. What was announced on October 6, 1979, was, of course, that the Federal Reserve was adopting a revised procedure of targeting bank reserves rather than interest rates. The view of many monetarists about the reform seems to be adequately captured in Lindley Clark's account:

> Over at the International Monetary Fund meeting in Belgrade last fall, the Europeans scared us to death. They didn't believe that we really cared at all about the value of the dollar. They were ready to dump every dollar they had.
>
> Well, Paul Volcker was over there and he got the message. He knew he had to do something drastic, so he rushed back

> and put together the program that he announced on October 6.[45]

Other monetarists, including some in official positions, have presented a similar account to me in confidential conversations, and others hint at this when they stress that the meeting of October 6, 1979, was very unusual.

It will come as no surprise to many to learn that board members disagree with this account in virtually every respect.[46] In particular, they maintain that international developments were not the only or even the dominant consideration in the decision. They stress that a small number of highly placed staff had been studying the possibility of such a change for some time, and that Volcker returned to the United States as scheduled. Governor Wallich found absurd the notion that such a reform would be contemplated without staff work, as the monetarist version suggested. Board members did agree that the changes took place more rapidly than one might have expected from the pace of prior major Federal Reserve reforms, and that district bank officials were largely in the dark until the last minute.

At least some board members were persuaded that an economic crisis was pending and that dramatic action was called for. Governor Partee, for example, said that "it seemed to me that we were on the border of an almost classic situation of losing confidence in the currency." It had become clear to the board that interest rates would have to be much higher in order to control inflation, but it was not entirely clear how much higher. This suggested two good reasons for adopting an aggregates target, one technical, one political. The technical argument was that if you do not know how high interest rates should be, then you cannot decide what the appropriate interest rate target should be. The political argument was that it was a bad idea for the Federal Reserve to be on record as having an interest rate target of 18 percent, especially given congressional sensitivity to interest rates. It was never the intent of the board, however, to cease to be concerned about interest rates.

The 1979 reforms did not reflect the kind of intellectual conversion that the monetarists have long hoped for. It was a decision forced on the Federal Reserve by external economic forces and political constraints; among the latter, count the monetarists. In this sense, the 1979 reforms were a classic example of Federal Reserve technical-political maneuvering. The Federal Reserve needed to solve several grave problems. It had to let interest rates rise to historically high levels without having to choose to do so explicitly. It had to do this in order to restore confidence in the dollar, in the government's willingness to fight inflation, and in financial institutions. So, the approach chosen was not surprising: Let interest rates rise – but don't let them fall too far. Keep the discount rate high, but much lower than market rates at their peaks. Focus on bank reserves. Try to influence congressional legislation so that new financial innovations come within the Federal Reserve purview.

Monetarists accuse the Federal Reserve of adopting only the form of monetary targeting, not the reality. This is a very complex issue. The Federal Reserve certainly was not lashing itself to the mast of the monetarist ship in 1979, so its announced retreat from aggregate targeting in late 1982 should not have surprised anyone. But in the eyes of many monetarists, the System was doing worse than that – it was actually making the economy less, rather than more, stable with its reforms. During the period in which the System claimed to be targeting monetary aggregates, volatility of monetary aggregates actually increased, rather than declining as might have been expected. For the ten quarters prior to October 1979, the standard deviation of the quarter-to-quarter growth rates of M1 was 2.55, and it was 1.32 for the monetary base. For the ten quarters after October 1979, the standard deviation of the quarter-to-quarter growth rates of M1 was 5.24, and it was 2.66 for the monetary base. That is, variability doubled despite small declines in the average.[47] However, nonmonetarist economists have argued vigorously that this variation can be more than accounted for by the unpredictable variation in various financial quantities and in the money multiplier, perhaps related to recent financial innovations.[48] In short, the debate continues unabated.

Conclusion

Henry Aaron argues in *Politics and the Professors*[49] that academic analyses critical of the 1960s social welfare programs had the effect of undermining the legitimacy of welfare state action and of encouraging a timid approach to positive policy. In the movement from the 1960s to the 1970s, he argues, the country learned that no expert conclusions could be trusted, that no findings were secure. In a parallel argument, Hugh Heclo argues that policy making increasingly has been dominated by networks of "issue-skilled" specialists who blur previously stable lines of political division and complicate policy debate, simultaneously making debate more controversial and less subject to conclusive resolution.[50] Heclo is disturbed by the way this makes democratic control more difficult.

The conflict between democratic control and domination by technical experts has been a long-standing source of tension in the case of the Federal Reserve. Developments since the early 1960s have increased the overtly technical nature of decision making. The System became, in large part, an arena for resolving academic disputes by political means. As with the issues Aaron analyzed, in monetary policy the intellectual consensus partially collapsed in the late 1960s and early 1970s. Issues of economic theory assumed a larger role in discussion and debate, and evidence of uncertainty among economists created new kinds of dilemmas for policy makers, leaving them to resolve cognitive dissonance as best they could.[51]

The fact that strong monetarists are a relative minority of economists points up the success and the importance of their political organization. The fact that they have managed consistently to influence the policy agenda is a remarkable tribute to their skills in dominating the critical communications channels.

The Federal Reserve has made a sophisticated response to the problem posed by the economic conflict during this period. The response, quite simply, has been to coopt serious critics. Thus, for example, the monetarists "have" the St. Louis Bank and the rational expectationists "have" the Minneapolis Bank. A traditional element of Federal Reserve responses to critics of their procedures has been to say, "we pay attention to all relevant variables, not to just a few." Bringing in the critics can be seen as an extension of this response. The hazard, of course, is that the critics will not be silent – as indeed, neither the St. Louis nor the Minneapolis bank presidents have been. Internalizing the critics means that the debate within the System remains lively – at least at a superficial level. Meanwhile, the System can reassure noneconomists that all points of view are represented. This may help to keep disputes out of traditional political arenas. Also, FOMC members can, if they wish, pick and choose from competing theories to legitimize their voting preferences.

The Federal Reserve has been drawn into a position such that it must be sensitive to important critiques from academic economists. Federal Reserve staff have been, and are, major participants in the economic debates. Because this development coincided with heightened controversy among academic economists, it has increased anxiety about policy errors and the contentiousness of debate, while subjecting the System to shrill criticism from outside economists who believe they are insufficiently heeded.[52] There has been a risk that issues that could be considered purely technical and, in principle, susceptible of resolution on some generally agreed-upon grounds would become hardened political positions. At the same time, obvious technical complexity has prevented the debate from opening the System up to meaningful influence by elected officials. On the contrary, it has increased the reluctance of many elected politicians to venture any opinions at all.

At the same time, it is doubtful that the Federal Reserve had a good alternative that would have allowed it to avoid this situation. The need for expertise certainly drove the Federal Reserve in the direction of economics, and its links to the discipline have been beneficial to the System. And it is almost certain that economists – including monetarists – have found the relationship to be beneficial as well, even if only in a small, self-interested way. Perhaps these controversies are in the public interest and will result in better policy. They are clearly not in the short-run political interest of the Federal Reserve, and they may not serve the public well, either. The politicized nature of the conflict leads both sides to search for allies, to maneuver for influence. That process guarantees that ideas will be oversimplified and that the benefits of technical reforms will be oversold. This consequence is of considerable interest, for it points out that in this case, expanding the conflict means running the risk that simple ideas might actually be adopted. Economists, monetarists and otherwise, advise an institution that operates in the real world of politics and finance. The stakes are high; the penalties for errors and for rigid indifference to the political consequences of a "correct" policy can be severe indeed.

6

The President and the Federal Reserve

With the rise of the managed economy after World War II, the presidency emerged as the foremost institution of macroeconomic policy. No others involved in macroeconomic policy are equally important in identifying problems and defining courses of action. One prominent study of the presidency argues that the concerns of macroeconomic policy have been second only to foreign policy for modern presidents.[1] Consequently, various issues of monetary politics arise clearly with respect to the president and his advisors, especially the question of what the objectives of policy should be. In short, presidents seem to be particularly likely to be the real, as opposed to the statutory, superiors of the Federal Reserve.

There are two primary reasons for presidential concern with monetary policy. First, although presidents have no legal authority with respect to monetary policy, they are charged under the Employment Act of 1946 and other legislation with general responsibility for macroeconomic management. Since monetary and fiscal policy are functionally interdependent, presidents have a continuing motivation to assure that monetary policy is consistent with fiscal policy. If presidential duties include stabilizing the economy, then presidents will want to influence all of the powerful instruments of macroeconomic policy.

Second, presidents are interested in monetary policy because of the link between macroeconomic performance and electoral success. It seems reasonably clear that the popularity and electoral success of contemporary presidents are affected by the state of the economy.[2] Thus, one would expect presidents to be interested in the behavior of the Federal Reserve generally, and their interest might intensify as elections approach. Since presidents are more likely than other actors to be able to define their objectives for monetary policy precisely and consistently, they may be more likely than others to be effective in pressuring the Federal Reserve. In periods prior to elections, the usual expectation is that presidents will seek expansionary policy.

Presidential relations with the Federal Reserve

In the relatively few studies on the question, there is a substantial consensus that presidents generally get the monetary policy they want from the Federal Reserve. Recent analyses by economists have stressed the conclusion that monetary policy is heavily influenced by pressure from the administration – I shall call it the "president as superior" argument. "[M]uch of the history of monetary policy can be explained just by noting who the President was when the policy under review was in effect."[3] Political scientist Nathaniel Beck argues that his analysis of the 1970s shows that the Federal Reserve "did appear to respond to the desires of the incumbent president."[4] Such analyses do not make it entirely clear how this compliance is brought about. Kane argues that the Federal Reserve does what the president wants because it needs presidential support to ward off attacks from Congress.[5]

My examination of the history of the relationship between the president and the Federal Reserve since 1965 has turned up only a small number of cases involving serious conflicts between the two.[6] Even with a very generous interpretation of the definition of independence suggested in Chapter 1, there have been only a few instances of independent action during the years 1965–82, these will be reviewed subsequently. This too appears to support the president as superior thesis.

Several chairmen of the CEA could also be quoted to support the proposition that the relationship between the president and the Federal Reserve is generally cooperative. For example, Paul McCracken: "On the whole, I think the coordination of monetary and fiscal policy over the years has been pretty good." Or Herbert Stein: "We didn't have any problems about what the objectives of [Federal Reserve] policy were, and I believe their objectives were pretty similar to ours." Arthur Okun wrote that the Federal Reserve was cooperative with the Johnson administration. These kinds of statements seem to provide still more support for the president as superior argument.[7]

The allegation that presidents dominate monetary policy is arresting given the more familiar analysis suggesting that presidential powers are limited in many policy areas, including fiscal policy. For example, it is the judgment of many students of the presidency that modern presidents are highly constrained in their ability to obtain from Washington bureaucracies the policies they desire. The best-known formulation of this argument is, of course, that of Neustadt, who proposes that presidential power is primarily "the power to persuade."[8] We know that there have been many cases in which presidents have found it difficult to control cabinet agencies – even in periods of highest crisis.[9] Another long-time student of the presidency, Thomas Cronin, has observed that the president has "very little influence over the Federal Reserve Board's policies on credit and money" – a sentiment that is echoed in other works as well.[10]

In ironic contrast to the president as superior notion is the argument that presidents have a great deal of trouble getting the fiscal policy they want despite the fact that in this area their authority is clearest. Presidents have to convince Congress to approve changes in taxes and spending, a process marked by long delays and many frustrations. Consequently, fiscal policy is often not an effective instrument of macroeconomic policy. Reformers of various ideological stripes mistrust and are impatient with congressional politics in economic policy making. For example, Okun wrote of the "defeat of the new economics by the old politics" in 1966; Congress would not take action to raise taxes.[11]

In fact, the president as superior thesis is *not* consistent with all of the evidence about monetary policy. Typically, this thesis has been supported with evidence showing that there is a general consistency between monetary and fiscal policy, or that policy shift points tend to coincide with changes in administration. This is not the same thing as saying that monetary policy is what the president wants, and it certainly does not mean that through some covert means, the president gives the orders and the Federal Reserve jumps to. Some of the same chairmen of the CEA could be quoted again to illustrate this point. For example, Paul McCracken: "for a very important instrument of macro policy, namely monetary policy, you don't have the dials in the President's office. Certainly, if Arthur Burns is chairman of the Fed, then you find that out quite explicitly!" Or Herbert Stein: "The relations were, however, always rather touchy because of the Federal Reserve's independence and the feeling that we should not intrude in it. . . . I would not regard [the Federal Reserve] as part of the President's team. It certainly was not hostile – Arthur was not hostile. . . . But he didn't feel any obligation to us; he operated in a very independent way." In an interview, Arthur Okun related tales of miscoordination and conflict in other administrations, some of which he found shocking. These statements do not exactly support the theme of president as superior.

One can think of the relationship between the president and the Federal Reserve as primarily a political struggle, so that apparent agreement on policy is really the result of one party successfully coercing the other. Alternatively, one could view the relationship as one in which both actors usually tend to be in agreement, with no coercion required. It is possible that there is frequent pulling and hauling behind the scenes that, for various reasons, nobody cares to reveal publicly. One supposes that if it ever came down to a pure conflict of political power, the president would surely win. But at the same time, the Federal Reserve is hardly defenseless. Often there is support for the Federal Reserve from financial and other anti-inflation groups. But, as we shall see, there are many factors that tend to lead to policy making without much overt conflict. Rather than conclude that presidents generally get the monetary policy they want, it would be more accurate to say that only infrequently are presidents extremely unhappy with the monetary policy they get.

Bases for mutual understanding

A high level of agreement between the Federal Reserve and the executive branch has been enhanced especially by three factors: exchanges of personnel, frequent and close interactions, and shared understandings of the problems – including the problem of congressional intransigence.

Personnel. Of course, one obvious link is economists. Informal communications networks link economists throughout the executive branch, especially those at the CEA, the Treasury, and the Federal Reserve. Both presidents and their advisors are drawn from the mainstream and are not likely to be very distant in ideology or economic theory from the Federal Reserve. These informal linkages have been reinforced by many exchanges of personnel between the Federal Reserve and the executive branch. This can be observed at the highest levels. The first post-accord chairman of the Federal Reserve, William McChesney Martin, had negotiated the accord for the Treasury. Truman's last appointee to the Federal Reserve, James Louis Robertson, was previously a career official with the Office of the Comptroller of the Currency – a division of the Treasury. The second post-accord Federal Reserve chairman, Arthur Burns, had served as chairman of the CEA for Eisenhower and as an advisor to Nixon. Paul Volcker, the fourth post-accord chairman, has served in the Nixon Treasury, where he played a major role in the transition to floating exchange rates in the early 1970s. A substantive token of the Treasury–Federal Reserve link is the Treasury's repeated expression of support for Federal Reserve freedom from closer congressional oversight.[12]

Most administrations, both Democratic and Republican, have included at least some top policy officials who have been close to the Federal Reserve. For example, under President Kennedy, Douglas Dillon and Robert Roosa (formerly vice-president of the New York Federal Reserve Bank) at the Treasury were quite close in outlook to Martin at the Federal Reserve. This closeness continued under President Johnson with Henry Fowler and Frederick Deming (formerly president of the Minneapolis Federal Reserve Bank). The Carter administration included two former top Federal Reserve staffers: Lyle Gramley at the CEA and Daniel Brill at the Treasury.[13] There have been direct loans of staff from the Federal Reserve to the CEA in several administrations, a practice that creates and preserves links between the two institutions. In at least some cases, CEA analytic work has been staffed out to the Federal Reserve.

Contacts. The president's top economic advisors interact frequently with Federal Reserve officials. Judging from the documents I have read and the reports I have received from various participants, it would be surprising if policy conflicts resulted from a lack of opportunities to exchange views. Others have adequately detailed the various mechanisms used over the years to bridge the institutional gaps between the Treasury, the CEA, and the Federal Reserve.[14] Since the Eisenhower administration, there have been regular meetings of the Quadriad – or an equivalent organization – involving heads of the CEA, Federal Reserve, Treasury, and Office of Management and Budget (OMB). In addition, there have been frequent telephone calls, weekly lunches, periodic meetings, interagency councils, and interagency staff groups to facilitate the exchange of views and the coordination of policy.

It is possible to draw rather strong conclusions about the communications and exchange of information during the Johnson years since so many sources are available. There were many, sometimes redundant, contacts between the Federal Reserve and the White House – some based on official and others on personal relationships. There was ample opportunity for both actors to know what the other was doing and to present their positions. The administration knew in some detail what was on the agenda for upcoming Federal Reserve meetings, and almost always had an opportunity to argue its position, at least with Chairman Martin. Despite the secrecy of FOMC meetings, the White House typically knew within hours what policy decisions had been made. The Federal Reserve and the president were scarcely isolated from one another.

In the Burns years, reports indicate that he monopolized communications with the executive branch. Whereas Johnson administration economists sometimes sought information through such board allies as Vice-Chairman Robertson or Sherman Maisel, the Nixon–Ford economists dealt almost exclusively with Arthur Burns. In many cases, Burns was a personal friend of particular CEA members, and the relationship seems to have been acceptable to both parties. The discussions of substantive matters were very broad between the White House and Burns, and the considerable exchange of information continued. But Burns was regarded in the Nixon years as being very reluctant to share Federal Reserve forecasts, and joint forecasting exercises were halted. However, in the Ford years, it is reported that sharing of forecasts was routine. Whereas Martin had always alerted the administration to pending discount rate changes well before the decision was made, Burns sometimes said nothing until afterward. As Stein put it, "they never described their future policy in terms that enabled us to criticize it." But of the period a few years later, Alan Greenspan said, "I could scarcely conceive of more discussion, more integration of policy overall, than existed with Arthur." Indeed, Greenspan reports, Burns had a "great deal of weight" and "very considerable input" in Ford administration policies.[15]

Carter appointed a former top Federal Reserve staffer, Lyle Gramley, to his CEA and then later to the Board of Governors. This appointment guaranteed that the Carter CEA was fully informed about FOMC decisions on a background basis. Given the number of appointments he made to the board, Carter had ample opportunity to establish close relationships with sympathetic board members. Indeed, for some time even Arthur Burns assumed a role of advisor to Carter, and they met privately on at least a monthly basis.[16] After G. William Miller was appointed chairman of the Federal Reserve, the Carter administration's contacts with the board became even closer, and these close contacts apparently continued under Volcker. Close relationships, of course, do not guarantee the delivery of preferred policy.

Reagan began his term with regular meetings with Chairman Volcker. White House interest in direct meetings then apparently flagged, and they became less frequent. There were still frequent, routinized meetings with the Treasury, the CEA, and at staff levels.

Same boat. In many respects, the president and the Federal Reserve are driven to cooperate simply because they are in the same boat. They are both trying to respond to the same economic crises; their economists analyze the options in similar terms. They both share the view that Congress constitutes an obstacle to swift and well-crafted policy and that to some degree the Federal Reserve can compensate for this shortcoming. As Okun noted in his discussion of policy making in 1966, when Congress was reluctant to act, the Federal Reserve was there, fortunately, to shoulder "the thankless burden."[17] Presidents are aware of the fact that economic sucess depends on receiving the support of the Federal Reserve's constituency – especially finance. This drives some presidents to reiterate their support for Federal Reserve independence. It shapes the appointments process, and it induces moderation in presidential criticism of unwanted Federal Reserve actions. So, for example, shortly after appointing Volcker, the Carter White House refrained carefully from any comment on monetary policy in order to avoid arousing the markets.[18] Presidents realize that they can benefit from the Federal Reserve's far-flung information network and its high-powered economic analysis. In turn, the Federal Reserve realizes the benefits of presidential leadership in making economic programs work. The Federal Reserve also knows that it may need administration assistance in resisting congressional attacks on its independence.

Presidential political resources

We have seen that there are many reasons for cooperation between the Federal Reserve and the president. In the absence of ready cooperation, however, a president is not helpless in dealing with the Federal Reserve. There are three main avenues of presidential influence on the Federal Reserve: assertion of the president's role as the single national elected official; use of the appointment power; and legislative leadership. Each of these forms of influence has considerable potential.

Most important, the president is able to use his resources to back clear, consistent policy preferences. A reference to "the president" often does not refer only to the incumbent, but the president plus his top economic policy advisors. Although all presidents have recognized the importance of economic issues, many have had relatively little interest in or understanding of them. Although the presidential establishment is quite capable of defining a clear, consistent position and pursuing it tenaciously, it is also capable of public divisiveness and conflict. In this regard, one thinks of the conflicts in the early Reagan administration between the supply-siders and the monetarists. Nonetheless, it is true that compared to every other group or institution involved in monetary policy, the president is the one most capable of speaking with a clear voice in support of consistent objectives.

Standing as the nation's leader. The most obvious of the president's resources is the fact that he can claim the democratic legitimacy that is in doubt at the Federal Reserve. One can easily conceive of the Federal Reserve as being reluctant to engage in clear-cut disagreements with presidents, even unpopular ones. The symbolic power of the presidency is immense, and a president's leadership, which is continually in question, can be no more clearly asserted than in a situation in which the "enemy" can be pointed out and personified.[19] Still, it seems reasonable that the value of the president's leadership should fluctuate with the president's own popularity and prestige. One is not surprised at reports during the late Nixon years that monetary policy was more independent than it had been in earlier periods.

The president's appointment power. The power of appointment is an important resource insofar as it determines the values and theoretical outlooks of Federal Reserve Board members. We have already seen that the party of the appointing president is useful in predicting the direction of dissenting votes of board members in the FOMC. However, if staff and peer influences pull members away from their apparent position at the time of appointment, the president has little means of exerting continuing influence over them.

The length of the term of Federal Reserve appointments is intended to limit the ability of any one president to shape the tone of the board. However, during the 1970s, average tenure on the board dropped precipitously. At the start of the decade, the cumulative years of prior board service shared by all members was around fifty. By 1978, this had dropped to around fifteen.[20] Thus, presidents in the 1970s had ample opportunity to shape the composition of the board. Carter was able to appoint a majority – and a new chairman – early in his term.

The most important single appointment the president makes is the appointment of the board chairman. The chairman represents the System to the outside world; he usually exercises a de facto veto over potential appointees; he is frequently the sole representative of administration viewpoints at board or FOMC meetings; he is capable of swaying votes in FOMC and board meetings; he allocates staff resources; he determines the agenda. Yet, as I pointed out in Chapter 4, in every recent appointment, the discretion of presidents in selecting candidates was restricted by the need to maintain the confidence of the financial markets. Chairman G. William Miller resigned when it became clear in 1979 that the markets no longer had confidence in the Carter administration's ability to master inflation.

Two brief anecdotes reveal the limits of the President's power of appointment. Walter W. Heller has recounted the story of a prospective appointee who was asked by the president: "When I call the signals, will you run to my goal or the opposite goal?" "Yours, Mr. President." Yet, Heller says, within six months, maybe even less, when the president called the signals, the new appointee promptly ran to the opposite goal.[21]

The second case has never been publicly discussed. Board Chairman William McChesney Martin, who had angered the president in December 1965 by running to the other goal, began cooperating openly with the president in early 1967 as his term as chairman drew to a close. Heller wrote to Johnson:

> A man who works closely with the Fed's economists tells me: They are now convinced that Bill Martin is "running for reelection." They judge this mainly from the fact that he's pushing so hard for further monetary ease, even to the point of expressing dissatisfaction with the last Open Market Committee decision of "no change" till the next meeting; he would have preferred slight easing. [Also, he has been] telling his staff that some "dramatic" move (such as cutting the discount rate or the reserve ratio for time deposits) is needed to signal the Fed's determination to keep on easing. (By the way this may happen in a couple of days.)[22]

At the same time, CEA Chairman Gardner Ackley was sending similar reports to the president, including one that "on several occasions Bill [Martin] has persuaded the Open Market Committee to go along with something 'because the President wanted it.'"[23] Obviously, Johnson's appointment power increased his influence over the Federal Reserve during this period.

During the Johnson administration, there was considerable emphasis on recruiting "Johnson men" for Federal Reserve appointments. The screening and interviewing procedures should have impressed any potential candidate with the fact that he was undertaking an obligation to the president. In the Nixon–Ford years, Arthur Burns, Nixon's appointee as chairman, played a major role in appointments. His role increased in importance during and after the Watergate crisis. It is clear from conversations with the Nixon–Ford appointees that their sense of being the President's appointee became much weaker following the initial (1972) appointments of Jeffrey Bucher and John Sheehan. Henry Wallich, appointed in 1974, was not even interviewed at the White House.[24] Robert Holland, who had been a top board staffer, was clearly Burns's appointee more than the president's. The same seems to have been the case with Philip Coldwell.

Although it is customary to believe that presidents are primarily concerned with the philosophy of their appointees and with their appeal to particular constituencies, some staff within the Federal Reserve suspected that Burns's choice of board members was intended primarily to reduce resistance to his preferred policy choices. It is impossible to know whether board members resisted Burns as firmly as they should have. Some evidence suggests that Burns did not do a very good job of suppressing resistance if that was his intent. Board members cast fifteen dissenting votes in FOMC votes on the monetary policy directive during the second four years of Burns's tenure and only five during the first four years.

Presidential use of legislative leadership. One of the most formidable resources available to a president is his ability to structure the legislative agenda. When the president identifies a problem as a major national issue, it will almost surely receive considerable attention in Congress. Any president who wanted to could easily put the question of the formal independence of the Federal Reserve on the legislative agenda. Without exception, recent presidents have chosen not to do so.

Proposals to alter the formal links between the president and the Federal Reserve have been quite familiar to students of monetary policy; indeed, almost every commission ever assembled to investigate monetary policy has considered such proposals.[25] During the period 1966–82, there is scant evidence of any sustained presidential interest in fundamentally altering this relationship or in bringing the Federal Reserve under direct presidential control.

President Johnson did not encourage the suggestion by others that he should consider reforming the Federal Reserve structure even after the famous conflict in 1965 over setting the discount rate.[26] Indeed, Johnson responded to a proposal from Senator William Proxmire to hold hearings on whether to make the terms of board members more coterminus with that of the president with a note to Joe Califano saying that "I don't quite understand it all."[27]

In his (lame duck) 1969 *Economic Report of the President*, Johnson advocated some modest reforms in Federal Reserve organization – making the terms of the chairman and the president coincide more closely, removing the geographical requirement for board representation, and asking for congressional review of the process of appointing Reserve Bank presidents.[28] Johnson's interest in reorganization stemmed, at least in part, from a 1968 CEA memorandum indicating that the Federal Reserve district banks were being uncooperative in lowering the discount rate as far and as rapidly as the board preferred.[29] The CEA provided Johnson with a far-ranging list of options. Most were rejected, but all would have been understood as attacks more on the district banks than on System independence per se.[30]

Not until mid-1971, when the Nixon White House wanted to let Arthur Burns know in no uncertain terms that they were displeased with him, were such reforms again publicly discussed.[31] Since that date, there have been no presidential attempts to alter the formal structural arrangements within which the Federal Reserve operates. However, in the early Reagan administration, Treasury Secretary Regan indicated at one point that the Treasury was studying options for limiting the independence of the Federal Reserve. This was apparently a reflection of the irritation of high-ranking monetarists in the Treasury with the inability of the Federal Reserve to keep the rate of growth of the money supply on target. The implication was, of course, that if the Federal Reserve didn't manage to get it right, then perhaps the Treasury could – and would. An alternative explanation was that the administration was trying to weaken congressional anger about interest rates by announcing "a study."[32] In any event, the Treasury retreated from this position within days, in part because "such a move is clearly not welcomed by Wall Street."[33]

The fact that presidents do not focus on this issue is partly due to the high level of policy coordination between the Federal Reserve and the administration. It is also due to the reluctance of presidents to exhaust their resources in combat over a matter that has considerable symbolic value to important constituencies – for example, the financial community. On several occasions, like that in 1982, discussion about altering the Federal Reserve's structure generated anxiety on Wall Street – anxiety that presidents have usually been very slow to encourage.

Conflicts

In only a few instances is it possible to point to particular time periods as obvious periods of conflict. These are important, however, because they confirm that the Federal Reserve does at least occasionally behave in a way that can unambiguously be labeled independent. It is possible in other instances to detect some ongoing tensions between president and Federal Reserve. Neither, of course, is consistent with the strong statement that the president is the superior.

There is no simple, ready method of determining the degree of agreement or disagreement between the Federal Reserve and the president. It is important to stress this point. There is no regularly available source in which to find administration statements of preferences about monetary policy that can be regarded as either clear or independent. One apparent candidate for such a source, one that has intuitive appeal, is the CEA analysis of monetary policy in the *Economic Report of the President.* Such statements could be compared to subsequent policy performance. There are, unfortunately, two serious problems. First, CEA statements are typically rather vague, especially concerning their expectations for monetary policy, and criticism is usually so veiled as to be invisible. Second, CEA statements about monetary policy are often negotiated with the Federal Reserve in advance; thus, they are not independent measures of preferences.[34] It is, of course, possible to describe the movement of policy instruments, but it is not possible to infer preferences from the movement of instruments alone. There is no good substitute for documentary evidence, insider reports, and journalistic accounts addressing the important political issues at stake. This approach gives a better sense of the limited but real independence of the Federal Reserve.

The basic factor producing conflict between the president and the Federal Reserve seems to be their differential responses to the economic conditions experienced in the late phases of economic upswings and downswings.[35] That is, the Federal Reserve is typically faster to switch to a restrictive policy and slower to move to an expansionary policy than the president. In this sense, the most important open conflicts have usually been about the timing of changes in policy direction. Less dramatically but more frequently, there are tensions related to the degree of stimulus or restraint. This occurs during periods when there is agreement that, for example, stimulative policy is in order, but there is not perfect agreement as to how rapidly monetary stimulus should be provided. Viewed in retrospect, the latter kind of disagreement has usually been discounted by participants as not having much significance. Consider the following cases.

December 1965

In late 1965 there was a much-noted dispute between the Federal Reserve and the president over raising the discount rate – an apparent switch in policy direction. The Federal Reserve Board, in a clear rejection of administration preferences, voted to raise the discount rate. There followed a brief public tempest. This is perhaps the best-known example of Federal Reserve conflict with the president, and since the period is very well documented, it merits a relatively detailed review.

At several times during the year, there was tension between the administration and Federal Reserve Board Chairman Martin over Martin's freedom to speak publicly about economic policy without prior coordination with the administration. The Quadriad – the Treasury, the CEA, the OMB, and the Federal Reserve – was reactivated by the Johnson administration in spring 1965 as a place where negotiations over macroeconomic policy could take place. Administration officials hoped that by involving Martin further, they could get him "on the team" and keep him from taking a public position at odds with that of the administration.[36] Early in the year, administration economic advisors began to worry that employment targets would not be achieved. They were anxious to assure that monetary policy accommodated their efforts to stimulate the economy, and consequently they were keenly alert for any signs of significant tightening in monetary policy. Documents show that administration economists believed that a primary indicator of tightening would be an increase in the discount rate.[37] Thus, for practically the entire year, the problem for administration economists was to ensure an adequate fiscal stimulus in the future and an accommodative monetary policy.[38]

So, for example, the concern about Federal Reserve cooperation and Martin's public statements resulted in calling a Quadriad meeting for June 10, only one month after the previous meeting instead of at the quarterly interval that had originally been anticipated.[39] White House worries about possible Federal Reserve tightening continued into early September, but the Federal Reserve still seemed to be cooperating with administration wishes.[40] By late September, market rates were moving up, leading many observers to expect a discount rate increase. Gardner Ackley, CEA chairman, warned the president then that "if there is to be a showdown with the Fed on monetary policy, it probably cannot be delayed much longer."[41] In order to avoid giving the Federal Reserve any official excuse for tightening monetary policy, the Bureau of the Budget decided in early October to withhold budgetary forecasts that would normally have been shared with the System on a confidential basis.[42] Through a series of meetings in the first half of October, administration economists made sure that Martin understood their preferences about monetary policy. Despite these pressures, Martin informed the Business Council – with Ackley present – that he believed interest rates should be raised. Ackley recognized that this was a "declaration of independence."[43]

Nonetheless, throughout November, White House officials received a number of indications of Federal Reserve cooperation. At the start of November, Treasury Secretary Fowler had a lengthy meeting with Chairman Martin to discuss "the credit situation and interest rates." Fowler informed the president that although Martin favored a discount rate increase, he was still willing to continue a policy of "steady in the boat."[44] On November 13, the president received a report of an interagency staff group including Daniel Brill, head of research at the board. Ackley described a staff consensus that "the best course is still 'watchful waiting' by the Fed, with no changes in the discount rate, the prime rate, and the ceiling rate on time deposits. Bill Martin is apparently ready to buy the report."[45] On this evidence, the White House believed that there was an agreement that monetary policy should not change until after the details of the budget were released in a few weeks.

At about this time, administration economists began to sound cautionary notes about the need for future restraint. In a December 1 missive, the Troika (Treasury Secretary, CEA chairman, OMB director) observed that "the case for monetary policy action early in 1966 should not be ruled out – it may, in fact, become persuasive."[46] But the administration economists did argue that later action should be coordinated. Years later, Okun suggested that the CEA wanted to use the threat of Federal Reserve action as a lever to persuade Johnson to act to control the budget.[47] This is not entirely implausible – the CEA tried this kind of maneuver in later periods – but Okun's interpretation has not been echoed in other accounts. Naturally, this kind of motivation would not be reflected in memoranda to the president. In any case, during November, administration economists modified their position that Federal Reserve action was undesirable.

A November 29 memo from Ackley made it clear that there had been further communications between the board and Secretary Fowler and between the CEA and Governor Maisel. Ackley reported on the contents of a discussion at the recent FOMC meeting, and he predicted accurately that a discount rate change was in the offing. The CEA economists were not yet prepared to argue for restrictive monetary policy, and Ackley instead proposed a political solution to the threatened Federal Reserve action. Ackley suggested that a member of the Federal Reserve Board, Dewey Daane, be directly lobbied concerning the discount rate vote. Such an approach has ordinarily been quite rare. Lobbying – that is, contacting members of the board about upcoming decisions – seems to have normally focused on members known to be sympathetic to the administration, and Daane was not regarded as an ally.[48] This occurrence is of sufficient interest that I have included as Exhibit 6.1 a copy of the memo advocating an approach to Daane as it was wired to LBJ at his ranch. It should be noted, as a matter of historical record, that Fowler did contact Daane, but he later voted against the administration.[49] In a December 2 memorandum, Joseph Califano suggested that the president have Fowler talk to Martin. I have found no evidence indicating that this was done,[50] but such a contact would not have been at all unusual. Within a few months, relations between the president and the Federal Reserve had returned to normal levels of tension. CEA economists were writing memos approving of monetary policy. Johnson probably conceived of the appointment of Andrew Brimmer to the board against Martin's wishes as a partial punishment, but no other retribution occurred. Eighteen months later, in fact, Martin was reappointed chairman by President Johnson.

Post-Johnson disputes

In interviews, Carter, Ford, and Nixon CEA members maintained firmly that there had been no significant disagreements with the Federal Reserve during their service.[51] It is clear, however, that there had been tension between the CEA and the Federal Reserve

√ 2 Fowler
Take action
if he thinks

Telexed to Sec Fowler
11-29-65 3P.
gg

EXECUTIVE
FI 8
FG 11-3
FG 233

EEA279
OO WTE10
DE WTE 468

FROM JOE CALIFANO
TO THE PRESIDENT
CITE [illegible]323

Received:
12:04 P.M. Monday 29 November 1965

//UNCLAS// [DECLASSIFIED]

THERE FOLLOWS THE TEXT OF AN URGENT MEMORANDUM TO YOU FROM GARDNER ACKLEY CONCERNING INCREASE IN INTEREST RATES BY FEDERAL RESERVE BOARD.
QUOTE

NOVEMBER 29, 1965

MEMORANDUM FOR THE PRESIDENT

SUBJECT: AVOIDING A DISCOUNT RATE RISE

1. AS JOE FOWLER HAS INFORMED YOU, THE FEDERAL OPEN MARKET COMMITTEE AT ITS MEETING LAST WEEK MADE NO CHANGE IN MONETARY POLICY. HOWEVER, CHAIRMAN MARTIN EXPRESSED HIS INTENTION TO VOTE TO APPROVE AN INCREASE IN THE DISCOUNT RATE IF IT IS PROPOSED BY ANY REGIONAL FEDERAL RESERVE BANK.

2. THREE OF THE REGIONAL BANK BOARDS ARE SCHEDULED TO MEET ON THURSDAY OF THIS WEEK. AT LEAST ONE -- IF NOT ALL THREE -- WILL PROPOSE A DISCOUNT RATE HIKE. BEFORE IT CAN BECOME EFFECTIVE, ANY SUCH INCREASE MUST BE APPROVED BY THE BOARD OF GOVERNORS. IF THE BOARD APPROVES ONE BANK'S PROPOSAL, THIS IS ALWAYS FOLLOWED AT ONCE BY THE OTHER BANKS, WITH APPROVAL TAKEN FOR GRANTED.

3. IN ADDITION TO CHAIRMAN MARTIN, TWO OTHER MEMBERS WILL SURELY VOTE TO APPROVE A DISCOUNT RATE INCREASE; THREE WILL SURELY BE OPPOSED. THE KEY VOTE WILL BE CAST BY GOVERNOR DEWEY DAANE.

4. GOVERNOR MAISEL BELIEVES THAT DAANE'S VOTE AGAINST A DISCOUNT RATE INCREASE CAN BE OBTAINED, ALTHOUGH HE NOW PROBABLY LEANS IN FAVOR OF IT.

DAANE REPRESENTS THE ADMINISTRATION IN A NUMBER OF INTERNATIONAL FORUMS, INCLUDING THE GROUP OF TEN. SECRETARY FOWLER COULD POINT OUT TO DAANE THAT IT WOULD BE INAPPROPRIATE FOR HIM TO CONTINUE TO REPRESENT THE ADMINISTRATION IF HE VOTES AGAINST A CLEAR ADMINISTRATION POLICY POSITION.

IF THIS FAILS, MAISEL BELIEVES THAT A CLEAR COMMUNICATION OF YOUR VIEWS TO DAANE -- PERSONALLY OR THROUGH AN INTERMEDIARY (E.G., DOUG DILLON, WHO RECOMMENDED DAANE'S APPOINTMENT AS GOVERNOR) -- COULD PERSUADE HIM TO WAIT UNTIL THE SITUATION CLARIFIES IN JANUARY.

5. THE BOARD WOULD NORMALLY CONSIDER A THURSDAY RECOMMENDATION AT ITS MEETING ON FRIDAY OR MONDAY. IF YOU SHOULD DECIDE TO MEET WITH THE QUADRIAD ON FRIDAY, YOU MIGHT BE ABLE TO PERSUADE CHAIRMAN MARTIN TO VOTE AGAINST A DISCOUNT RATE INCREASE AT THIS TIME. HOWEVER, BECAUSE HE IS ALREADY ON RECORD WITH HIS COLLEAGUES AS PREPARED TO VOTE IN FAVOR, I BELIEVE THAT IT IS PRUDENT TO TAKE OUT INSURANCE BY WORKING ON GOVERNOR DAANE.

Nothing else sent to Central Files as of 2-14-66 LB

SIGNED
GARDNER ACKLEY

UNQUOTE [UNCLASSIFIED]

Exhibit 6.1. Memorandum, Gardner Ackley to President Johnson concerning a pending Federal Reserve discount rate change.

during the first Nixon administration. This tension, like those later during the Reagan administration, reflected the concern of monetarist presidential advisors with the fact that the money supply did not appear to be growing fast enough. Burns made his displeasure with CEA complaints clearly known, and no further incidents occurred (see Chapter 8).

There have been some reports from onlookers that there were clashes during the Ford years, but none of the immediate participants have confirmed this in retrospect. There was apparently some concern at staff levels that Federal Reserve policy in 1976 was not vigorous enough to support the recovery. However, this appears not to have troubled officials at the top levels.[52]

Carter took office in 1977 while Nixon's appointee as chairman, Arthur Burns, was still serving. Their relationship was apparently strained, and the press paid close attention to evidence of conflict. One incident generated particular excitement. A CEA memorandum critical of monetary policy was posted in the White House press room. Although the CEA maintained later that this was an innocent blunder by inexperienced officials, it was a sharp departure from the normal circumspection affected by administrations in their dealings with the Federal Reserve. Since this was a period when many observers saw tension between the Federal Reserve and the president, the action instantly drew the attention of the press. It became a substantial event that required days to cool down.[53]

Similarly, during the opening months of Miller's tenure at the Federal Reserve, the financial press carefully charted the ups and downs they saw in the relationship.[54] There were further reports in May 1979, prior to Volcker's appointment, that the Carter administration, and in particular the Treasury, was urging the Federal Reserve to tighten further than the Federal Reserve was prepared to go – an interesting reversal of the expected relationship. Carter's Treasury officials apparently believed that the economy was overheating, but the Federal Reserve thought further tightening was inappropriate. In this case, the dissatisfaction seems not to have included the CEA. The situation was even more confused because, as the *Wall Street Journal* observed, "some of the monetarist economists . . . are calling for more ease than Mr. Miller has supplied."[55] In any event, the public squabbling embarrassed the president, who called a halt to it in a matter of weeks.

It appears that when an apparent turning point precedes a presidential election year, top elected officials, who want to avoid a downturn close to an election change their normal attitude with respect to the timing of policy tightening. In such circumstances, disputes would reflect the desire of elected officials for tightening *now* rather than later. The events of 1979 may be paralleled by a dispute in 1955 in which Federal Reserve policy was apparently easier, not tighter, than the administration desired.[56]

Finally, in the waning moments of the 1980 presidential campaign, Carter and Treasury Secretary Miller attacked the Federal Reserve for high interest rates. It is easy to accept the notion that this scapegoating represented last-minute electioneering aimed at traditional Democratic constituencies. What is more telling is that Carter resisted the temptation to attack for so long.

The first two years of the Reagan administration involved two kinds of disagreements with the Federal Reserve. One was a dispute over budget deficits similar to ones that had occurred in previous administrations. But this issue was particularly acute for Reagan given his deep commitment to a supply-side strategy of cutting taxes. The Federal Reserve argued, as it often had before, that reducing the deficit through spending cuts should precede any tax cuts. The administration disagreed. The second dispute involved monetary targeting. Treasury officials repeatedly criticized the Federal Reserve's inability to hit its monetary targets – whether by undershooting or by overshooting. At the same time, officials in both institutions repeatedly stressed their view that the administration basically agreed with and supported what the Federal Reserve was trying to do.

Every administration has experienced some dissatisfaction with the Federal Reserve. It is difficult to believe that the dissatisfaction has not been genuine, and in many cases that displeasure has been publicly understated. This does not mean that disagreements have been fundamental. They have often been focused on the speed, not the direction, of policy action. In some cases, the Federal Reserve has been criticized for economic outcomes it was trying to avoid. However, if it is true that Federal Reserve policy is generally close to what the administration desires, this result is not automatic. It is, in particular, not the product of a relationship between superior and subordinate.

Elections

Few research enterprises have captured the imagination of political scientists in recent years like the demonstration of the link between the timing of presidential elections and macroeconomic policy.[57] Most of the research on the United States has been guided by a single, central, and rather simple hypothesis: The president wants good economic conditions prior to elections, and he achieves them by stimulating the economy before elections. After elections, he undoes the inflationary damage by adopting restrictive policy. The result is a politically generated economic cycle referred to as the "political business cycle" (PBC).

It has not always been obvious to observers that things work this way with monetary policy. Many observers have believed that the Federal Reserve System was likely to create *recessions* at election periods, not booms. Thus Nixon firmly believed, and thus were Lyndon Johnson's economic advisors warned about the Federal Reserve by outsiders.[58] In short, the view in official circles in the mid-1960s was that monetary policy could *not* be counted on to support stimulative fiscal policy.[59]

The PBC hypothesis has been subjected to vigorous criticism, based on the weakness of the empirical findings cited in support of the theory and on conceptual shortcomings in the theory itself.[60] Different studies have produced contradictory results concerning the same countries and even the same elections. Only the 1972 election, which is discussed in Chapter 8, clearly fits the expected pattern in the United States. One possible reason for the absence of good fit in the United States could be that institutional obstacles to rapid changes in fiscal and monetary policy limit the president's ability to manipulate the economy for electoral purposes. The independence of the monetary authority is one such obstacle. Tufte deals with this by suggesting that monetary policy is a participant, often willing, in election-year economic manipulations.

Evidence on monetary policy

Nordhaus has presented no evidence bearing specifically on monetary policy. Still, it is interesting to note that he discovered evidence of "very marked" electoral economic cycles only in Germany, the United States, and New Zealand.[61] Since the central banks of Germany and the United States are often characterized as being independent, Nordhaus's suggestion that it may be possible to diminish PBCs by depoliticizing central banks is somewhat baffling.[62] Tufte presented data on observed growth rates of M1 over the two years before and after presidential elections. He reported that in six of seven postelection biennial periods during

1948–76, M1 grew more slowly after the election, and in four of seven, M1 grew more rapidly before the election – apparently in confirmation of his expectations about PBCs.[63]

My attempt to reproduce Tufte's findings using a slightly different measure, the compound annual rate of change in the detrended monetary base, completely failed to reveal Tufte's pattern.[64] Golden and Poterba estimated reaction functions for the inflation-adjusted money supply to see if it varied in a pattern consistent with the PBC. They found no statistically significant results.[65]

It is more appropriate, surely, to test the PBC hypothesis by looking at the instruments policy makers are actually trying to control rather than at variables, like the money supply, which they cannot control in the short run. Results of this sort are generally quite negative as well. For example, the appropriate PBC hypothesis would probably be that in election years interest rates should decrease or should increase at a rate slower than or equal to the rate of increase in the previous year. If bank reserves are being used as an operating target, they should grow at a rate faster than or equal to the growth rate in the previous year. My examination of those monetary instruments, which, to spare the reader some rather tedious work, is not reported here, shows that trends are about as likely *not* to fit as to fit the PBC hypothesis. On the contrary, monetary policy makers have been as willing to begin a policy of restriction in election years as in nonelection years.[66] In another reaction function study, this one focused on policy instruments, Beck reports that even for the 1972 election there is no econometric evidence consistent with the PBC hypothesis.[67]

Lying low

Sherman Maisel wrote that "Federal Reserve policy has always been to avoid, if possible, taking any major monetary actions as elections approach."[68] This conclusion was echoed in several interviews with Federal Reserve officials. As Governor Partee put it, "if you were to ask a central banker about what he would want to see in a period prior to an election, he would say he wanted to have stability." Stability in interest rates and the money supply would presumably keep the central bank from being dragged into partisan politics.

As far as I know, no discussion of the PBC hypothesis has used this idea to explain why monetary policy might contribute to an observed cycle even though monetary policy instruments do not

Table 6.1. *Highly visible policy moves and election timing, 1955–77*

	Number of highly visible moves occurring in:	
	Even years	Odd years
Easing	19 (61%)	20 (42%)
Firming	12 (39%)	29 (58%)

Notes: Chi square = 4.2 (significant at 0.05 level).
D.f. = 1.
N = 80.

reveal a strong policy thrust. This might have the consequence of producing the PBC pattern if fiscal policy was simultaneously shifting to a very expansionary stance – for example, as in 1972. Such a pattern would, in any case, clearly demonstrate the sensitivity of the Federal Reserve to partisan politics.

To see if quantifiable measures coincided with the anecdotal accounts, I examined the timing of highly visible Federal Reserve actions such as changing the discount rate and reserve requirements. The PBC hypothesis would suggest that in election years (even-numbered years), visible moves should be more toward easing than toward firming, and that there should be fewer actions of any kind in even-numbered years than in odd-numbered years.

Table 6.1 summarizes two kinds of Federal Reserve actions during 1955–77 that are generally regarded as being highly visible and that can be given a straightforward directional interpretation: increases and decreases in the discount rate and reserve requirements.[69] The tendencies are as expected. In even-numbered years, visible actions are more likely to be in an easing direction, and in odd-numbered years to be in a firming direction. Sixty percent of highly visible actions occurred, as anticipated, in odd-numbered years. In short, the Federal Reserve does seem to try to lie low in election periods.

The key policy instrument, the Federal funds rate, has been no more stable in presidential election years than in nonelection years. Over the years 1958–81, the average within-year variation in the monthly average federal funds rate, as measured by the standard deviation, has been 0.819 in presidential election years and 0.892 in odd-numbered years.[70] Obviously, whatever the reality underlying the PBC hypothesis, recent periods are not adequately captured by any relatively simple behavioral expectations. Elections are no doubt very important for monetary policy. They are important not because of political business cycles but because elections determine one set of constraints on policy choice – the identity of the president.

Conclusion

Several important conclusions emerge from this analysis. Rarely have there been lengthy or serious disputes between the president and the Federal Reserve. On the other hand, neither has the relationship been devoid of tensions and uncertainty as to what monetary policy should be. Obviously, the Federal Reserve is not independent in the large, and perhaps absurdly unrealistic, sense of pursuing its own policy objectives oblivious to the preferences of the president. But by the same token, neither is it the president's subordinate. In terms of elections, it is very clear that the Federal Reserve is not indifferent to what is going on. There is almost no persuasive evidence that the Federal Reserve is actively engaged in partisan manipulation, at least not of the sort that can be readily detected. But the Federal Reserve is anything but oblivious to elections. It tries to lie low, to avoid being made the political issue, and this could well lead it to pursue a policy course rather different from the one economists would recommend. If indifference to partisan events is the hallmark of independence, then the Federal Reserve is not independent.

Presidents have political resources they can use to influence the board, and occasionally these have been important. William McChesney Martin's "reelection campaign" of 1967 was a period in which, in retrospect, one can see that policy was overly stimulative. Similarly, the Federal Reserve has its share of political resources, too. Its expertise is genuine and important in a city hungry for expert analysis. Its information network produces knowledge that presidents and their advisors want to have. The confidence of its financial constituency cannot be ignored by any president.

Because the president does not have legal authority over the Federal Reserve, he can function as its superior only through political domination. The fact that the Federal Reserve possesses valuable political resources suggests that both actors may be led to negotiate if they disagree. The common economic analyses, the shared personnel, and the realization that they are in the same boat all tend to encourage agreement. One can also imagine both preferring not to have any disagreements become publicly known. No actor who values his reputation for power wants to be perceived as losing a dispute. No economic policy maker who is committed to achieving good economic performance wants to shake the confidence of financial markets unnecessarily.

There is some fairly clear evidence from the Johnson years that explicit bargaining took place between the president and the Federal Reserve.[71] This is, however, a luxury that is possible only with a very strong president who can count on congressional support. By the mid-1970s, there was very little bargaining, partly because the participants on both sides were less enthusiastic about the prospects for fine tuning the economy and partly because of presidential weakness. Fiscal policy is not controlled solely by the president. Even if the president agreed with the Federal Reserve about policy, it is questionable whether he could deliver. Indeed, this is one reason why presidents are driven to cooperate with the Federal Reserve.

Finally, it is worth noting again that both the president and the Federal Reserve are solidly in the mainstream. There usually *is* a mainstream consensus on the nature of the economic problem. The objective of the president and the Federal Reserve is to establish the details of their own consensus. One consequence of the processes of recruiting and selecting both presidents and Federal Reserve officials is that they will rarely be far apart, and when differences occur they will not be profound. So, it should be neither a surprise nor evidence of nonindependence if, as far as president and Federal Reserve are concerned, monetary and fiscal policy move together.

7

Congress and the Federal Reserve

In a formal sense, Congress is the Federal Reserve's superior. Members of Congress have jealously asserted their right to guide the System, and have occasionally aided the Federal Reserve in fending off administrations seeking a larger role in monetary policy. Members of Congress have repeatedly demanded a pledge from members of the Board of Governors that the Federal Reserve is responsible to Congress. In one exchange in the 1950s, Board Chairman William McChesney Martin was provided with a slip of paper reading "The Federal Reserve is an agency of Congress" and asked to tape it to his mirror so that he could see it each morning as he shaved.[1]

In the early 1980s, the combined effects of high interest rates and high unemployment provoked considerable anger and concern in Congress. Many bills and resolutions were introduced to instruct the Federal Reserve about the conduct of policy. Some of those proposals were sponsored by influential members of Congress, including members of the leadership of both parties. If adopted, some of this legislation would have had the effect of completely removing the autonomy of the Federal Reserve and of substituting for it congressional determination of monetary policy objectives and, in some cases, operating procedures. This move followed a decade of growing congressional attention to and concern about the Federal Reserve. In turn, growing congressional concern produced a clear uneasiness at the Federal Reserve about congressional intent.

Is it plausible that Congress is a threat to the autonomy of the Federal Reserve? How likely is it that Congress would take action either to instruct the System on policy or to subordinate it directly to the president? Some of the comments of high System officials suggest that they perceive Congress as basically unpredictable, rather whimsical, capable of practically *anything* – even destruction of the Federal Reserve.

Despite this perception, congressional action has been notable primarily for its failure to sustain attention to the Federal Reserve's conduct of policy. In contrast to the president, many voices in Congress have regularly advocated alteration in the structure (the independence formula) of the Federal Reserve. More recently, there have been periodic efforts to give policy instruction to the System. These latter efforts have been episodic and, as I shall show, occur in a predictable pattern. However, as events from the mid-1970s demonstrate, even when these efforts have been successful in the legislative arena, there has never been the concerted, persistent, clearly focused action required to significantly shape the behavior of the Federal Reserve.

Congress: capabilities and incentives

Capabilities

Congress is capable of affecting the Federal Reserve in several important ways. Indirectly, Congress can affect the System through fiscal policy, housing policy, laws affecting the functioning of the financial system, and other similar initiatives. All of these may be of considerable concern to the Federal Reserve insofar as they affect monetary policy. Congressional actions may confront the System with a political dilemma. The Federal Reserve has to decide how to respond to budgets it considers too stimulative. Pursuing a more restrictive monetary policy may lead members of Congress to question the legitimacy of the System's actions. By what right does it contradict congressional policy? Other kinds of congressional policy do not pose this dilemma so directly, although the System does have to frame an appropriate response.

Congress can attack the System directly. One means of confronting the System is through the appointments process. Congress can reject appointees or delay approval until policy direction changes. More vigorously, Congress could prescribe monetary policy in great detail. Congress could subordinate the System to the president. It could remove the symbols of independence the System cherishes – relative insulation from the budgetary process, relative secrecy, the private status of the district banks, lengthy terms of appointment, and so forth.

Congress can take more routine kinds of direct action. For example, it can hold oversight hearings and conduct investigations of the Federal Reserve. Congress can provide a highly visible forum for criticism of the System. Hearings and investigations may raise doubts about the System's technical competence or about its willingness to consider the decisions of elected officials as binding. These may be occasions to harass and embarrass the System's representatives.

Incentives

Many recent studies of congressional behavior are based on the relatively simple assumption that members of Congress are primarily (although not exclusively) motivated by the desire for reelection.[2] From this perspective, one would expect action with respect to monetary policy whenever members of Congress could reasonably anticipate an electoral payoff. For example, one might expect action when particular constituent groups are harmed by monetary policy (i.e., especially when money is tight) or when beneficial publicity could be generated by well-timed hearings.

A second line of analysis stresses that "the electoral motive" needs to be supplemented by other motives in order to make sense of important historical developments in Congress as an institution. Most prominently, Dodd speaks of the "power motive."[3] Usually this implies a struggle between the president and Congress, but obviously the Federal Reserve could be involved in a broader attempt to assert congressional power. Dodd argues that congressional attention must be directed periodically toward maintaining the external authority of the institution.

The banking committees

It is almost a cliché to say that the work of Congress is carried out in committees. In a direct confrontation over the conduct of monetary policy or an attempt to reduce the System's autonomy, the Banking Committees of the House and Senate would usually be the source of action. Fiscal policy, of course, is the responsibility of the Budget and Appropriations committees. The Joint Economic Committee regularly holds hearings on all aspects of economic policy, including monetary policy. Occasional action of importance to the Federal Reserve has originated in the Government Operations Committee. In this chapter, attention is focused primarily on the Banking Committees.

Congressional scholars have been less successful in moving from an examination of the motives of individual members of Congress to an understanding of the functioning of specific committees such as the Banking Committees. The most important characteristic of the Banking Committees seems to be the relatively modest quantity of highly selective pork barrel material benefits they control and, probably as a consequence, their generally low prestige and power. Powerful committees such as Appropriations, House Ways and Means, and Senate Finance all have substantial ability to distribute benefits and influence policy. The Banking Committees, with their relatively meager capacity to bestow benefits widely, have been less attractive assignments.[4] Lower power and prestige are associated with high rates of turnover because members attempt to move to more desirable posts.[5] Most members seem to have little interest in the substantive policy issues before the committees.[6]

In summary, the nature of the committees suggests that members will often be new to the substantive area and technically uninformed. Members of Congress seeking primarily to gain control of distributive benefits will find that there are relatively few such benefits associated with service on the Banking Committees. This may further lower their interest in the issues at hand.

The partisan and interest group context

Although the policy issues the Banking Committees consider are challenging and complex, they are, by and large, not central to contemporary partisan conflict. Money and banking were once the commanding issues of the day, but, by the early years of the twentieth century, most of those issues had been settled.[7] In recent years, banking and financial issues have achieved prominence during crises and during periods in which financial innovations have threatened to alter traditional market shares in the industry. However, the alternatives debated usually have not been divisive in partisan terms. In the absence of clear partisan guidance, one would expect the Banking Committees to be heavily influenced by the executive branch and interest groups.[8] In particular, the committees should be responsive to the changes in patterns of mobilization and demobilization by groups intermittently harmed (or helped) by monetary policy. This uneven pattern of influence, together with the fact that many of these issues lie outside the basic partisan cleavage, explains why otherwise liberal members of Congress often vote for pro-banking positions (in violation of the hopes of some liberal researchers).[9]

The interest group context within which the Banking Committees operate is complex, involving as it does the construction industry, banks, savings and loan associations, labor, consumer finance, and industries dependent on consumer finance (e.g., automobiles). In many cases, the issues before the committees involve difficult zero-sum tradeoffs between segments of the financial industry, for example, banks versus savings and loans or money market mutual funds versus banks. Here we see another reason why members of Congress who are not intrinsically interested in these policy questions might find the Banking Committee assignment relatively unattractive.

It is difficult to assemble thorough information on the relationship between members of the Banking Committees and the many interest groups they deal with. Still, it may be of interest to examine the relationships between committee members and the banking industry since banking is the Federal Reserve's main constituent group. We have seen in Chapter 4 that banking interests are highly organized and are often represented by lobbyists with close links in Congress.[10] However, neither House nor Senate committee members have frequently been owners of stock in financial institutions.[11]

There is information available about contributions by financial Political Action Committees (PACs), but it is ambiguous regarding the extent to which such contributions obligate members of Congress to financial and other interest groups. Bank PACs have not been among the top PAC contributors to election campaigns.[12] On the other hand, financial PACs do concentrate their activities on the Banking Committees. One study of five financial PACs show that at least four of them made contributions to the same twenty-five candidates; of these twenty-five, seventeen were members of the House Banking Committee.[13]

Of course, the banking industry is not the only industry attentive to the Banking Committees. For example, the savings and loan associations are also highly organized. In a recent year, between 33 and 69 percent of Senate Banking Committee members have been recipients of honoraria from banking or savings and loan interests (the mean percentage is 48).[14] Officials of banks and savings and loan associations make substantial personal donations to Banking Committee members; in dollar terms, these have been twice as large as the contributions of banking PACs.[15]

In summary, conventional partisan divisions have not clearly shaped the debate on many issues the Banking Committees consider. Consequently, one expects that members' decisions will be shaped more by their personal ideologies and the nature of the pressures from interest groups and constituents. Available evidence suggests that financial interest groups are well staffed, well financed, and make carefully targeted financial contributions to members of the Banking Committees in efforts to win access.

Committee floor success and divisiveness

Insofar as the Banking Committees resemble the Education and Labor Committee of Fenno's analysis, committee voting decisions should be marked by a sharp division.[16] Members should prefer to insist on good policy rather than to compromise. As a result, the committee should have less success in passing its bills on the floor than committees such as Appropriations that are preoccupied with achieving power in the House.

In fact, several of Fenno's expectations seem to be confirmed. In particular, the Banking Committees are more liberal than their respective houses and are sharply divided internally. They apparently have only modest success in passing legislation.[17] Low success would be expected, too, for any legislation attacking an institution such as the Federal Reserve, valued by conservatives and viewed by many moderates as vital to the stability of the economy.

Incentives and oversight

We expect actors external to the Federal Reserve to be successful in shaping its behavior only if they are able to specify their policy preferences in the appropriate technical language and to do so persistently in a consistent, clear way. The president appears to be able to do this, as do monetarist economists and, at a very general level, bankers. Nothing so far suggests that Congress or the Banking Committees have this capability. The reasons for this inability may be found in the kinds of incentives that members of Congress face. These incentives have usually discouraged congressional oversight of the sort that would be required to influence monetary policy.

Studies of oversight have agreed on one conclusion: Oversight is pursued insofar as it pays off for the legislator relative to alternative uses of his or her time.[18] In an analysis of committee review of independent regulatory agencies, Scher called oversight "a spasmodic affair."[19] Bibby observed that the Senate Banking Committee's interest in oversight was aroused "only in special circumstances, such as a major scandal."[20] Scher's concluded that there is not more oversight for several reasons:

1. Oversight provides fewer electoral benefits for members of Congress than does constituent service.
2. Members of Congress are afraid of looking ignorant.
3. Members of Congress are reluctant to disrupt mutually beneficial relationships with agencies.
4. Personal contacts are more effective than congressional hearings in serving constituent needs.
5. Oversight investigations may provoke reprisals from the agency's constituency.
6. Members of Congress avoid embarrassing presidential appointees if there are potential payoffs for supporting the president.
7. When oversight is not part of committee routine, it tends to be ignored.

Naturally, the opposite conditions should encourage oversight. Congressional staff interviewed for this study characterize the members of the Banking Committees in terms that are remarkably similar to those used by Bibby and by Scher. Staffers say that members do not understand monetary policy, do not really care, and therefore are willing to listen to the Federal Reserve on policy. Senator William Proxmire flatly pointed out that congressional influence on the Federal Reserve is "extremely thin":

> And it's not hard to understand why. Monetary policy is considered to be extremely complicated by most Senators. The influence of policy on the economy is indirect, and the lags are long – and the length of lags is controversial. How surely monetary policy will affect things like unemployment, inflation, economic growth, and so forth is very hard to say . . .
>
> If things get too extreme, however, there is more of an interest – if, for instance, tightening monetary policy results in making things very uncomfortable for home building. . . . Congressmen have many other obligations and interests. And other things don't require the preparation and technical analysis that monetary policy does.

One could hardly ask for a more succinct restatement of the kinds of factors Scher identified.

Agencies can also engage in positive activities to discourage oversight. These actions are clearly illustrated in the case of the Federal Reserve. The Federal Reserve has tried to encourage congressional good will by providing expert advice and commentary to members of Congress interested in economic reforms. The Federal Reserve courts members with frequent small private breakfasts. At these breakfasts, the chairman provides them with specialized financial and economic information about their districts as well as the latest inside word on the course of macroeconomic policy.[21] The ultimate effect of these activities is to reinforce the System's reputation for power and expertise. By providing favors for members of Congress, the Federal Reserve helps create the barrier that must be overcome prior to effective oversight – the "aura" of which congressional staff speak. The aura is that projected by the master of a vast and arcane science, and it is cherished by the Federal Reserve.

Patterns of interaction with the Federal Reserve

There are two readily observable aspects of the Federal Reserve's relationship with the Banking Committees that can be examined. The first involves the frequency with which members of the Board of Governors appear before the committees to testify. The second involves the timing of congressional efforts to alter the course of policy or to discipline the Federal Reserve by reducing its independence.

The frequency of testimony by members of the Board of Governors is influenced largely by personal factors and by the rhythms of congressional life rather than by policy considerations or the condition of the economy.[22] Figure 7.1 plots the frequency of appearances by board members before Banking and other congressional committees. The major breaks in the series involving the Banking Committees occur in 1970, when Arthur Burns became the chairman of the Federal Reserve, and in 1975, when new, more aggressive chairmen assumed control of each Banking Committee. There may be another break developing in the mid-1980s following another change in the chairmanship of the Banking Committees. Also, note that in the 1970s there is a clear drop-off in appearances during election years, when time for hearings is more limited.

Legislative challenges, by contrast, are linked in a general way to economic conditions. A House Banking Committee staffer offered the following summary of the committee–Federal Reserve relationship: "Whenever things are going well, nobody really raises

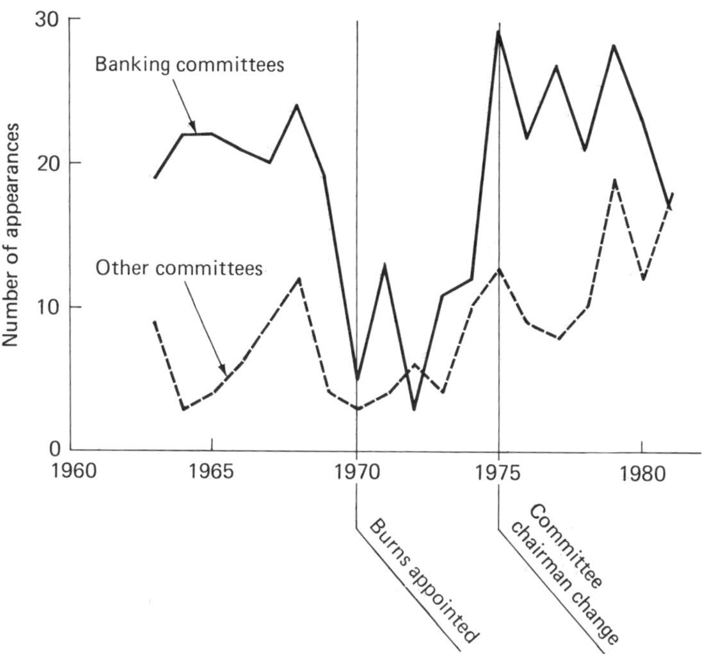

Figure 7.1. Appearances by members of the Board of Governors for testimony before the Banking Committees and other committees, 1963–81.

hard questions. When they go badly, all institutions are subjected to questioning." And evidence seems to confirm this notion. The most serious challenges to the conduct of monetary policy occur in periods when interest rates are high and interest-sensitive industries are hurt.

Various actions have been taken to confront the System directly and may have been perceived as a threat by the Federal Reserve. There have been three general approaches:

1. Structural reforms of the System, such as audits by the General Accounting Office (GAO); subjecting the System to the congressional budget process; altering the composition of the FOMC; and reducing Federal Reserve secrecy.
2. Credit allocation to protect those sectors vulnerable to restrictive monetary policy.
3. Direct instruction of the Federal Reserve regarding tar-

Table 7.1. *Legislative actions concerning the Federal Reserve, 1970–80*[a]

	Structural reforms					Credit allocation					Conduct of monetary policy				
Year	0	1	2	3	4[b]	0	1	2	3	4	0	1	2	3	4
1970	–	–	–	–	–	–	–	–	–	–	–	X	–	–	–
1971	X	–	–	–	–	–	X	–	–	X	X	–	–	–	–
1972	–	–	X	–	–	–	–	–	–	–	–	–	–	–	–
1973	–	–	X	–	–	–	–	–	–	–	X	–	X	–	–
1974	–	–	–	X	–	–	–	–	–	–	X	–	–	–	–
1975	X	X	X	–	–	–	X	X	–	–	–	X	–	–	X
1976	–	X	–	X	X	–	–	–	–	–	X	–	–	–	–
1977	–	–	–	X	X	–	–	–	–	–	–	–	–	–	–
1978	–	X	–	–	X	X	–	–	–	–	X	–	–	–	X
1979	–	–	X	X	–	–	X	–	–	–	X	X	–	–	–
1980	–	X	–	–	–	X	–	–	–	–	X	–	–	–	–

[a]Both House and Senate Banking Committees and Banking Subcommittees and, in 1977, the Government Operations Committee. See also Appendix B.

[b]Key to entries

0: Investigatory hearings other than routine oversight (i.e., after 1975); no bill considered.

1: Hearings on proposed legislation.

2: Legislation reported out by committee.

3: One house passes legislation.

4: Both houses pass legislation.

gets it should achieve, such as for interest rates or monetary aggregates.

During the late 1960s and throughout the 1970s, there was legislative activity in each of these areas. At the very least, hearings were held concerning each kind of threat. The frequency and disposition of those actions are summarized in Table 7.1.[23] If hearings may be taken as an indicator of minimal levels of legislative concern, there was continuing concern about the Federal Reserve in the 1970s. Action of all sorts peaked in 1975, when the economy was just recovering from a deep recession. However, giving direct instructions about the conduct of monetary policy has until recently been the least popular congressional approach. Congress has overwhelmingly preferred structural approaches to reforming the Federal Reserve, with intermittent interest in schemes for credit allocation. Comparative study suggests that such a structural approach is not likely to be fruitful in shaping Federal Reserve behavior.[24] Of course, since behavioral independence has often been assumed to be a function of organizational factors, the congressional approach is not unreasonable.

Avenues of reform

With the exception of action taken in 1975 (considered subsequently), legislation that actually passed between 1970 and 1980 did not address the conduct of monetary policy directly.[25] In 1971, credit allocation provisions were inserted by the House Committee in HR 11309, a bill to extend the Economic Stabilization Act, under which President Nixon was then carrying out wage and price controls. The mild language required the president to control interest rates whenever prices were controlled – if he determined that control of interest rates was necessary to stabilize the economy.[26] If this was perceived as a threat to the Federal Reserve, it was minimal.

The "Sunshine Act" of 1976 (HR 11656) did threaten to reduce the secrecy at the Federal Reserve. The System fought successfully for exemptions. The Federal Reserve Reform Act, passed in 1977, continued the quarterly oversight first required by a concurrent resolution in 1975; required Senate confirmation of nominations to the chairmanship and vice-chairmanship of the Federal Reserve Board; prohibited discrimination in the selection of regional Federal Reserve Bank directors; and required consideration of broader economic interests in the selection of bank directors representing the public.[27] In 1978, the much compromised Humphrey-Hawkins Act required the Federal Reserve to report on its projections for various economic quantities in the upcoming year and to justify any projections that seemed inconsistent with those of the president. The FOMC has adopted relatively wide bands for these projections, bands that reflect the range of views within the committee, virtually precluding any clear disagreement with the president. Finally, also in 1978, HR 2176, requiring a limited GAO audit (excluding the details of monetary policy), was passed. In short, by 1978, most of the reform agenda dealing with the structure of the Federal Reserve had been adopted, but only in name. In substance, the reforms were quite modest.

The politics of congressional control of monetary policy

Many obstacles lie in the way of effective congressional supervision of monetary policy. The strategy most frequently used has been one of post hoc discipline of the Federal Reserve by structural reforms attacking the System's independence. To recall the discussion in Chapter 1, this is exactly the kind of strategy one would expect from an institution that is decentralized and difficult to coordinate, and whose members are uncertain of their expertise. However, the timing of this kind of action has not been closely related to economic performance. In other words, congressional dissatisfaction is hard to link to specific policy performance. The recent history of structural reforms suggests the importance of the power motive in this area of reform; that is, these reforms reflect the time-tested concern for congressional prerogatives.

These efforts have occasionally generated some lively political maneuvering by supporters of the Federal Reserve – principally bankers. These supporters value the symbolism of an independent institution dedicated to inflation fighting. So, on at least a few occasions, when Congress has threatened that independence, the Federal Reserve's constituency has rallied to its defense. The clearest example of this occurred in the early 1970s and involved attempts to subject the Federal Reserve, including the district banks, to a GAO audit. In response there was a substantial lobbying campaign, partly organized by the district banks, which aided in bringing about the defeat of the audit legislation proposed by Wright Patman.[28] The effect of the campaign was to guarantee that monetary policy was exempted from subsequent bills.

The more serious attempts to take control of monetary policy, or at least to instruct the Federal Reserve about how to conduct it, have been post hoc responses to high interest rates and the collapse of the housing industry. In that these responses are prompted by the problems of constituents, they can probably best be explained by the election motive. To indicate the timing of these events, Figure 7.2 plots the condition of the housing industry as measured by the number of housing starts at an annual rate. Since 1967, the housing industry has hit bottom in early 1970, early 1975, and late 1981. At approximately those dates, Congress took special steps to alert the Federal Reserve that it was very concerned about the consequences of high interest rates. In 1969 Congress passed a law (PL 91–151) granting the president stand-by authority to control

Figure 7.2. New private housing starts, 1968–82 (millions, annual rate, log scale). (Source: Business Conditions Digest, *October 1982, p. 25.)*

interest rates. Politically, this was an attempt to remove any excuse that the president might have for limiting the harmful consequences of Federal Reserve policy. The power was not used until 1980, when President Carter temporarily imposed controls on consumer credit. In 1970, hearings were held on legislation to require a rollback in interest rates. In 1973, when price control legislation was under review, Congress flirted with the idea of controlling interest rates, but eventually decided against it. In 1975 the response of Congress was to pass a resolution urging the Federal Reserve to maintain a steady rate of growth of the money supply. At the time, it seemed clear that if the Federal Reserve had kept monetary growth higher in 1974, the recession would not have been so severe and interest rates would have been lower. This action, which I will discuss in more detail subsequently, was quite consistent with the usual interest rate-related pattern of post hoc rebukes of the Federal Reserve.

Finally, in the period 1980–2 there was a flood of resolutions and bills concerning monetary policy and the Federal Reserve, most of them clearly reflecting congressional frustration about high interest rates. For example, one bill, Senate Joint Resolution 120 (from 1982), requiring the president to assure an adequate flow of affordable credit to small borrowers, secured thirty-five cosponsors. By the end of 1982 there had been hearings and threats of floor amendments, but only a token resolution actually passed as a rider to other legislation. There were reasons to expect that, as in previous similar cases, Congress would not be satisfied until some stronger symbol of its dissatisfaction had been produced.

The congressional challenge of 1975

Conditions in 1975 were ripe for an attack on the Federal Reserve. The economy was bad; new members of Congress had recently been elected who took a very aggressive stance toward the executive branch; and both Banking Committees had new chairmen who were relatively hostile toward the Federal Reserve. However, as we shall see, the action taken was vague and compromised, and the follow-up was half-hearted. In this area, members of Congress opted for symbol rather than substance.

The 1974–5 recession (officially lasting from the fourth quarter of 1973 to the first quarter of 1975) seemed at the time to be particularly devastating. In President Ford's inflation conference in September 1974, heavy criticism was directed at the Federal Reserve by many economists,[29] and Arthur Burns appeared to defy their advice to ease monetary policy.[30] At that time, interest rates in the secondary mortgage market hit 10.4 percent – the highest rates ever in the post–World War II period, and the housing industry was crashing into depression. The federal funds rate in February 1975 had dropped to around 9 percent, down from the July 1974 high of almost 13 percent – another postwar high.

The 94th Congress was marked by the arrival of the "Watergate class." In 1975, over 45 percent of the House Banking Committee members were new – the highest percentage in the period from the 88th to the 94th Congresses; they were inexperienced, inexpert, and Democratic. In the Senate, by contrast, Banking Committee turnover (23 percent) was lower than average. The influx of new members seems not to have produced an especially liberal Congress,[31] but the new members were more aggressive toward the executive branch or, in Dodd's terminology, more concerned with the power motive. At about this time, accusations were published suggesting that Federal Reserve policy in 1972 had been motivated by partisan politics, possibly helping to justify further congressional skepticism about Federal Reserve behavior.[32]

Wright Patman, the autocratic chairman of the House Banking Committee, was one of three chairmen removed by the Democratic caucus under recently adopted reform rules. His successor, Henry Reuss, was generally known as a liberal, less preoccupied with the evils of banking, and very concerned about exerting congressional dominance over the Federal Reserve. Legislatively, Reuss was more flexible than Patman, more willing to compromise. He was thus able to produce more viable legislation containing a threat to the Federal Reserve.[33]

Also in 1975, John Sparkman resigned his chairmanship of the Senate Banking Committee in order to become chairman of the Foreign Relations Committee. Sparkman had been a personal friend of Arthur Burns and a protector of the Federal Reserve. He was succeeded by William Proxmire, a liberal maverick, who was confident of his ability to understand economic policy and the Federal Reserve.

One study has shown that congressional oversight increased in the 1970s largely due to an increase in staff resources.[34] However, this factor cannot account for congressional action in 1975 or for the subsequent increase in oversight of the Federal Reserve – although the lack of growth of specialized staff may account in part for the failures of oversight. On the Senate Banking Committee there was steady growth in the size of the staff between 1972 and 1977 – but not in staff specializing in monetary policy.[35] One professional economist was on the staff during this period, and a former Federal Reserve economist was hired after 1975. In fact, subsequently, the handful of professional staff have complained of being hampered by the lack of trained economists on the Banking Committee staff and in Congress generally. In this respect, matters have not changed significantly since Bibby's study nearly two decades ago.[36]

Seldom have conditions seemed more conducive for a broad-based attack on the Federal Reserve than in 1975. A Democratically controlled Congress faced an appointed Republican president. The economy was staggering through a bitter recession that had throttled the construction industry. Many Democrats felt that they had a mandate to revive the economy. An expert consensus laid much of the blame for the recession at the doorstep of the Federal Reserve. There was new, more effective Banking Committee leadership and a new Congress populated with members eager to discipline a runaway executive branch. When, if ever, would the Federal Reserve be more vulnerable?

HCR 133: Legislative monetarism?

In February 1975, both Proxmire and Reuss introduced legislation to give specific policy direction to the Federal Reserve and to increase congressional oversight. Reuss moved first with HR 212, specifying the rate of change in the money supply (6 percent) the

Federal Reserve should achieve and calling for credit allocation to "national priority uses." Following hearings at which Burns vigorously opposed the proposed legislation, Patman and cosponsors introduced two bills that revised HR 212 and split it into two parts – HR 3160 and HR 3161. Instead of specifying a money growth target, HR 3160 directed the Federal Reserve to lower interest rates. HR 3161 vested credit allocation authority in the president rather than the Federal Reserve.

Hearings were hastily called on these two bills for the evening of February 19, with Arthur Burns as the only witness. Burns's spirited attack on those bills effectively immobilized the committee. In the course of the hearings, Burns proposed two routes for further action: voluntary "affirmative action programs" in bank lending rather than credit allocation, and periodic Federal Reserve consultations with Congress about the conduct of monetary policy.[37] The next day, the committee reported out a new piece of legislation, largely authored by Thomas Rees (D., Calif.), House Concurrent Resolution 133 (HCR 133), directing the Federal Reserve to lower long-term interest rates and to report quarterly to Congress on its progress.

Proxmire introduced his own resolution, Senate Concurrent Resolution 18 (SCR 18), on February 12. In contrast to the House approach, Proxmire's proposal directed the Federal Reserve to expand the money supply for the first half of 1975 so as to facilitate prompt recovery; maintain long-run growth in the monetary and credit aggregates commensurate with long-run potential output growth; and appear semiannually before Congress to discuss plans for the next six months. Eventually, after amending the bill to incorporate the House's references to lowering long-run interest rates, Proxmire's version was substituted for, and passed in late March as, HCR 133.[38] Burns was somewhat less successful in opposing the more monetarist thrust of the Senate's version.[39]

Thus, Congress moved from considering aggressive legislation in the form of HR 212 to two less aggressive bills (HR 3160 and HR 3161) and ended up with a relatively mild resolution. Several liberal Democrats opposed the House version because they thought it was too weak. Despite attempts to characterize the legislation as a "directive from Congress," it clearly was not strong action. Nor would anyone with a knowledge of the history of congressional reluctance to take strong action in this area have expected anything different. Obviously, there were some members of Congress who would have preferred more forceful moves. But even the House Banking Committee, more liberal than the House as a whole, was unwilling to report out that kind of legislation.[40]

So, despite the innovation of attempting to give instructions to the Federal Reserve, and despite the monetarist tone, HCR 133 was toothless and compromised. It indicated some congressional concern about money supply growth rates, and it suggested that perhaps members were paying more attention to M1 than in the past. But even in this respect, the legislation was flawed. HCR 133 explicitly permitted the Federal Reserve System to deviate from announced target ranges.[41] Moreover, neither HCR 133 nor the process of debate preceding it produced a clear signal from Congress that it cared about monetary aggregates more than interest rates. The compromise language of HCR 133 explicitly incorporated references to interest rates. Reuss referred repeatedly to interest rates in his presentation of the compromise legislation to the House, assuring members that their earlier "language and intent" had been retained. And, of course, earlier House language and debate referred almost exclusively to interest rates.[42] For years, it had seemed that Congress became upset when high interest rates shut down the housing industry. A prudent policy maker, faced with all this information, might reasonably have concluded that Congress's political demands had not really changed. Mainly, HCR 133 required the appearance of the Federal Reserve chairman at regularly scheduled hearings. This was an *opportunity* for fruitful exchange, nothing more.

When opportunity knocks

After HCR 133 passed, Milton Friedman wrote that it was a "major change," and speculated that it would make the Federal Reserve more accountable, more likely to produce the policy it had announced.[43] Many, like Friedman, were optimistic at the time. What did Congress do with this opportunity? For Congress to have been effective in enforcing its will, members would have needed to demonstrate persistent concern. Different committees dealing with similar topics would have needed to have demonstrated similar, if not identical, concerns about policy. There were actions that tended to support the monetarist tone of HCR 133, but interest was neither persistent over time nor consistent across committees.

Lack of interest. Measures of the level of congressional information about and interest in specific issues are rare, to say the least. One cannot know with any certainty that members of Congress are better informed about monetary policy now than before HCR 133. However, Banking Committee staff economists report that in their view the hearings have served the useful function of focusing congressional oversight on measures of Federal Reserve monetary policy action and have raised the level of debate in Congress.[44]

Data on attendance at regularly scheduled oversight hearings, however, indicate that members of Congress have regarded routine oversight as a rather low priority. In contrast to Bibby's expectation, routinizing oversight appears not to have resulted in a significant change in the members' calculus about how best to allocate their time. Attendance at regular oversight hearings is sharply affected by the identity of the witnesses appearing, with attendance much higher when the chairman of the Board of Governors is in the chair. Between 1975 and early 1982, average attendance at Senate Banking Committee hearings more than doubled when the chairman appeared, and, on similar hearing days, attendance increased by 40 percent in the House Banking Committee. These findings do not indicate high levels of concern about policy. Rather, they suggest nothing so much as a well-developed sense for the location of a good media event.[45]

I am not aware of figures for attendance at oversight hearings in other committees that could show whether the members of the Banking Committees do better or worse than their colleagues in other areas. There were so few similar Federal Reserve oversight hearings involving the Banking Committees prior to HCR 133 that a before and after comparison is also ruled out. There have been a few other Federal Reserve oversight hearings during this period in the House Banking Committee, and those cases suggest that nonroutine oversight hearings produce more interest than the routine kind. This reinforces the conclusion that routine oversight is a very low priority for committee members.[46]

Lack of consistency. Largely through the efforts of former House Banking Committee staffer Robert Weintraub, there was some success in creating the presumption of congressional support for monetarism.[47] As table 7.2 reveals, appearances to testify before the House Banking Committee by all economists increased dramatically after Weintraub began to serve (1975). Not coincidentally, Weintraub also increased substantially the probability that

Table 7.2. *Appearances before the House Banking Committee (HBC), Senate Banking Committee (SBC), and JEC by monetarists and nonmonetarists, 1970–9*

	HBC		SBC		JEC	
Year	Mon.	Nonmon.	Mon.	Nonmon.	Mon.	Nonmon.
1970	0[a]	0	0	2	1	3
1971	0	2	0	1	2	6
1972	0	0	0	0	0	14
1973	1	6	1	5	0	9
1974	1	0	0	2	0	10
1975	3	5	9	1	0	15
1976	3	3	2	4	0	10
1977	7	4	1	3	0	6
1978	3	4	1	4	0	11
1979	2	3	2	4	3	6
Total	20	27	16	26	6	90

[a]Tallies are limited primarily to academic economists and economists with independent research organizations such as Brookings and the AEI. Economists employed primarily by business and testifying primarily on the effect of policies on particular industries are excluded, as are trade association economists. (Exceptions were made so as to favor the monetarists: Beryl Sprinkel, Jerry Jordan, and, perhaps implausibly, Alan Greenspan). Also excluded are economists testifying as government officials. Counted as monetarists appearing before the House Banking Committee are Brunner, Meltzer, Christ, Dewald, Jordan, Laidler, Meigs, Meiselman, Poole, Sprinkel, and William Fellner, Darryl Francis, and John Lindauer. Counted as monetarists when appearing before the JEC are Brunner, Weintraub, Christ, Alan Greenspan, and, again perhaps implausibly, Herbert Stein.
Source: Lists of appearances and information on substance of testimony are drawn from *CIS Annual Abstracts,* 1970–9. JEC counts are based only on testimony at hearings on the *Economic Report of the President.* House and Senate Banking Committee counts refer to all hearings dealing with macroeconomic policy and the performance of the Federal Reserve.

monetarists would be called to testify before the committee. One can also perceive Weintraub's monetarist influence in the Senate Banking Committee figures for 1975, when he worked briefly for that committee. Otherwise, in both the Senate Banking Committee and the Joint Economic Committee (JEC), monetarists and monetarism still played a very minor role (Table 7.2). For the period covered in Table 7.2 when Weintraub was employed only in the House Banking Committee (1976–9), monetarists constituted a *majority* of the economists who were called to testify. In the other committees, their proportions more nearly approached their degree of representation in the economics profession.[48]

The monetarist approach of the House Banking Committee strengthened in the late 1970s and was plainly evident in the reports issued by the committee commenting on monetary policy.[49] But since this had a highly personal cause, the particular committee chairman and his staff, when the chairman and staff changed in the early 1980s, so did the content of the reports.[50] After 1981, when the leadership and staff of the Senate Banking Committee changed, the monetarist tone of their monetary policy reports increased markedly.[51] During the same period, the content of commentary on monetary policy in the JEC reports on the *Economic Report of the President* never was monetarist. The committee's reports for the entire decade of the 1970s were marked by concern about interest rates; the money supply was discussed as if it were an instrument for influencing the short-run behavior of interest rates. The recommendations of the JEC for 1978 were typical and scarcely monetarist: "The growth of the money supply should be such that the rise in short term interest rates is reversed. Policy in 1978 should tend to move short-term rates toward their 1977 levels. Short term interest rates should be maintained at these lower levels in 1979."[52] No matter how monetarist the Banking Committees may have become, other influential committees have been giving the Federal Reserve sharply conflicting instructions. By 1982, members of Congress were rushing to introduce legislation to force the Federal Reserve to begin targeting interest rates.

Given the language of HCR 133, the history of debate preceding its passage, and the history of prior congressional interest in interest rates, there was little reason to expect that it would cause much change in behavior at the Federal Reserve. As it became clear that members of Congress were not interested in monetary policy on a continuing basis, it should have been even more obvious that HCR 133 would do little to change Federal Reserve behavior. And indeed, it appears that this is exactly what happened. Nonetheless, economists who had believed that HCR 133 would change Federal Reserve behavior were disappointed.[53]

In fact, the Federal Reserve responded to HCR 133 overwhelmingly as a problem in congressional relations, not as a directive requiring a change in operating procedures. In April 1975, the FOMC discussed at length how it should respond to the HCR 133 challenge.[54] In that meeting, there was only a hint from FOMC members that the legislation might require a change in operating procedures.[55] After all, the FOMC's view was that it had been specifying monetary targets internally for several years. The problem, as its members perceived it, was how best to announce their targets to Congress.

The discussion focused on several questions. For which aggregates should targets be announced? Should point targets or ranges be used? If ranges, how wide should they be? Some members argued for announcing only one target for a quantity closely controlled by the central bank such as bank reserves, and then announcing ranges for other aggregates believed to be consistent with that target. There was also an argument that rather narrow ranges should be announced (e.g., 1 percent) to avoid suspicion that the Federal Reserve did not take targeting seriously.

Eventually, however, the argument that won the day was that the FOMC should try to satisfy members of Congress. This meant that ranges should be 2 percent wide because that was what Burns believed a committee chairman expected.[56] This meant that targets should be announced for the familiar aggregates M1 and M2 because this was what members of Congress expected. It meant that a target for M3 should be announced because this involved funds for the housing industry, which so interested Congress. In a later meeting, this kind of argument caused the FOMC to decide always to announce targets for the next twelve months (i.e., for the next year) rather than only for calendar years.[57] This decision, made to satisfy congressional onlookers, obviously provided the opportunity for "base drift," or acceptance of past target misses, which some observers believe to have been one of the major shortcomings of Federal Reserve operations during the late 1970s.[58]

Two things seem clear about Federal Reserve behavior in the period following HCR 133. First, the Federal Reserve did not relegate interest rates to a secondary position. As critics have pointed out, the Federal Reserve hit its interest rate targets regularly and missed its monetary targets. In early 1977, the Federal Reserve actually reduced the range of fluctuation permitted in the Federal funds rate rather than increasing it.[59] Second, the Federal Reserve did not ignore its monetary targets despite the limits it set on interest rates. One study of the period shows that no variables account for movement within the system's chosen funds rate range except for changes in the monetary aggregates in relation to the targets set by the FOMC.[60] Moreover, when monetary targets were overshot, there was an additional upward shift in the Federal funds rate. In light of these findings, it would seem inaccurate to argue that the Federal Reserve ignored the monetary aggregates, although it is unclear whether that was due in any significant degree to HCR 133.

It is obviously important that for most of the 1970s the FOMC constrained interest rate movements within a narrow band. These constraints were partly in response to perceived congressional pressures. They were partly a response to demands from the financial sector for financial stability. And they were partly a response to administration demands for a policy to support economic growth. In short, the obstacles to dramatic change in Federal Reserve behavior were much too substantial to be overcome by a limp congressional resolution. The Federal Reserve's change in procedure in 1979 came despite Congress, which has subsequently made its displeasure with the lack of attention to interest rates very clear. Like many, perhaps most, dramatic policy departures, it came when many participants believed they confronted a deep crisis (see Chapter 5).

Conclusion

As a routine matter, members of Congress have relatively little interest in the Federal Reserve. When their interest does increase, they stop short of taking strong, forceful action. Interest in guiding monetary policy in any detail is intermittent, usually linked in a fairly predictable way to high interest rates and a lagging housing market. When Congress tries to give orders, as opposed to merely complaining, it speaks with a babble of voices.

Although intermittent, however, congressional interest is quite real. Congress possesses the capacity to force great changes on the Federal Reserve and in the way it conducts monetary policy. The Federal Reserve obviously respects this capacity and fears that Congress might, in the heat of the moment, take action largely for symbolic reasons that would later, again for symbolic reasons, be very difficult to reverse. Fear and respect seem to lead to Federal Reserve efforts to defuse congressional ire, not least by facilitating the decline of interest rates around the time Congress has worked up the anger necessary to take action. It is a move that comes naturally since it usually coincides with a business cycle trough when interest rates fall of their own accord. Politically, this is a risky maneuver, but as of the early 1980s, it seems to have carried the day.

The Federal Reserve also fears and respects the fact that Congress is constitutionally the final arbiter in the conduct of monetary policy. Behavior blatantly inconsistent with the idea that the Federal Reserve is a creature of Congress and is responsible to Congress could bring down punitive legislation on the Federal Reserve. In practice, this leaves the the Federal Reserve with considerable leeway since Congress has a difficult time defining what it prefers. As we have seen, congressional ambivalence has precluded the taking of strong action. The difficulty Congress has in acting is partly the consequence of Federal Reserve efforts to build good will, and partly due to the respect of members of Congress for the Federal Reserve's financial constituency. However, after several years of monetary targeting and increased congressional attention to monetary policy, some members of Congress have become more confident of their ability to understand monetary policy and to deal with the Federal Reserve. Consequently, the threshold of offense required to provoke congressional action may be lower. However, it is difficult to prove this in the early 1980s, when occasions for grievance have been so many and so widespread.

The fact that members of Congress continue to perceive problems with monetary policy despite their actions in 1975, despite repeated efforts at structural reforms, and despite regular oversight hearings suggests that there is room for further reform. No matter what effects the oversight process may have had in exposing the Federal Reserve to expert criticism and in creating more knowledgeable members of Congress who specialize in the area, it has not precluded periodic congressional dissatisfaction with monetary policy. Congress may desire to do no more than register its unhappiness about the bad news the Federal Reserve periodically delivers. However, if Congress wants to avoid hearing the bad news, it will have to find a more effective way to punish. There is little question that Congress can find that method, but it is doubtful whether the Federal Reserve will permit the necessary conditions to last long enough to provoke that kind of congressional anger.

8

Making Monetary Policy in a Political Environment: The Election of 1972

The preceding chapters have examined the setting in which the Federal Reserve operates. We have seen how the System interacts with other actors and the factors that condition those interactions. This chapter focuses on the System's response to its environment in 1972. The case of monetary policy in that year is an especially interesting one, for some have suggested, and many have accepted as true, that Federal Reserve policy during 1972 had a clearly partisan motivation. The most frequently cited source of these allegations is an article by Sanford Rose, a well-known and respected economic writer, published in July 1974 in *Fortune* magazine. In the opening sentences, Rose bluntly defined the issue: "One of the controversies swirling around the battered Nixon Administration has been of special interest to the economics profession. The issue, in brief, is whether the Federal Reserve Board went on a 'monetary binge' in 1972 in order to guarantee President Nixon's reelection."[1] After devoting over five pages to the argument that monetary growth had been excessive during 1972, Rose answered his own question in the affirmative: yes, policy had been shaped for partisan purposes.

> Burns's arguments, [for continued stimulus throughout 1972] were impressive, but not impressive enough to sway the FOMC. . . .
>
> In the circumstances, the dispute between Burns and the FOMC majority became fairly tense at times. At one point, frustrated at his inability to convince the committee of the need to hold down interest rates, Burns left a meeting in obvious anger. He returned in an hour, announcing: "I have just talked to the White House." . . . The committee got the idea: the White House was determined to keep rates from rising.[2]

Rose speculated that the FOMC might have had an additional incentive to support the White House in order to preclude Republican cooperation in efforts by southern Democrats to limit Federal Reserve independence.

Others have agreed with Rose, too. Tufte's analysis of the PBC relies heavily on the 1972 case, and he accepts the notion that partisan concerns motivated monetary policy in 1972. Tufte notes that the case is still the subject of controversy, but he states flatly that "the 1972 election was nothing special" – that is, it was not atypical.[3] Tufte's account has, unfortunately, been widely accepted as authoritative.[4] My analysis in Chapter 6 should have cast doubt on the notion that the pattern of monetary policy in election years is sufficiently clear that we can confidently speak about the "usual" role of monetary policy in creating electoral economic cycles.

As for 1972, the confluence of pressures on the Federal Reserve was unusual and probably extreme. Thus, 1972 may constitute a limiting case and, therefore, a particularly illuminating one in terms of Federal Reserve relationships with the president and Congress. Although many observers have concluded that the "lesson of 1972" is that the Federal Reserve is likely to be involved in clear preelection stimulation of the economy, I shall argue that the story is much less clear. I shall argue that it is at least equally plausible that monetary policy in 1972 reflected FOMC calculations about the most effective way to defend Federal Reserve autonomy. During 1972 the FOMC was keenly sensitive to dangers in its political environment, and FOMC members were trying to anticipate those dangers rather than merely react to them.

The stimulative monetary policy of 1972 was real, and it does appear to have been important in influencing subsequent economic performance.[5] Many observers have attributed a large part of the accelerating inflation in 1973 and 1974 to this stimulation. The extent to which the later inflation should be attributed to the devaluation of the dollar and to price shocks in food and oil remains a controversial issue.[6] It seems reasonably clear that the acceleration in inflation beginning in late 1972 was due in part to monetary policy. (See Figure 8.1, which plots inflation and unemployment for 1971–4.) So, it is also of considerable historical interest to examine this particular period.

The plausibility of the charge of election-year misbehavior

Close observers of American economic policy making may have been entertained by Rose's charges, but they were not likely to have been surprised. There were several reasons for this. The idea that elections are critically affected by the state of the economy

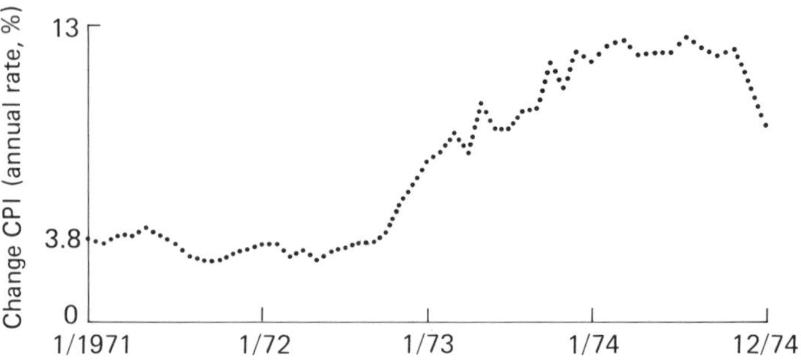

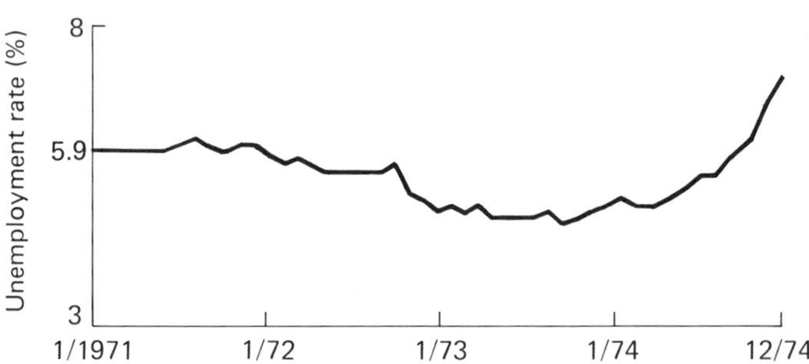

Figure 8.1. Unemployment (percent) and inflation (percent change), 1971–4, based on monthly data. (Source: Business Conditions Digest, *1977, tables 43, 320-C.)*

and that politicians try to promote an economic conjuncture beneficial to their elections was certainly nothing new in 1972.[7] Moreover, the conventional wisdom was sustained, in part, by a well-known anecdote about the 1960 election that involved the two protagonists of the 1972 tale, Arthur Burns and Richard M. Nixon.[8] The Burns–Nixon relationship was widely known to be a long-standing and cordial one.[9] The clincher of the story about monetary policy in 1972 is that Burns and Nixon were very close and thought alike on electoral–economic matters. Under the circumstances, would it not be illogical to believe that Burns would not be willing to help Nixon win reelection by generously boosting the money supply?

It was clear to several observers at the time that Nixon's major concern as 1972 approached was his reelection. It was also clear that economic policy was being shaped with that goal in mind.[10] The issue was raised in a *Business Week* article early in 1972:

> With business still dragging and the November election coming into view, President Nixon has determined to lash the economic system to a gallop.
>
> [The administration] has lined up the cooperation of the Federal Reserve Board, headed by the President's old friend, Arthur Burns. The Fed has been trying to push money into the economy by every means but assault and battery.[11]

The issue was also raised twice during the year in JEC hearings by Senator Proxmire, and other observers remarked on the electioneering aspects of economic policy as well.[12]

Discordant notes: Burns versus the White House, 1970–1971

This view ignores the tensions between the White House and Burns during the eighteen months prior to 1972. At least as early as May 1970, Burns publicly urged consideration of some kind of incomes policy; at that time, the idea was anathema in the White House.[13] By the end of August 1970, tension between Burns and the administration had spilled out into the press.[14] Despite White House pressure on Burns and Nixon's public claim that Burns was cooperating with his plan, Burns continued both publicly and privately to advocate an incomes policy.[15]

The public coolness between Burns and administration did not diminish as 1971 began. At the outset of 1971 in hearings before the JEC, Burns announced that "it is the considered judgment of the Federal Reserve Board that, under present conditions, monetary and fiscal policies need to be supplemented with an incomes policy."[16] He also firmly disagreed with the administration's GNP projection, volunteering that Federal Reserve economists considered it to be "very optimistic."[17]

Shortly thereafter, Burns was irritated by two instances of perceived direct pressuring of the Federal Reserve by the White House. The first involved a meeting with White House advisor Peter Flanagan, who was overly persistent, Burns believed, in inquiring into the future course of monetary policy.

> Then shortly after that, I had lunch with Shultz, who started out asking about the money supply and saying it wasn't behaving right. I said, "This is the second time today that I've

> heard this from the White House. Once is too many, and twice is completely unacceptable. I'm going to tell the President that if he ever again sends one of his assistants to talk to me on this question, I'll throw him out bodily." And I told Nixon that. (It was the day he was leaving for Tom Dewey's funeral [March 19, 1971].) I told him exactly that in no uncertain terms. And it never happened again after that.[18]

By mid-1971 the split had apparently deepened.[19] Burns made another strong statement at midyear economic review hearings in Congress. Shortly thereafter, Charles Colson, a presidential aide, unleashed an attack on Burns and the Federal Reserve that Burns bitterly resented.[20] Burns informed the Nixon administration of his feelings through old friends. Shortly thereafter in a phone call, Nixon retracted the attack, and did so publicly at a press conference, saying that Burns had received "a very unfair shot."[21]

It may be that the president's apology and his decision to impose wage and price controls in August 1971 wiped away all of this tension and animosity. Perhaps it made a team player of Arthur Burns again. It is important, however, that the verdict on the policy of 1972 not be based on a false view of Burns as Nixon's lackey.

The alternative view: the pressure of controls

The basic alternative to the simple partisanship interpretation is that 1972 was a year of wage and price controls, and in this new political and economic environment, monetary policy went awry. One variation emphasizes the importance of Burns's contradictory roles during that period. In addition to his role as Federal Reserve chairman, Burns was the chairman of the Committee on Interest and Dividends (CID), which was responsible for monitoring dividend payments and interest rates. The CID's objective of holding down interest rates, it is argued, conflicted with the appropriate monetary policy, letting interest rates increase.[22]

This view is certainly correct in part. The CID was worrisome to FOMC members, and the topic arose several times in FOMC discussion. Burns struggled repeatedly with some members of the FOMC to win their agreement to a policy of limiting the upward movement of interest rates. However, this view overly personalizes these events. Monetary policy in 1972 was not merely the reflection of Burns's personal weaknesses or his inability to resolve the role conflicts in which he found himself. FOMC members had good reasons to be cautious about interest rates independent of Burns's role conflicts. There were political risks associated with letting interest rates rise during a period of generalized economic controls. These risks were not something Burns invented. They could have been ignored if the Federal Reserve were an invincibly independent institution. Given the reality of the Federal Reserve's relationships to Congress and the president, it is hard to imagine contradictory action during this particular period.

The general setting

The period leading up to the election of 1972 contained some interesting parallels to a period a decade later, when economists and policy makers seemed to have lost confidence in their ability to restore economic order. It was a period when received economic wisdom seemed not to be so wise. It was also a period when Richard Nixon's determination to be reelected produced unexpected controls and anticipated fiscal stimulus.

Controls.

> . . . if the Fed helps to plan a wage–price or credit policy, it is more difficult to adopt a conflicting monetary policy, even though, in the course of debate on the final overall program, Fed representatives may have been overruled at many crucial points and even though the Board as a whole was not sufficiently integrated into the decision process.[23]

There can be little dispute about whether Nixon's decision to institute wage and price controls in August 1971 was political. Presidents, like all politicians, operate in a world of uncertainty regarding their support. Everything they do, like it or not, has a political aspect if it bears on their popularity, their chance for reelection, or the cohesion and solidarity of their coalition in government. A decision to impose wage and price controls is clearly political in many senses. For example, not everyone is equally controllable. Further, the timing of the controls in relation to Nixon's reelection campaign was certainly no coincidence. An incomes policy is political, and it was clear to all that this was the case in 1971.

One measure of Nixon's political skill was his ability to choose a course of action that could not be opposed by his critics or potential critics in terms of its basic design. Since the Federal Reserve had been on record for months prior to August 1971 as favoring an incomes policy, and since Arthur Burns had been an active and cooperative participant in the planning sessions at Camp David immediately prior to Nixon's announcement, there was little question that the Federal Reserve would cooperate, at least in the initial phases.[24]

There was a recurring threat that interest rates might be frozen, and this created a very difficult dilemma for monetary policy. During this period, monetary policy operated primarily through setting short-term interest rates. Control over interest rates would have struck directly and fundamentally at the Federal Reserve's autonomy. Also, Federal Reserve officials believe strongly in the virtues of a freely functioning money market. On purely ideological grounds, they would have found controls on interest rates objectionable. As we have seen in Chapter 7, rising interest rates are viewed with hostility by members of Congress – especially when they are seen as harming local constituents or as evidence of unjustified bank profiteering. The fact that interest rates were *not* controlled might reasonably have been expected to provoke congressional concern. If interest rates *rose* during a period of controls, one might have expected Congress to be further aroused.

Fiscal stimulus. Monetary policy during 1972 was also operating in an environment of substantial fiscal stimulation. Current dollar budget deficits for 1971 and 1972 exceeded those for any postwar year except 1968; in that period, large deficits had never occurred in consecutive years.[25] Another measure of fiscal stimulus, the full-employment surplus (or deficit), also shows that 1972 was a year of very stimulative fiscal policy. Blinder estimates that fiscal policy raised the rate of growth of the real GNP by one-third above what it would otherwise have been in 1972.[26]

One reflection of this stimulus was the boom in the housing industry. Long-term interest rates – especially mortgage rates – were regarded as politically crucial in 1972. In FOMC meetings there were repeated references to fluctuations in these rates. Construction of all sorts flourished. Residential fixed investment grew during 1971 and 1972 at rates unmatched since 1950.[27] Mortgage debt also expanded at record rates in both years.[28] This expansion was important because a booming demand for mortgages would be expected to put upward pressure on the rates. It was also important because increased construction is a powerful stimulus for many related industries – which is of considerable interest to policy makers trying to decrease the unemployment rate.

The growth in construction was substantially encouraged by public policy. Estimates of direct cash subsidies for housing show increases in 1972 over 1970 of over $2 billion; estimated subsidy benefits from housing credit programs during this period were over $1 billion.[29] Between 1970 and 1972, federal ownership of mortgages expanded by over $7 billion. In this period, a secondary market in conventional mortgages (i.e., mortgages not federally insured or otherwise subsidized) was begun by the Federal Home Loan Mortgage Corporation and the Federal National Mortgage Association. The effect of the secondary market was to further increase the liquidity of mortgage lenders.[30] It is clear that the Federal Reserve was aware of developments in mortgage markets during this period, but it is not clear if the Federal Reserve was interested in restraining this stimulus or could have done so readily had it so desired.[31]

Inside the FOMC in 1972

The phone call

Let's dispose of the most exciting allegation first. Was there a heated meeting in which Burns persuaded his opponents by citing White House support for his position? One thing is clear: *All* persons with whom I have spoken, which includes all but one voting member of the FOMC that year plus about ten others regularly in attendance, fail to recall such an incident; most insist that such a blatant tactic would have been strongly repudiated.[32] On the other hand, at least one staffer recalled that as he observed Burns in action, he remarked to himself, "damn, he's being heavy-handed." Readers will recall from documents quoted in Chapter 6 that Chairman Martin had on occasion used references to the White House to influence FOMC actions. Doubtless it would not have been rare for Burns to do this either. However, any such references suggesting that the Federal Reserve should act in some sense because of White House orders would have been an offense, doubly so if there were any partisan overtones.

No incident like the one Rose reports is recorded in the *FOMC Minutes*, but suspicious observers, especially those who read the discussion of data sources in Appendix A, will not regard the *Minutes* as conclusively ruling out the event. Rose has recounted conversations with a then governor who suggested that something like "the incident" took place during a break in a meeting. If so, that would put it outside the formal record.[33] The fact that this story could create such a flap is testimony to the strength of the norms of nonpartisanship governing Federal Reserve activities.

Several members recalled a break in a tense meeting when Chairman Burns was not getting his way. As former Governor Robert Holland explained,

> We were having a hard time reaching a consensus. Burns got up and left the room. . . . Burns said he would confer with the staff and bring back something we could vote on. He came back with a rather different proposition than they might have expected. And there might have been speculation around the table as to *why* he came back with what he did.
>
> I know that such a phone call [to the White House] wasn't made. I went with him, and what was done was to work out a proposal that most of the members could agree with.

The same general pattern of events has been recalled by George Mitchell and Philip Coldwell.[34]

There were several heated moments during the year; the months of August and September particularly stand out. In both months there were explicit references to the CID during committee debate; indeed, in August, there were references to possible "political constraints on interest rates."[35] In both meetings, Burns linked monetary policy to the controls program by arguing that rising interest rates could harm efforts to limit rises in other controlled areas. In both meetings, Burns had to fight for specifications on the directive that were clearly different from those preferred by a *majority* of the members present. In both cases, the specifications were more stimulative and involved less range for interest rate increases than the majority preferred. Despite these disagreements, there were no formal dissents by members in August, and in September there were only two dissenting votes (cast by Bruce MacLaury, president of the Minneapolis bank and J. L. Robertson, vice-chairman of the board).

Overview of FOMC strategies in 1972

FOMC policy making during the period of wage and price controls (through the end of Phase II) can be divided into three periods with distinct political strategies. These periods and the associated strategies are outlined in Table 8.1. Figures 8.2 and 8.3 plot the movements of two interest rates that figured prominently in policy discussion. Figure 8.4 plots the growth rate of M1.

Table 8.1. *FOMC political strategy during the 1972 period: a summary*

Period I

August 15–October 31, 1971 (dates are approximate)
Objectives: break inflationary expectations
Tactic: avoiding any appearance of support for expansionary policy
Primary audience: the market
Change in M1 over period (simple percent annual rate): −3.1 percent
Change in federal funds rate over period: −0.48 percent

Period II

November 1, 1971–March 31, 1972
Objective: signal that policy is not being restrictive
Tactic: rapidly increasing monetary aggregates and bank reserves
Primary audience: Congress and the president
Change in M1 over period: 6.7 percent
Change in federal funds rate over period: −1.25 percent

Period III

April 1, 1972–January 1973
Objective: avoid interest rate increases that might provoke political controversy
Tactic: focus on interest rates rather than monetary aggregates; avoiding increasing discount rate; "jawbone" the banks
Audiences: Congress, the president, banks
Change in M1 over period: 11.4 percent
Change in federal funds rate over period: +1.29 percent

Source: Statistics based on data from *Federal Reserve Bulletin*, various issues, 1971–3.

In the initial period, from mid-August through October 1971, the FOMC was casting about for an appropriate policy strategy for the period of the wage and price freeze. The strategy chosen was to try to lower inflationary expectations by making it clear that monetary policy would not be vigorously stimulative. As Burns put it in the August 24th FOMC meeting:

> . . . if interest rates – particularly those over which the System had the most control – were to move lower immediately after today's meeting, observers would conclude that the System was taking a deliberate step toward ease in order to encourage still faster growth in the monetary aggregates. The effect, in his judgment, would be to nullify the favorable impact that the announcement of the new economic program had had on confidence. He thought the System would have to exercise great care if the change in expectations which the program was designed to produce was to take hold.[36]

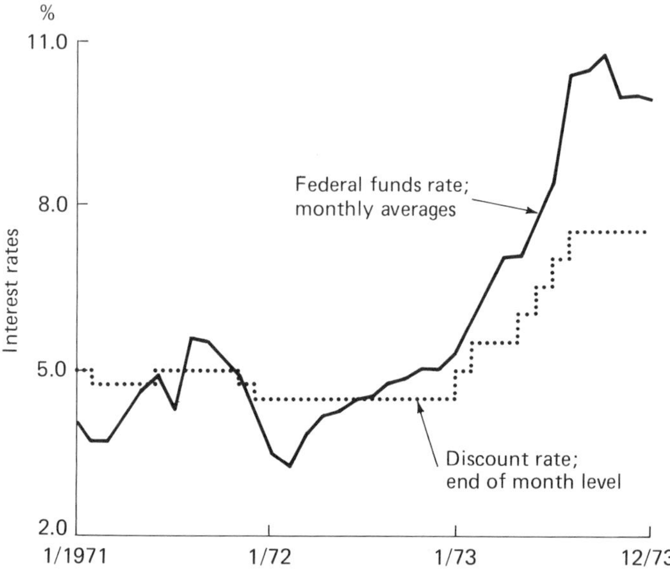

Figure 8.2. Federal funds rate and the discount rate, 1971–3. (Source: Federal Reserve Bulletin.*)*

FOMC members were also interested in avoiding an increase in interest rates that might be interpreted as financial sector profiteering from the controls program. Such an increase might provoke members of Congress, already suspicious about the exclusion of interest rates from the controls program, to require that rates be controlled. Thus, for the first controls program, the FOMC decided to accommodate declines in the federal funds rate but to avoid openly signaling that there had been a move toward ease.

The second period started approximately in November 1971 and lasted until sometime in late March 1972. In this period, policy was dominated by a desire to demonstrate that the System was stimulating the economy. During the first six weeks of the controls program the money growth rate decreased, continuing a decline that had begun earlier in that year. The decline had been worrisome to the White House, which had lectured Federal Reserve staff on the matter.[37] It had begun to appear to some observers that the Federal Reserve might be undercutting the opportunity for noninflationary expansion provided by the controls program. Thus, the FOMC chose to try to walk a fine line between appearing to pursue a tight policy and appearing to pursue a policy that was too easy.[38] As Burns put it in the December meeting: "in light

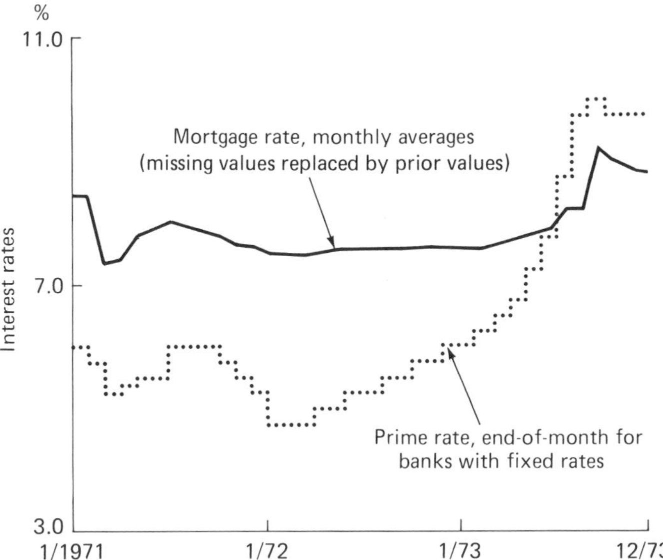

Figure 8.3. Prime bank lending rate and the FHA secondary market mortgage rate, 1971–3. (Sources: Mortgage rate: Business Conditions Digest, *1977, table 118. Prime rate:* Federal Reserve Bulletin, *February 1974, p. A32.)*

of the behavior of the aggregates some people were now asking whether the Federal Reserve was deliberately moving to a restraining policy so as to nullify what the Administration, with the support of Congress, was attempting to accomplish."[39] The FOMC adopted a policy of rapidly supplying reserves to the banking system despite negative reactions from Wall Street and the financial press. Foreign central bankers complained vigorously that this was weakening the dollar further at a time when they expected action to try to strengthen it.[40]

The third period lasted from late March 1972 until the end of the year. Policy was dominated by a concern that interest rates (especially the prime rate) should not move above the rates prevailing at the start of controls, and that open market policy should not be conducted in such a way as to require a change in the discount rate. Again, Burns's statements in the FOMC were quite clear on the policy risks of having increases in some prices, especially food and utility prices, accompanied by increases in interest rates.[41] This policy came under stress repeatedly as the staff projected future increases in inflation and rapid rates of growth of the

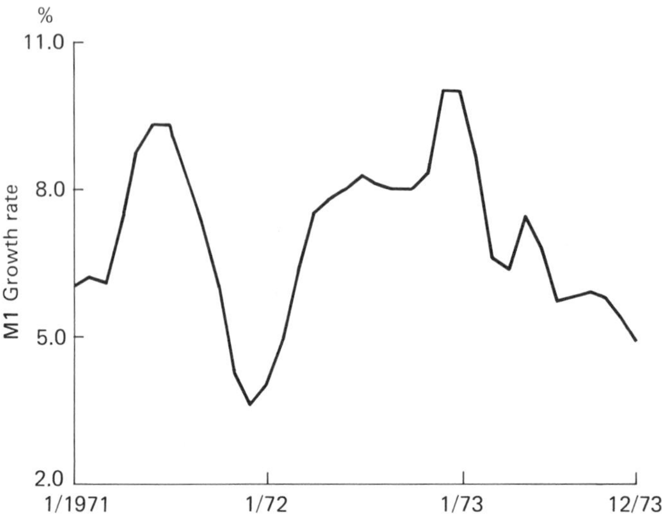

Figure 8.4. Growth rate of the narrow money supply (M1, seasonally adjusted, simple percent change over level six months earlier), 1971–3. (Source: Calculated from data in Federal Reserve Bulletin.*)*

GNP. Challenges came particularly in response to reports of high money growth rates and similar projections for the future. This occurred in August, when the staff announced that the July rate was 15 percent and that third-quarter estimates were 9 percent. There was conflict again in September, when the estimated M1 growth rate for the third quarter was increased to 10.5 percent. In both months, the estimated rates were well above the FOMC's targets. Conflict declined in October as the estimates of M1 growth for the third quarter were lowered.

Composition of the FOMC

The combination of policy views and personalities represented on the FOMC during 1972 probably facilitated Burns's efforts to have his view prevail. Among Federal Reserve Board members, Dewey Daane believed that financial markets were rather fragile and could not withstand sharp interest rate fluctuations. This view often brought him into agreement with Burns. Andrew Brimmer advocated a relatively expansionist policy as long as estimates of future unemployment seemed high. This view often aligned Brimmer with Burns in FOMC voting, but in board meetings in the second half of the year, Brimmer repeatedly cast a solitary vote in favor of increasing the discount rate.[42]

John Sheehan, who joined the board in January 1972, came into the organization with a deep admiration of Burns and little experience with monetary policy. The *FOMC Minutes* for 1972 reveal him to have been a reliable defender of Burns who often echoed Burns's arguments.[43] Jeffrey Bucher replaced Sherman Maisel in mid-1972. Maisel had backed Burns because of a strong belief that the Federal Reserve should support any administration's policy direction. Bucher, as the newest, most junior, and least experienced board member, was unlikely to oppose Burns, and in fact never did.

George Mitchell reports that he never believed in shifting policy sharply before the direction of the economy was relatively clear.[44] Since 1972 was a year in which uncertainty was abundant, his support for Burns should not have been a surprise. Mitchell also seemed to share Burns's sensitivity to political dangers, possibly as a consequence of his broader political experience. The only board member to oppose Burns forcefully in 1972 was J. L. Robertson, who had emerged as a strong inflation fighter in the late 1960s. In sum, a majority of board members (Daane, Brimmer, Sheehan, Bucher, and Mitchell) was unlikely to vote against the chairman in 1972. Internal FOMC dynamics suggest that such a group could very likely define the final decision, and their choice would usually be supported unanimously.[45]

As for the district bank presidents, Burns was frequently opposed in debate by Bruce MacLaury of Minneapolis, who dissented once. Philip Coldwell of Dallas also dissented once and made it clear several times that he would have preferred a tighter policy. David Eastburn (Philadelphia) also provided some strong vocal opposition to Burns late in the year. Alfred Hayes (New York) had a reputation as a "hawk" in monetary policy and was not reluctant to dissent from a policy with which he disagreed. Hayes dissented twice during 1972, both times at the first of the year, on the issue of reserve targeting. Hayes opposed Burns in debate later in the year, but did not dissent. Hayes, MacLaury, Coldwell, and Eastburn, together with Robertson, represented considerable experience with monetary policy. They might have been expected to provide more effective opposition if there had been fundamental disagreements about policy. The lack of such opposition suggests either that these FOMC members shared Burns's perception of the political risks or that the situation was sufficiently ambiguous that they judged it best not to make an issue of their misgivings.

1972 in retrospect

The contemporary view of experts

There was some dissatisfaction with monetary policy among the experts in 1972. Objections were strongest at the first of the year, when the Federal Reserve was vigorously adding to bank reserves, but Democratic economist Arthur Okun argued in February that the stimulus was not adequate.[46] Some dissent began to be voiced later in the year, but with vigor only after the election. Among monetarists, the group most likely to criticize policy in this period, commentary varied during the year. In March, monetarists were reported to be urging more expansion. In April, June, and September, they were reported to be against the heavy monetary expansion. But in December, the monetarist-leaning Argus Research Corporation praised U.S. success in slowing monetary growth, complimenting the "steady course" of policy.[47]

The Red Book, distributed prior to each FOMC meeting, includes reports prepared by each district bank about the economic conditions in that district. The Federal Reserve Bank of Boston included among its 1972 reports the observations and advice of prominent "correspondent" economists. The composition of the group varied from month to month but included Paul Samuelson, James Tobin, Otto Eckstein, Eli Shapiro, and Henry Wallich.

A clear note of caution began to creep into the advice of the Boston bank's correspondent economists in August, and sharpened in tone in subsequent months as the economists urged moderate monetary growth.[48] It was evident to them that the Federal Reserve was reluctant to see interest rate increases, and they criticized both the failure of the Federal Reserve to raise the discount rate and the attempts to "jawbone" interest rates down. However, for most of the year, the comments of these economists were relatively positive and, as late as August, quite complimentary. In August, for example, Eckstein and Samuelson warned that returning to the orthodoxy of monetary restraint would abort the recovery. Still, there was some consensus among these economists as early as October that monetary growth rates should be lowered by one or two percentage points and that interest rates should increase.

Blinder notes that econometric estimates at the time showed much greater scope for noninflationary economic stimulus than have subsequent estimates dealing with the same period.[49] Perhaps this explains why Democratic economists such as Heller and Samuelson were publicly warning in late July against "repeating the mistakes of the sorry Eisenhower decade" or choking the expansion off "in its infancy."[50] Perhaps this also explains the optimistic economic forecasts for 1973 that were being reported in late November.[51] In short, it is not at all clear that there was a strong consensus among outside economists that policy was badly off the track at any time in 1972 or that the economy was in danger of exploding into inflation.

Federal Reserve staff had occasionally warned the FOMC of the dangers of overdoing the stimulus. For example, as early as March, the staff urged that "it is becoming more important that monetary policy avoid a defense of any particular structure of interest rates at the expense of too swift an expansion of the monetary aggregates."[52] Throughout the year, the staff's estimates of future inflation were gradually increased. Internal documents suggest that the staff was ready to tell attentive board members that policy was not turning out to be exactly what the Federal Reserve was publicly announcing.[53]

Commercial bankers had an opportunity to express their views in Federal Advisory Council (FAC) meetings during the year. In the last three meetings of the year (May, July, and September), bankers in the FAC were urging greater restraint, pointing out that current expansionary policy could not long be sustained. In an interesting maneuver, Arthur Burns put the FAC members on the spot in September 1972, asking them to indicate by a show of hands whether they felt that policy was then too easy, should be tightened immediately, or should be tightened several months hence. Only one member out of twelve agreed with the first option, only two with the second, and all with the last. At least as late as September, the bankers were not firmly convinced that monetary policy had been overly expansionary.

Similarly, prominent business executives on the Business Council twice passed up the occasion during 1972 to make any sort of critical statement on monetary policy. Their second opportunity came relatively late in the year, in October.[54]

Interest rates and the CID

The most important consideration shaping monetary policy was the fact that interest rates were not included in the controls program. The Federal Reserve was eager to assure that they did not become the object of controls. There were several periods when it would have been reasonable for Federal Reserve officials to conclude that interest rates might be subject to controls. At the start of the wage and price control program, monetary policy might have become dominated by an outsider – perhaps John Connolly – or a deep conflict might have developed with the administration over policy. In any case, it is clear that Arthur Burns and other FOMC members did not want to risk opening what they perceived as a virtual pandora's box – controlling interest rates. Consequently, this led to a series of "preemptive strikes" on the issue of controlling interest rates whenever the threat of controls seemed to loom. Burns has explained that he viewed the entire period as one of danger to the Federal Reserve.

> My whole purpose was to protect the Federal Reserve's independence in the sphere of monetary policy during a very difficult period when we had general price and wage controls along with persistent calls for controls on interest rates. . . . I took on the job of Chairing the Committee on Interest and Dividends in order to protect the Federal Reserve. With someone else in charge of that Committee, the Fed could have lost its independence in the sphere of monetary policy, which is exactly what happened during World War II.[55]

From the earliest days of wage and price controls, it was clear to Arthur Burns and the Federal Reserve that the decision *not* to control interest rates would be controversial. Burns raised this issue in the August 24, 1971, FOMC meeting.

> Questions were being raised in many quarters as to why the 90-day freeze had not been extended to cover interest rates – in effect, why financial institutions had not been asked to join in what was intended to be a common sacrifice. During the White House meeting last week with the bipartisan leadership of the Congress, which he [Burns] had attended, a number of the legislators had indicated that they were troubled by the omission; and the matter was certain to be discussed in the Congress when it reconvened in early September.
>
> The possibility of including interest rates in the freeze had been considered at Camp David, Chairman Burns noted, and the decision not to do so had been made deliberately. In his

judgment that was the proper decision. Insofar as the wage–price freeze tended to curb inflationary expectations, it could be expected to release powerful forces tending to reduce interest rates, since recent rate levels clearly included a substantial inflation premium.[56]

Congress was indeed concerned about the exclusion of interest rates from the Phase I controls. Beginning in late August and continuing intermittently for a month, the JEC held hearings on the controls. Several witnesses were concerned about the exclusion of interest rates and dividends from the freeze. Administration sources told reporters in early September that interest rates remained as "ground that can be plowed" in Phase II.[57]

Throughout September 1971, concern about interest rates surfaced repeatedly in the financial press. The FOMC's decision to begin trading in all Federal agency issues was interpreted by financial observers as a means of trying to exert more direct control over politically sensitive long-term interest rates.[58] The associations representing mutual savings banks and savings and loan associations announced that they would not increase their loan rates during the wage–price freeze and the subsequent follow-up program[59] – probably an effort to defuse efforts to include interest rates in controls. At the end of the month, Burns made a point of noting that interest rates had remained level in the freeze thus far.[60] During this period, prior to the establishment of the CID, Bruce MacLaury, president of the Minneapolis bank, stated in an FOMC meeting the rule of thumb that appears to have guided monetary policy for the next fourteen months – that interest rates should not move above their mid-August levels in order to avoid political problems.[61]

In early October, the White House decided to ask Congress for authority to control interest and dividends, but to hold the authority in abeyance.[62] Part of the Phase II program announced subsequently was the formation of the CID with Burns as its head. The CID was to be a watchdog organization, monitoring and restraining increases in corporate dividends and interest rates. The CID's first action, taken in late October, was to issue a notice instructing lenders to assemble data on the interest rates they charged.[63]

Subsequent accounts suggest that Burns's role in the CID was viewed with suspicion from the outset by some FOMC members. Certainly, Burns's awareness of the political problems that could be caused by increasing interest rates was clearly communicated to the FOMC. In one of the few published accounts of the operation of the CID, Paul Horvitz characterized the way the CID viewed its role in terms that clearly coincide with Burns's understanding of the political circumstances at the time.

> The CID concluded that a successful voluntary program would be essential to head off public and congressional pressures for mandatory controls. In an important sense, the interest rate control program was similar to the dividend program: both were designed (a) to convince the public and Congress that an effective, equitable program was being enforced, yet (b) simultaneously to avoid the distortions that would inevitably be produced by a rigid, mandatory system.[64]

That is, Burns was attempting simultaneously to execute a symbolic policy and to defend against the imposition of mandatory controls.

By mid-December 1971, Congress had completed legislation extending the president's authority to impose controls. This legislation did not require interest rates to be controlled. On the contrary, it gave the president the discretion to determine that controls on interest and dividends were not required. Obviously, this gave the president the power to decide to the contrary as well. Only days later, the Cost of Living Council and the CID jointly announced that mandatory regulation of interest rates and finance charges was not necessary at that time. Instead, the CID was to focus on a program of voluntary restraints on interest rates.[65]

Did this effectively remove interest rates from the congressional agenda? Certainly not in the mind of Arthur Burns. However, subsequent media attention to the issue of control of interest rates appears to have been stimulated by the administration and the CID, not by Congress. Administration efforts were almost certainly an attempt to derail congressional interest in controls. Arthur Burns participated by encouraging banks and the FOMC to try to keep interest rates down and by persuading Congress that interest rates were not a problem.[66] In early July 1972, for example, as interest rates were trending upward, a correspondent for the *New York Times,* citing unnamed administration economists, wrote that "the possibility of direct controls of . . . the cost of credit . . . appears to have increased significantly in recent weeks."[67] The article went on to specify that it would be particularly critical if long-term rates began to exceed the levels existing at the outset of controls. The prime rate was "considered of major importance, if mainly psychological, to the outlook for controls," with 6 percent (the precontrols level) being the "nonviolable level."

During the difficult August 1972 FOMC meeting, Burns warned about the possibility of controls on interest rates and stressed that it was important that monetary policy avoid provoking any such action.

> Given the framework of the Government's incomes policy, Chairman Burns continued, there was widespread opposition to higher interest rates. Thus far the record on interest rates had been extraordinarily good, and while the System could claim only a small part of the credit for that record, it had made its contribution. Nevertheless, voices had been raised to advocate ceilings on interest rates. Fortunately, resistance to ceilings had come from the President, from the Secretary of the Treasury as well as from himself, and so far resistance had succeeded. . . . In the circumstances, the Federal Reserve should not be eager to raise interest rates.[68]

Later, in early October, with the election approaching, market pressures on interest rates again increased. Banks moved the prime rate up to 5¾ percent. In reaction, economist Pierre Rinfret, principal economic spokesman for Nixon during the campaign period, warned that this move could provoke the administration to impose controls on interest rates.[69] There immediately followed a flurry of concern about controls, including a statement by the president of the ABA that controls were likely.[70] The CID also issued a statement attacking the increases in the prime rate: "The Committee reminded commercial banks and other financial institutions of the importance of relatively stable interest rates in the success of the Economic Stabilization Program. The Committee also announced that it was extending its surveillance of interest rates to the earnings of financial institutions."[71] This fed speculation that controls on interest rates were pending.[72] However, since much of the concern was generated by administration spokesmen, it is likely that this was a preelection ploy to preempt congressional criticism about interest rates.[73]

Interest rates stabilized in November, and the attention of top administration officials shifted to the problem of what to do at the end of Phase II of the controls program. As one commentator noted, "the fact that interest rates are not controlled has led to political criticisms that the inflation-control program is 'rigged' in favor of the banks and other lenders at the expense of the man in the street."[74]

The reality of this political criticism became evident in early 1973 as the president's plans for Phase III were being debated. Congress began active debate on the Phase III controls authority in late January 1973 and completed action by the end of April. During this period, interest rates again begin moving upward. That movement again provoked congressional discussion about controlling interest rates. At virtually the same time that congressional hearings began, administration officials, especially Burns of the CID, again began to confront major banks about announced increases in the prime rate.[75] The coincidence of these events cannot be purely chance. The banks appeared not to realize the elements of political strategy behind the criticisms made by the CID, and there ensued prolonged controversy that was resolved, remarkably enough, on the same day that it became clear that neither the House nor the Senate would vote to impose controls on interest rates.[76]

In the intervening weeks, however, there was strong validation for Burns's earlier worries that Congress would try to control interest rates. The Senate narrowly rejected a proposal to require controls on March 20, 1973.[77] In early April, legislation to require controls was reported by the House Banking Committee. Rules Committee maneuvering produced a different bill that still involved controls. However, in floor action the interest rate controls, as well as other major revisions of the president's plan, were rejected in a series of complex maneuvers that surprised observers.[78]

Burns told an interviewer that in his view the CID and his role in it cannot bear much responsibility for 1972 policy.

> I would say that Federal Reserve policy was not affected, except possibly in a subtle, psychological way; in a way that I couldn't put my finger on – and I doubt if a roomful of psychologists could either – by the existence of the CID.
>
> It took a tremendous amount of energy continually to remind everybody on the FOMC, in the banking community, in Congress, that the Federal Reserve was not affected by this; that the ability to control money and credit was in no way affected by the Committee on Interest and Dividends.[79]

Contrary to Burns's recollection, policy *was* affected by the CID. The policy record for April, August, September, and November surely shows that it was worrisome to FOMC members. In FOMC debate, Burns himself acknowledged that his participation in the CID complicated his policy calculation.[80] The record also shows that in appealing for a moderate Federal Reserve policy, Burns did not hesitate to link moderation to the responsibilities of the CID. Whether in a literal sense the *ability* of the Federal Reserve to conduct policy was affected by the existence of the CID seems beside the point. The Federal Reserve feared the possibility of formal interest rate controls and pursued a related political strategy of trying to control interest rates informally.

Congressional support for stimulative monetary policy in 1972[81]

The president was not the only enthusiastic supporter of highly stimulative policy during 1972. That year, the most obvious congressional action was not a call for controls on interest rates.[82] On the contrary, Congress encouraged a strong monetary stimulus throughout the year. There was much on the congressional agenda, and there was little explicit concern about interest rates during the particular periods when the FOMC was struggling most to justify keeping interest rates down.

In January 1972, at a FOMC meeting called earlier than scheduled (as members had agreed in December should happen if growth of monetary aggregates was inadequate), Burns stated his concern about congressional pressures for more stimulus. "In his view . . . it was important that the performance of monetary policy improve rather promptly." Burns was worried about the reception he would get at the JEC in February.[83]

In the February JEC meetings, Senator William Proxmire quizzed Burns about his planned economic policy for the year, and warned him that if monetary policy became restrictive in the second half of the year, that action would lend itself to a partisan political interpretation. Burns assured Proxmire that the degree of stimulus would vary with the economic circumstances.[84]

> At this stage of the business cycle it is essential to pursue a monetary policy that will facilitate good economic recovery. Supplies of money and credit must be sufficient to finance the growth in consumer spending and in investment plans that now appears in progress. Let me assure this committee that the Federal Reserve does not intend to let the present recovery falter for want of money and credit. And let me add, just as firmly, that the Federal Reserve will not release the forces of a renewed inflationary spiral.[85]

The JEC noted in its February *Report* that "fairly rapid money growth will also be needed if recovery is not to be choked off by rising long-term interest rates." The committee recommended that

M1 growth be about 6 percent.[86] The JEC was obviously not urging a policy of monetary restraint at this point.

During hearings held as part of the JEC's midyear economic review (in July), Proxmire again closely questioned Burns on his plans for monetary policy in the coming months. Proxmire asked whether he had Burns's assurance that

> all your decisions between now and November will be made without regard to politics, and whatever advice you may be called upon to give the President will be objective and not political, and that your public statements will not be slanted so as to in any way obtain a more favorable economic picture than the facts merit?[87]

Burns told Proxmire firmly that this would be so for as long as he held his current post. Proxmire replied that Burns's statement had "cleared the air; . . . I think it is a situation that is clarified by the kind of assurance you have given this committee."[88]

Proxmire went on to argue that the economy needed further stimulation. He pressed Burns for his response to a situation "which it seems to me is inadequately stimulative to get unemployment down."[89]

> *Proxmire:* Now do you see any actions that we should take or that you should take in the Federal Reserve Board to try to reduce the unemployment rate, in view of the fact that historically, as you say, it has not recovered the way it has in the past, we have had a sluggish recovery? What can we do about it?
> *Burns:* I think Congress has done a great deal to stimulate the economy. And results are now being achieved. At the moment I am confident that enough stimulative action has been taken.[90]

Following those hearings, the JEC again stressed that monetary tightening should be avoided. "Many observers predict that monetary policy will tighten in the coming months and that interest rates will rise, and some are urging this as a policy course. Such a policy would be extremely damaging."[91] This warning could only have reinforced other indications to the FOMC that it should move with great caution with respect to raising interest rates.

The politics of hindsight

For most observers, the Federal Reserve's 1972 policy errors have been seen much more clearly in retrospect than they were at the time. At the time, observers believed that the controls would be much more effective than they now appear to have been. Many observers then took a much less monetarist view of events than they do now. Also, econometric estimates suggested more scope for noninflationary stimulus than appears to be the case in retrospect. The ABA criticized 1972 monetary policy only in its 1975 statement to the JEC. Rose published his allegations only in 1974. Wright Patman discovered the Federal Reserve's 1972 misdeeds in an article published in February 1975.[92] Other liberal congressional critics were also late in attacking 1972 policy.

Reuss and Proxmire originally praised the Federal Reserve for its policy in 1972 rather than criticizing it. In hearings before the Senate Banking Committee in February 1973, Proxmire reminded Burns: "We on the Joint Economic Committee were holding hearings every month on unemployment, complaining about a lack of effective action on it. *Your monetary policy did respond to an unemployment situation that no other aspect of our economic policy seemed to take cognizance of.*"[93]

Again in February 1973, Proxmire and Burns met at JEC hearings. Also participating in the questioning were Wright Patman and Henry Reuss. Proxmire's questions included almost no discussion of current monetary policy or the course of policy over the prior year.[94] Nor did Patman assail Burns for an election-biased policy. Representative Reuss roundly complimented Burns for the previous year's monetary policy:

> [To Burns:] Do you not see something ironic in your testifying, as I think you have to, that you intend to make monetary policy tighter, create less new money than the 7.4 percent which you created last year? Frequently that was in defiance of the mandate of the committee, which said, "Do not create more than 6 percent," *and I congratulate you on defying us.*[95]

Both Reuss and Proxmire subsequently changed their minds about 1972. In remarks on the Senate floor on November 9, 1973, Proxmire pronounced 1972 monetary policy to have been "reckless."

> Throughout 1972, when the economy was picking up an inflationary head of steam, the pace of money growth continued at a reckless speed. It did, indeed, slow down from quarter to quarter, but the pace was still breakneck throughout the year. After the money supply was expanding in each quarter of the year at more than 7 percent, a rate that was feeding, not restraining, inflation. [sic]

> About all that can be said of that policy is that it served a useful political role. Unlike another election year, 1960, when a restrained monetary policy against Burns' advice may have cost the incumbent Republican Party the wafer-thin majority by which they lost the election, the 1973 monetary policy gilded the economic expansion lily and helped assure the Nixon landslide. It also converted a year of strong economic progress into a serious inflation.[96]

In a February 1975 meeting, Reuss confronted Burns about the "harm . . . done to the nation's economy" in 1972, 1973, and 1974 by monetary policy. "The Federal Reserve, over the repeated objections of many Members of Congress and others, expanded money and credit at rates which we felt, and in the event proved so to do, would stimulate inflation." When Burns pointed out that Reuss was changing his earlier position, Reuss modified his criticism to refer only to 1973–4.[97]

Proxmire, clearly enough, had been suspicious about the Federal Reserve's monetary policy from the outset of 1972. But the pattern of policy that Proxmire and others came to criticize could be described equally accurately as a response to congressional concerns about unemployment as to Nixon's reelection program. The belated raising of the accusations about 1972 must be seen in the context of tight money in 1974 and the desire of congressional liberals to attack the System.

In fact, the Federal Reserve acknowledged subsequently that policy was too stimulative during 1972. As one might expect of policy makers who stress expertise in justifying their actions, none of these acknowledgments has ever explicitly mentioned political constraints. Perhaps the closest one can expect to that kind of a statement came when Burns confirmed the System's special concern with developments in long-term interest rates during 1972. In an exchange with Proxmire concerning policy in 1972–3, Burns argued:

> The severe rate of inflation that we have experienced in 1973 cannot responsibly be attributed to monetary management or to public policies more generally. In retrospect, it may well be that monetary policy should have been a little less expansive in 1972. But a markedly more restrictive policy would have led to a still sharper rise in interest rates and risked a premature ending of the business expansion, without limiting to any significant degree this year's upsurge of the price level.[98]

Conclusion

The best explanation for the policy of 1972 is the Federal Reserve's perception of a political threat to control interest rates and its desire to avoid criticism for not supporting the controls program. This policy has been criticized, primarily in retrospect, as being full of error. In my view, both the policy and the critique are to be understood as being political.

The process of making policy was clearly political. Conflicts were sharp, and economic expertise often gave way to calculation of how best to protect the institution. The policy's consequences were political. The policy supported an economic expansion that aided Nixon's reelection whether that was the intention of Federal Reserve officials or not. The System's way of avoiding externally imposed interest rate controls was to attempt to control them anyway. This did contribute to the problem of inflation in 1973 and 1974 that was itself "solved" by creating a bitter recession with monetary policy. These events produced an impression of technical incompetence that clearly damaged the System's credibility with economists (among others) and provoked an attack from Congress.

At the same time, the course of action taken has been easy to interpret as partisan. The superficial plausibility of that story has also detracted from the System's legitimacy. It is common now to see news articles during election periods speculating on the possible political motivations for monetary policy actions; this is clear evidence of damage done. The fact that liberal observers applauded the Federal Reserve's actions at first and then deplored them later – at a time when different types of political consequences were being created by monetary policy – is not surprising. But it did further embroil the Federal Reserve in ordinary politicking. In short, the defensive policy of 1972 did not contribute further to the institution's political strength. In the pursuit of long-run political autonomy, Federal Reserve officials may have inadvertently increased the Federal Reserve's short-run political responsiveness in a more or less permanent way.

There is an important moral to this tale. If we measure policy by standards of performance that could be attained only if actors systematically ignored any future political repercussions of their actions, we will always find that policy has failed or is in some sense corrupt. Such an approach is itself political in that it tends systematically to undermine the legitimacy of state actions by showing them to have been either incompetent or misguided. This, however, is precisely the political problem confronted by an institution that is legitimized on grounds of nonpartisan, technical expertise. This is a continuing problem for the Federal Reserve in its relationship with economists. It is obviously very difficult for an analyst to say what political consequences an institution must anticipate in order to remain viable. This means that there is no clear-cut, neutral standard against which to evaluate such behavior. In short, evaluation itself is unavoidably political.

The notion that such an important institution could *not* be involved in politics is simply a delusion. To believe that the Federal Reserve could have chosen not to adjust its policies to the politically charged conditions of 1972 and survived unchanged is extraordinarily naive. In saying this, I do not excuse monetary policy that may have been technically incorrect. Rather, I want to stress that it is analytically incorrect to limit our definition of the "monetary authorities" in 1972 to the Federal Reserve. If there is guilt, it is widely shared. In doing policy research, it is essential to define the research problem so that the political problems policy makers face are, as a matter of course, incorporated as part of the substantive problems they must solve. In important areas such as monetary policy, there is no analytic justification for or advantage gained by acting as if political calculations can be overlooked.

9

Monetary Politics: A Summary

One of the greatest difficulties a political scientist faces in trying to study monetary politics is finding a productive way to analyze the issues that dominate public discussion and debate. For many political scientists, the basic questions motivating their inquiry have to do with the way the clash of interests in political arenas produces allocative consequences. The traditional emphasis on such questions, even in behavioral political science, has been substantial.[1]

In trying to comprehend monetary policy, then, many political scientists would naturally inquire about distributive issues and would examine the process of policy making for signs of conflict related to these issues. The search would be a frustrating one. A great deal of the most visible debate about monetary policy is not explicitly about distributive issues. It is a battle of technicians, and the stakes are not at all obvious to those not among the congnoscenti. As we have seen, there are important distributive consequences associated with different positions in the technical debate. For example, the monetarists argue that distributive considerations must be subordinated to the fight against inflation.

It is true that the distributive implications of different kinds of monetary policy actions are difficult to sort out in this area. It is frequently not clear who benefits or loses – which sectors of business and finance, which income classes, which parts of income classes. The fact of that uncertainty is, no doubt, politically significant because lack of clear information discourages consideration of distributional choices and makes it more difficult to mobilize affected groups. This uncertainty may even reflect efforts of gainers to hide their winnings. Because policy impacts are produced through market processes, the independent contribution of policy to outcomes is often not obvious to those who feel them. Moreover, the technicians involved in the more visible debates have no particular commitment to enlightening us about the distributive implications of monetary policy choices. If they did, it would undoubtedly contribute to creating a broader, more informed, and more meaningful debate.

This is not to say that distributive consequences are completely ignored or that they are politically irrelevant. Periodically, we observe lively assaults on the Federal Reserve by Congress. The most important of these assaults have been in reaction to the distributive consequences of high interest rates. These reactions reveal the elements of conventional interest group politics working through established links with Congress. However, for reasons elaborated in Chapter 7, this is a relatively ineffective means of influencing monetary policy. Congress reacts to policy choices made long in the past, rather than shaping future policy. Further, it is very difficult for Congress to define a consistent, clear policy preference extending for any meaningful time period.

Here again, we see the importance for monetary policy of the distinction drawn in Chapter 1 between technical discourse and ordinary political discourse. Not all debates are the same. Some types are of more consequence in shaping policy than others; some are more likely to raise distributional issues. The more consequential debates are not distributional debates.

In the technical realm, debate focuses on control issues such as the implications of selecting different kinds of instruments; the implications of setting instruments in different kinds of ways; the nature of the relationship between monetary and fiscal policy; the role of optimal control theory and optimal policy; and the implications for policy of actions being taken by actors in the private sector. Analysts focus on the need to identify reliable indicators on the current state of the economy that could show that economic trends have changed and, thus, that policy should change. They are concerned with showing under what conditions policy actions might so disrupt markets that overall economic stability would be threatened. Typically, dense technical debates about policy tactics "crowd out" debates about which ultimate targets to select and which values of those targets should be achieved.

Various aspects of technical discourse are of interest to political scientists. In technical discourse about monetary policy, normative issues are usually introduced only implicitly, often by way of assumptions that are treated as being noncontroversial. One such assumption is that efficiency is desirable above all else. Such assumptions are political in that they embody judgments about the desirability of the status quo or implicitly favor some interests (e.g., the efficient) over others. At a less basic level, I have pointed out that different positions in the monetarist–Keynesian debate about *how* control should or could be exercised have political implications because of the consequences each considers as important or unimportant. They are also politically important because they identify parties responsible for the success or failure of policy.

There are other ways in which technical debate is of interest to political scientists. Many analyses of why there may be problems in controlling the economy point directly or indirectly to political factors. For example, analyses tracing the loss of monetary control to financial innovations such as Eurodollar markets, NOW accounts, electronic funds transfers, and so forth frequently identify some policy decisions that preceded or provoked the innovations. Political scientists may usefully and interestingly direct attention to the political conditions that produced the earlier destabilizing reforms.

Ordinary political discourse is less precise and rigorous; it is empirically and theoretically casual. Compared to technical discourse, it is more explicitly normative, more concerned with distributive issues, and more concerned with assigning responsibility for undesired distributive outcomes. With the exception of the question of the independence of the Federal Reserve, no issues have dominated this area of discourse in recent years as the monetarist debate has in the technical realm. Interest in monetary policy is episodic and reactive. Ordinary political discourse changes with the changing impacts of current economic performance. Typically, discourse is dominated by negative reactions to undesired economic conditions.

Ordinary political discourse is often preoccupied with assigning responsibility. Whose actions led us to our current dire straits? Government? Business? Labor? Congress? The Federal Reserve? Thus has the independence issue emerged, and thus has Congress been led to attack the Federal Reserve's structure, which has been seen as permitting and facilitating ill-conceived policy. Assigning blame may be effective symbolically, but it usually has not led to the serious analysis that might eventually confront distributional issues, with possibly radical conclusions. This means that the control issues of technical discourse dominate most debate that has a serious chance of influencing events.

Note that questions about the Federal Reserve's independence have been raised in both realms but largely for different reasons. As a technical issue, independence is evaluated in terms of its consequences for maintaining more effective, rational control of the economy. In the realm of ordinary political discourse, independence is considered in assigning responsibility. The latter process has not involved sustained, systematic attempts to alter outcomes.

As we have seen, the two realms are somewhat separated institutionally. Technical discourse, partly for reasons related to a desire to sustain System autonomy, is the preferred mode of debate in the FOMC. Actual behavior may not match the ideal, but the technical ideal governs. It dominates exchanges between the Federal Reserve, the CEA, and the Treasury. This seems to be less so with presidents and members of Congress, among whom ordinary political discourse is much more likely to predominate.

Each realm has limitations, and different issues tend to be overlooked in the different realms. Whereas ordinary political discourse may appear to be naive, uncritical, and inconsistent, technical discourse seems to rule out classes of issues from debate that can, at least occasionally, emerge in ordinary discourse. Technical debate often appears to take efficiency as its primary virtue and to subject that standard to little critical scrutiny. Distributive issues are either ignored or obfuscated. In order to define tractable analytical problems, participants find it convenient to take the status quo largely for granted. And of course, technical discourse restricts participation to the technically adept. By contrast, ordinary political discourse opens up debate to a wider range of participants and issues, but often at the cost of oversimplification and petty finger pointing.

Political scientists will note that technical discourse tends to exclude as a legitimate policy objective the need to defend against criticisms emerging from ordinary political discourse. Nor have outside critics of the Federal Reserve who are engaged in technical discourse fully taken into account the fact that their technical criticisms will be exploited, and perhaps distorted, in the realm of ordinary political discourse. The former means that any policy moves suspected of being politically motivated are automatically categorized as unjustifiable. Such criticism, in turn, provides ammunition for critics operating within the terms of ordinary political discourse.

Students of political economy make an error in defining their point of departure in such a way that they rule out as illegitimate any political survival strategies. It is analytically misleading and unnecessarily contentious to define the study of political economy in terms of some supposed set of errors in economic policy that are then attributed to politics. Policy, whether governed entirely by standards of technical efficiency or not, is always good or bad in relation to specific categories of people.[2] For whom policy is good or bad is what politics is all about. Politics is inevitable in this sense, and there is nothing gained by setting up the "problem" in such a way that the answer is always knowable well in advance. That is, by taking politics as bad compared to some ideal counterfactual policy, we will always discover that policy has been corrupted by politics. Surely this conclusion is no longer interesting. The objective of understanding policy choice is, in fact, impeded by such an approach because it substitutes labeling of a residual category for serious analysis of the reasons for behavior.

Political economy approaches

In the past few years, there has been a remarkable surge of interest in the politics of economic policy. Among political scientists interested in this area, there have been efforts to supplement standard policy studies approaches with other approaches more specifically concerned with economic policy. Two approaches have been particularly influential and have generated large bodies of research – the politico-economic approach and the neo-Marxist approach.

The politicoeconomic literature, highly quantitative in orientation, has focused on the impact of electoral politics on economic policy making. The findings and the assumptions used have been quite diverse. For example, there are studies showing that the interests of a government's electoral coalition predict its macroeconomic policy.[3] Other studies show that the partisan orientation of governments has little explanatory value, but that, for example in the United States, presidential administrations are decisive.[4] Still other research based on the PBC hypothesis suggests that governments use macroeconomic policy instruments primarily to engineer economic conditions favorable to their reelection or their short-run popularity.

By contrast, the neo-Marxist literature typically treats electoral politics as relatively insignificant. More important from this perspective are the "real" and constant obligations of governments in capitalist societies – promoting conditions favorable for private capital accumulation.[5] In most of this literature, the research focus is not on the question of whether governments in capitalist societies ignore or attend to this ultimate objective. Rather, research explores the mechanism by which private capital accumulation is publicly protected. Is the mechanism *structural* in the sense that any government eventually realizes that it must cater to the needs (not necessarily the wants) of private capitalists in order to get good economic performance? Or is it *instrumental* in the sense that private capitalists use their disproportionate control over the state apparatus to win attention for their preferences?

Conclusions relevant to politico-economic studies

This study includes findings relevant to both of these approaches. For example, with regard to the politico-economic approach, I have found that the instruments of monetary policy have not been used in the way predicted by the PBC hypothesis. This conclusion reinforces conclusions reached by others using other methods and approaches.[6] However, the Federal Reserve does try to avoid dramatic policy actions during election periods – proving that it is not independent in a strong sense. On at least two occasions, presidents appear to have urged a restrictive policy on the Federal Reserve in years prior to the election year in order to approach the electorate during a period of recovery rather than recession. In 1972, the year of the most blatant politico-economic manipulation, the Federal Reserve's performance cannot adequately be understood by the simple hypothesis of partisan manipulation. Such a hypothesis fits the facts in a crude way, but badly misperceives the way policy was actually being made and greatly oversimplifies the nature and sources of the political pressures on the Federal Reserve.

However, I do not conclude that electoral motivations are unimportant for monetary policy. Thus far, the discussion of the PBC has tended to be dominated by an overly simplified kind of hypothesis. That is, policy instruments (or even policy outcomes) must move in a strictly defined way or the hypothesis is not confirmed. Alternatives are, one can readily see, much more difficult to study. For example, one alternative might be that policy makers have to continually try to solve short-run optimization problems when the electorate's weights on objectives are changing. "Good" economic performance is not stably defined for all time, as proposed in the basis PBC hypothesis, but changes. In short, even all of the negative results produced to date do not add up to a conclusion that governments (or the Federal Reserve) are indifferent to electioneering opportunities.

Monetary policy has not been a major partisan issue. However, it is marked by a liberal–conservative dimension underlying most debate; this suggests that debate could become more partisan. Also, it is clear that partisan differences are useful in predicting the direction of FOMC dissents by board members. In a political system like that of the United States, the major means for reflecting partisan differences in monetary policy is the president. There have rarely been sustained clashes between the Federal Reserve and the president. Despite evidence of tensions concerning the speed of policy action, presidents and their advisors are not usually dissatisfied with the outcomes of their negotiations with the Federal Reserve. In short, the conditions for expecting to find presidential influence on monetary policy seem to be met. The degree to which *partisan* effects can be identified in monetary policy depends on the degree to which partisanship has a relatively stable meaning at the presidential level.

Conclusions relevant to neo-Marxist studies

The text does not deal explicitly with the neo-Marxist approach, not because I have any fundamental hostility to it, but because it proved to be of limited help in the analysis. Because this conclusion may not be obvious to all readers, and because of the current popularity of neo-Marxist approaches, I want to explore this negative finding in more detail. The case *for* the neo-Marxist approach, or something like it, might take note of some of the following points.

For many observers, the most important feature of monetary politics is the absence of so much that one might expect to find in examining a key political process. For example, it is important that monetary and banking issues are *not* basic partisan issues. It is important that members of Congress do *not* have incentives to become deeply involved with monetary policy and that congressional initiatives with respect to monetary policy tend to avoid core policy issues. It is important that the short-run distributive impacts of policy are very unclear and that identifying precisely who gains and loses, in what amounts, from what actions, even in the long run is very difficult to do. It is important that most interest groups find themselves unable to define effective strategies for dealing directly with the Federal Reserve.

The recruitment process also has important consequences from this perspective. The overwhelming majority of recruits for top Federal Reserve offices have been members of mainstream financial networks working in government, the private sector, the Federal Reserve, or academia. They have been drawn from an upper- or upper-middle-class milieu. In many basic respects, their outlooks have been very similar. Typically, appointees have had a substantial personal stake in the status quo. One probable consequence is a narrower range of debate and a greater willingness to limit debate to the realm of technical discourse.

These observations are interesting for the neo-Marxist approach because they show why, in an institution of such importance to the economy, it is not necessary for elites to exercise constant, detailed oversight of ongoing decisions. Officials are selected who are naturally very concerned about the continued health of American capitalism. Most others who might aspire to be participants are ruled out in the recruitment process, and they do not have the kind of information and expertise that would be necessary to change the focus of current debate from technical to distributional issues.

The history summarized in Chapter 2 demonstrates that the Federal Reserve was established to guarantee that certain interests were automatically represented in national policy. To a substantial degree, this structuring of interests has persisted. In part, this is reflected in the high level of access by and the casual contact with bankers. This structuring of interests does not refer merely to the interests of bankers, but also in a larger sense to the interests of those who benefit the most from the working of the U.S. economy. The Federal Reserve is part of a larger system of power that is dedicated to maintaining an economic system producing vastly disproportionate distributions of wealth. This is precisely the point of interest to many neo-Marxists.

In the context of preserving a capitalist economic system, the characteristics that restrict monetary politics to a relatively narrow, technically skilled community are extremely important characteristics for a central economic regulatory agency to have. If the American state is to perform its functions of regulating the economy, and if it is to do so in a fashion that permits it to behave with relative autonomy from societal groups, the Federal Reserve needs precisely these characteristics to insulate it effectively. In this view, the Federal Reserve and the economic system benefit from the prominence of technical debates focused exclusively on the problem of control; they benefit from having policy debates uncontaminated by distributive issues.

Unfortunately, the evidence presented in earlier chapters does not support this view so neatly. The evidence from 1972, for example, reveals a Federal Reserve that is sensitive to external pressures, not the well-insulated, autonomous protector of the interests of the capitalist system described in the prior paragraph. The analysis of bankers and the Federal Reserve suggests that bankers do not always put their long-run interests first, and this ordering of priorities has been reflected at the Federal Reserve. The discussion of Congress shows that congressional pressure can be strong and may provoke, at least temporarily, responsive Federal Reserve policy. This is not to say that the Federal Reserve has been contaminated with anticapitalist sentiment. Far from it. There is little about the Federal Reserve that is particularly hospitable to liberal, much less radical, sentiments. But despite all the characteristics that combine to make the Federal Reserve a "class agent" of the first rank, it is possible for short-run forces to distract it from its larger cause for significant periods of time.

Perhaps more important, the debates with the monetarists and the periodic conflicts with the president show that even actors who agree on the long-run objectives identified by the neo-Marxists (e.g., preserving a viable capitalist system) may disagree strongly on the appropriate short-run means. Indeed, if there is no technical consensus on the ideal means to accomplish those agreed-upon ends, then decisions must be made politically, even if the debate is couched in largely technical terms. Under such circumstances, however, short-term political forces become more important in shaping decisions.

Despite the fact that the Federal Reserve's larger role is apparently sustained by its political circumstances, the actual performance of that role is contingent on permissive short-term political forces. The Federal Reserve need not be pressured to regulate the economy in the interests of preserving corporate capitalism, but it can be pressured to take actions that may, in the long-run, make the stability of the corporate system uncertain. In this respect, if the Federal Reserve desires to underwrite the corporate order, it must attempt to preserve its ability to act correctly whenever short-run pressures are relaxed. The evidence examined here fully supports the conclusion that this has, indeed, been the basic Federal Reserve strategy. Whether the Federal Reserve has been successful, and whether it has in fact enhanced its ability to focus only on long-run issues, is much less certain.

Patterns of mobilization and monetary politics

Neither the politico-economic nor the neo-Marxist approach is successful in informing us about the full range of monetary politics. If the objective is to understand the ongoing conduct of policy, as opposed to alerting us to important considerations that may influence policy from time to time, much of interest is overlooked by these approaches. The politico-economic approach is useful in understanding the conduct of policy in a continuing sense only if electoral considerations are dominant and if those considerations imply an unambiguous monetary policy strategy. Similarly, the neo-Marxist approach is helpful only if there is an unambiguously correct policy strategy for protecting the capitalist system. Often, however, perhaps usually, there are no such clear strategies. That is why other views are needed of the ongoing political relationships of the Federal Reserve.

My approach has been to analyze relationships in pairs – the Federal Reserve and bankers, the Federal Reserve and economists, and so on. In each case, I have examined each actor's resources and objectives, and the factors that might enable an outside actor to mobilize effectively to influence the Federal Reserve. The objective has been to determine the degree to which an external actor has succeeded in obliging the Federal Reserve to attend to his objectives. Of course, it is not adequate simply to examine pairwise relationships. We need to complicate the analysis in a way that brings in several actors at once.

Kane's analysis of the Federal Reserve, which has been discussed at several points, including his scapegoat hypothesis, has been perhaps the most interesting attempt to achieve this complexity.[7] Kane's argument involves some ambiguities, but with some liberal supplementation, I reconstruct it as follows. This interpretation emphasizes a consensus among major governmental participants that monetary policy must be protected from the short-run pressures of political processes – especially the demands of interest groups for protection from the costs imposed by stabilization policy. The relationship between the Federal Reserve and the administration is seen as largely one of agreement. It is, in effect, a tacit conspiracy to discourage congressional participation in the monetary policy game, and it allows the president the opportunity to use the Federal Reserve as a scapegoat.

At the same time, Congress welcomes the fact that there is an "independent" Federal Reserve that can be blamed for economic difficulties. Few members of Congress really want to control monetary policy or believe that it would be wise to try to do so. They realize as well as anyone that it is important to have experts managing policy in this area. Similarly, members of Congress are reluctant to give further control over economic policy directly to the president because they find it very useful to have the Federal Reserve's independent analyses to contrast to the president's.

In summary, independence and occasional independent action are welcomed by the Congress and the administration because: (1) The president recognizes the desirability of having one macroeconomic policy instrument that can more or less respond solely to the technical requirements of the economy without congressional interference, and (2) members of Congress like deflecting the political costs of unpopular policy choices to an "independent" central bank and away from elected officials. Everyone agrees on the commitment to a free market in credit and money, which is reinforced by an independent central bank. The result of this is private agreement and public disagreement. It is clear from the discussions in Chapters 6 and 7 that considerable evidence could be produced to support this interpretation. There is much to encourage agreement between president and Federal Reserve. Some members of Congress talk a great deal about controlling the Federal Reserve, but Congress does very little.

If this interpretation presents an accurate picture of the relationship of the Federal Reserve with government, then the relationship is a very delicate one. In order to perform the political function of diverting criticism for an unpopular policy, the central bank must be perceived as having some genuine degree of independence. It can, however, never be seen to be so independent and its policies so harsh that it provokes a genuine attack that destroys the illusion. It must avoid being formally subordinated to the executive branch or having policy dictated by Congress. On the other hand, the more the central bank cooperates openly with the government or openly responds to congressional demands, the less plausible it is for others to point the finger when policy tightens. And the less likely it is that attentive groups will be fooled by the illusion of independence – and if they are not fooled, why bother with the charade? Thus, the ideal public relationship would be one of studied distance and intermittent squabbling. Such a relationship would be expected to produce policy in the long run very similar to the policy that would result from a fully subordinate central bank subject, like the fiscal authority itself, to political pressures from various groups in society. The primary differences would be that policy might respond somewhat less quickly to political pressures, and that considerable energy and inventiveness would be invested in protecting a facade of independence that primarily serves to let elected officials evade responsibilities for policy.

Entertaining though this interpretation is, it fails to capture accurately what is really going on. One can maintain one's cynicism about the capacity of officials to dissemble publicly and still believe that behind the facade of independence some real independence exists. If, as Kane concedes, the organization of Congress makes it very difficult for it to attack the Federal Reserve, might we not suspect that the goat is a real goat, not simply a scapegoat? If presidents are reluctant to alienate the Federal Reserve's financial constituency, especially when it is united and concerned, perhaps the System's room for maneuver is larger than one might suspect from the scapegoat hypothesis. There is too much evidence that the intermittent conflicts and frustrations are real. There is too much evidence that the Federal Reserve really does possess important political resources beyond the mere indulgence of president and Congress. There is too much consensus among attentive elites that the Federal Reserve chairman is powerful.[8] To accept this interpretation, we must willingly ignore too much contradictory evidence.

Fortunately, we are not obliged to make an either-or choice in this case. In rejecting extreme versions of independence, one is not obliged to accept extreme versions of Federal Reserve subordination. Federal Reserve policy is not, in fact, *easily* determined by short-run political pressures, but it *can* be influenced by such pressures especially when there is a substantial congruence of forces pushing in the same direction. What matters is that for most of the relevant actors, the degree and nature of their interest in monetary policy and their capacity for coherent mobilization vary systematically through time.

In several important cases, it appears that both the political capacity and the nature of interest vary with the business cycle. So, in the case of Congress, we see that attention varies with the condition of interest-sensitive sectors of the economy such as housing. When the housing sector is in a depression, congressional attempts to instruct the Federal Reserve about the conduct of policy increase, as does congressional willingness to contemplate credit allocation schemes. High interest rates provoke a negative congressional reaction. This reaction has been observed repeatedly and is well understood at the Federal Reserve.

In the case of bankers, evidence suggests that there may be a conflict between bankers' short-run concerns for profitability and competitive advantage and their long-run concerns for low, or at least stable, rates of inflation. Unified pressure from the financial sector focusing on long-run rather than short-run problems is expected only when inflation has unambiguously become a problem for most financial sector participants. Similarly, there is some evidence that conflicts between the president and the Federal Reserve about policy objectives are more likely to occur around turning points in the business cycle, when economic conditions are extreme, than at other times. In short, the nature of the short-run political forces focused on the Federal Reserve are linked in a regular way to the performance of the economy.

These short-run forces are not mobilized simultaneously, and they are not consistent. For example, with the possible exception of a president highly concerned about inflation, there is ordinarily no highly mobilized anti-inflation coalition with political power. Monetarists are always mobilized, but not always allied with officials in power. Financial interests are always concerned about inflation, but are often more concerned about some other problem in the short run. However, inflation fighting is intermittently the consensus of all, or almost all, highly mobilized groups. The Federal Reserve may anticipate this consensus and make policy moves prior to the emergence of organized pressure. One can be sure that the inflation objective will become primary under those circumstances – but not necessarily at other times.

This provides a political explanation for the observation of economists such as James Pierce that the Federal Reserve engages primarily in "fire fighting" – focusing on one pressing problem at a time.[9] Pierce argues that fire fighting "gets in the way of pursuing policies that are sustainable over the longer run" – which is not surprising since policy made with a short-run focus is rarely the same thing as policy with a long-run focus. Pierce's complaint echoes the long-standing frustration of many economists with the Federal Reserve's inability to adopt what they believe is the appropriate long-run focus. The correct explanation for fire fighting is not to be found in the conceptual weaknesses at the Federal Reserve but in political weaknesses. The cyclical mobilization and demobilization of political forces provokes shifting responses from the Federal Reserve. When the political environment is such that long-run problems are regarded as the dominant issues, then the Federal Reserve will surely be focused on long-run problems.

There is no doubt that the Federal Reserve will continue to have to walk a fine line between the correct policy from any technical viewpoint and the correct policy from a political viewpoint. Technical errors can create political problems, and political errors can create technical problems. It is important for analysts not to neglect political errors and political problems in their efforts to understand how this institution behaves.

APPENDIX A

A Note on Data Sources

This research is based on several sources of information. First, and most important, is the public record. There is a vast amount of public information about monetary policy making. Probably most important are the various kinds of records of the FOMC. Detailed *Minutes* of the FOMC have been made public with a five-year lag and extend through 1976. With the onset of pressure for greater openness in policy making in 1976–7, the Federal Reserve responded by shortening the time in which it released the record of policy actions from ninety to thirty days and discontinued the practice of keeping "almost verbatim" minutes. Instead, it now publishes a longer policy record in the *Federal Reserve Bulletin,* a record substantially less revealing than the detailed *Minutes,* a tradeoff of rapid availability for detail. I am assured that the published record accurately and fairly reflects the issues discussed in meetings. However, for purposes of political analysis of the FOMC, the new procedure is significantly less revealing.[1]

Accuracy of the pre–1977 *Minutes*

The pre–1977 *Minutes,* which as of this writing are available through 1975, are in an edited, semiverbatim form, based on transcriptions of tape recordings of meetings. Copies are available to the public at Federal Reserve Board offices and at all Federal Reserve banks, and microfilm copies may be purchased from the National Archives. Debate is reported in the third person. For example, "Mr. Daane said that given the current state of the financial markets, he believed it would be advisable to avoid sudden interest rate movements." Some members prepared written statements for meetings, and these, as well as previously prepared presentations by the staff, are often included verbatim in the record.

It is important to know how reliable this record is as a document of divisions, debates, and intensity. Editorial revisions were made in preparing the *Minutes* – which took place in the days immediately following each meeting – and they may not always be regarded as minor. One former governor described this as "toning down words" and making debates sound less emotional. A further and equally important part of the editorial process consisted of giving more coherence to the statements of some governors and presidents than had actually been true in debate. The same former governor reported going to Arthur Broida, then FOMC secretary, to congratulate him on his editorial skill: "I didn't say that, but that's what I meant!" In some cases, details of politically interesting discussions are simply omitted. Thus, for example, in the February 1972 meeting, the *Minutes* recount the following:

> The chairman then summarized the discussion on two subjects at the Joint Economic Committee hearings – profits of Government securities dealers and proposals for GAO audits of the Federal Reserve. After some discussion of these matters, the Chairman invited Mr. Maisel to comment on the directive committee's latest report.[2]

Broida discussed the editorial job with me. It was permissible for members to make off-the-record comments in FOMC meetings, but these had to be so identified at the time. Comments would not, he said, be taken from the record later. Obviously, comments made during breaks in meetings or in other nonmeeting settings are not recorded. The sharp edges were taken off exchanges on the grounds that it would not be fair to report verbatim statements that would leave a different impression in writing. Some discussion was rearranged in order to provide a more coherent flow to the record of the meeting, especially by juxtaposing related comments. Further, "we tried to put good English into the mouths of people." An example? "The case of the guy who had just flown back from Rome and was badly jetlagging and was just incoherent."

A more interesting example of revisions relevant to a political scientist came from another informant who demanded strictest confidentiality. He noted that "you'll never find this in the *Minutes*, but . . . " and others have alluded to the incident as well. The case involved Arthur Burns's first meeting of the FOMC after assuming the chairmanship (February 1970). He was convinced that policy had to be changed, and a reading of the *FOMC Minutes* shows him weighing into battle with an apparent eight to four majority against him. The informant says that the *Minutes* in no way reveal the actual bitterness of the exchanges involved, especially between Burns and New York Bank President Alfred Hayes. Burns, it is reported, eventually silenced his opposition by arguing that his opponents could have said everything they were saying "in September 1929."[3] As I read the *Minutes,* the meeting was marked by a lengthy period of negotiation, but there is no evidence of any especially bitter exchanges.

Broida stressed that in substance the record is "pretty damn straight." This was an issue, he reported, of considerable sensitivity to all concerned. "Nobody tried to cook the record." In part, this was guaranteed by the fact that all members had the opportunity to read the edited *Minutes* and object to any inaccuracies.

As is clear in Chapter 8, the record after editing is still very informative. Not all indicators of the intensity of debate have been expunged. Such a record vastly exceeds that available for the Supreme Court, for example. But those using the record must be aware that it overstate the actual quality of economic analysis in debate and understates the degree of division. The *Minutes,* thus, must be seen as partially manifesting the System's political strategy of conveying an impression of indifferent technocracy.

Congressional hearings

Congressional publications dealing with the Federal Reserve are similarly vast. The hearing records provide an opportunity to review statements of Federal Reserve positions under questioning ranging from the very hostile to the very friendly. Many of the most useful hearings are cited in notes to various chapters. Staff studies for congressional committees have also occasionally proved to be quite informative sources.

Unpublished sources

I received access to two major sets of unpublished records that are not routinely available to the public. The first were minutes of meetings of the FAC for 1968–72. I was told at the time that the minutes had never been made public before; they had been edited, with certain passages deleted. Most of the deleted sections involved discussions of specific banks. Board Secretary Theodore Allison reviewed for me various deleted passages of interest, in all cases revealing their general nature and in some cases a good deal more. I am confident that no key passages were removed. The *FAC Minutes* are abridged in a similar fashion to the *FOMC Minutes,* except, it seems, that they are somewhat more truncated.

The second set includes copies of staff background reports to the FOMC for 1972. This included the Red Book containing statements from each district bank on conditions in the district; the Green Book containing general staff economic projections for the next several quarters; and the Blue Book containing the staffs' most current analysis of the short-term financial effects of possible alternative policy choices. At the time of each meeting, the Blue Book is *the* central policy memorandum, and it is treated as highly confidential. It is available on special request to researchers at the Federal Reserve Board's offices for years for which the *Minutes* have been made public. It is an essential source.

Another important source of unpublished documentation is the White House files available through the Lyndon Baines Johnson Library in Austin, Texas. In recent years, many highly confidential documents have been opened to the public, including memoranda from the CEA commenting on current policy (including the Federal Reserve) and memoranda from important interagency staff members dealing with economic policy (the Quadriad and the Troika). Other valuable documents include those relating to the selection of appointees to the Federal Reserve. Comparable papers for the Nixon years had not been made public at the time of my research, and the most interesting documents probably will not be made available for some time.

I also received access to the James Louis Robertson collection of papers at the Library of Congress. These papers include some additional internal Federal Reserve documents of interest and help provide a fuller account of several interesting events.

Interviews

Over a period of several years, I interviewed sixty current or former officials and close observers as background for this research. Several were interviewed twice. Included were sixteen of twenty-three members of the Board of Governors between 1966 and 1981, representing about 80 percent of the "man-years" served. Also included were five district bank presidents; four members of the CEA, many staffers at the Federal Reserve Board, the district banks, the IMF, the Treasury, and Congress, and one senator. Some interviewees had occupied several positions during their careers, and thus the coverage of roles was somewhat greater than the number of interviews. I had telephone conversations with three other current or former officials. Also, I had access to transcripts of interviews in the oral history collection of the Lyndon Baines Johnson Library, as well as Vanderbilt University's Institute of Public Policy oral history interviews with chairmen of the CEA from Heller to Greenspan.

Although the coverage of relevant positions was reasonably extensive, there was in no sense a sample drawn of various personnel. My objective, quite simply, was to interview as many current and former incumbents of key positions as possible, given the limits of time and resources.

The questions asked varied from person to person. Partly, this was done to accommodate the differences in roles and in the events in which different individuals had participated. Partly it reflected my own cumulative learning about the institution. Some lines of questioning proved not to be fruitful and were dropped. As I learned about new issues and events, they were included. These were not attitude interviews. Although many interviewees were asked very similar questions about the same topics, they were regarded more as providing information than as reflecting distributions of opinions. Interviews are often quoted for illustrative purposes.

I believe that various lines of attitude research would be interesting, including questions about the theory and boundaries of monetary policy. Important studies of the attitudes of political and administrative elites in the United States and Europe have generally excluded central bankers, so there is no systematic evidence on their attitudes on general questions about politics. However, in this research I faced a basic choice of whether to stress general questions or to rely more on unstructured – but, I hope, focused – interviews intended to reveal how the respondents viewed the world in which they operated and the problems they faced.[4]

This goal, of course, presented its own research problems. At least 90 percent of the respondents were Ph.D. economists or had some other postgraduate social science training. They were interested in the questions motivating the research, and they were very sensitive to political charges that had been made about the Federal Reserve in the past. It became obvious that the most fruitful strategy was to assure interviewees that I had no axe to grind, and that I was trying to conduct a serious and informed investigation of issues that we both realized might be controversial. I would be reluctant to claim complete success, but I think the strategy was correct.

Since there is often a fairly rich documentary record relating to most issues and events covered here, I have rarely been obliged to rely solely upon interview reports. In most cases, specific events and topics have been discussed with several respondents. However, many insisted on anonymity or consultation before explicit attribution. I have tried to honor all such requests. As a consequence, there are unattributed quotations in the text. All quotations from interviews with Arthur Burns were approved by him prior to publication. Quotations from the Vanderbilt oral history collection are used with permission of each interviewee.

In this kind of interviewing, it is inevitable that respondents will try to guide the researcher toward a particular kind of conclusion. At best, as a researcher, one can try to be aware of this possibility and to report one's subjective estimate of an informant's reliability. In the case of an institution such as the Federal Reserve, which is known for its secrecy, such problems might seem especially likely. Any powerful, long-lived institution is bound to have developed a set of justifications and ideologies to use in explaining itself to the outside world and resisting challenges. I am not sure how to avoid asking questions that remain grounded in the concrete language policy makers use but that do not elicit "System defenses." One tries to learn to identify such responses and to probe past them. Consequently, of course, to the extent that I have relied on interviews for evidence in controversial matters, the exercise of my own judgment is much more obvious than might be the case in a more quantitative study. I believe that this difference is more in form than in degree.

In preliminary investigations, I was warned that current officials would be very reluctant to be interviewed. This proved not to be true, although in fact the majority of the individuals contacted were former officials. Only one person refused an interview (a member of Congress), and only one other (a district bank president) was obviously reluctant to schedule a meeting. Most interviews were scheduled by phone, and my calls were invariably returned. Interviews typically lasted for about an hour, although a few lasted considerably longer. The shortest interview, with Senator Proxmire, was thirty minutes long. Senior staff (but never governors) sometimes invited me to lunch in the Federal Reserve dining rooms, a pleasant corruption. The overwhelming majority of interviews took place in the offices of the officials interviewed.

Probably my biggest advantage in gaining interviews at the outset of the work was sponsorship by the Brookings Institution. Other factors may have been at work as well. Most interviews were conducted during the chairmanship of G. William Miller, who was strongly supportive of openness. I also detected a sense on the part of some officials that the Federal Reserve System could not avoid scrutiny by outsiders and that despite that scrutiny, it could continue to conduct policy with reasonable autonomy. The Federal Reserve has subsequently adopted guidelines intended to alert the Office of the Staff Director for Monetary Policy of contacts by outsiders with staff. The effect is to reduce researchers' control over their own interview program.

Access

In an effort to encourage more openness, I deliberately avoided delving into current policy issues in any precise way. Having access to individuals is obviously not the same thing as having access to important information. Others no doubt can judge better than I how much access I gained. In some sense, outsiders can never *really* have access to the Federal Reserve. The outsiders most likely consistently to reach inside are economists who have personal and professional contacts at high staff levels. There are many.

For at least two reasons, few economists have undertaken studies such as this, even though many have made contributions to it. First, the Federal Reserve has, or at least has a reputation for having, dealt harshly in the past with insiders who become critics. Second, there are almost no professional incentives for economists to produce such a study. On the other hand, there are obvious disincentives, primarily in the form of potentially being cut off from future data sources. Thus, one observes a vast disjuncture between the way economists discuss policy-related issues professionally and the way they discuss them informally.

The evidence of such hazards comes mostly from certain prominent cases often cited as being instructive by interviewees. The most obvious example of an insider who drew fire from the Federal Reserve for his sins is Sanford Rose, an economic journalist who, in 1974, authored an article alleging partisan motivations behind policy in 1972. According to Rose, the Federal Reserve organized a campaign directed at Time Inc. executives seeking a retraction. These executives communicated to Rose their fear that without a retraction, it would be impossible in the future for *Time*-

affiliated reporters to get any information from the Federal Reserve.[5] It is widely believed by close observers that a St. Louis Federal Reserve Bank vice-president was eliminated as a serious contender for the bank's presidency because of a suspicion that he was involved in discussing those events with Rose. I have also been told of an economist who was invited to the Economic Consultants Group and later publicly revealed some of the discussion – all of which is confidential. He was never invited back.

Sherman Maisel embittered many in the System by publishing *Managing the Dollar* shortly after leaving his position as governor. He was accused of revealing portions of what were still confidential *Minutes*. He clashed with Arthur Burns over a section of the book that presents Burns as indiscreetly advocating Nixon's reelection after his appointment to the chairmanship of this "nonpartisan" board. Maisel also reports altering sections of the book with which former Chairman Martin took exception, despite Maisel's own feeling that the account was accurate – if unflattering.

I asked many respondents about Maisel's book. Very few had praise for it, and several raised points of disagreement. One well-read former Federal Reserve economist who suggested many other published sources on the System rather implausibly stated that he had never taken the time to look at it. Another, who by one report had circulated a lengthy critique, professed to having had only a "couple of points" of concern. One respondent, in what strikes me as at least a vast exaggeration, denegrated Maisel as "incoherent. . . . He lives in a world of total confusion." I attribute much of this kind of sentiment to residual anger over Maisel's real or imagined inaccuracies in the book and his betrayals of confidence.

Such behavior at the Federal Reserve is quite revealing. These incidents did not expose the Federal Reserve to be riven with corrupt, ill-intentioned, or incompetent officials. Nor, indeed – and this is really the point – do these incidents differentiate the Federal Reserve from other large, self-protective organizations. Indeed, they seemed simply to *reveal*. More than anything, they revealed a System filled with human beings who sometimes made mistakes, who sometimes did not have very good reasons for what they did, and who sometimes manuevered politically to achieve their objectives. On the one hand, it seems as if the System has been unnecessarily preoccupied with confidentiality per se; it is the method of operation. But the System is also very concerned with its image. In this case, the revelations that provoked retaliation eroded the preferred image of the neutral, dedicated, competent technocrat.

APPENDIX B

Legislation Included in Table 7.1

The following legislative actions are included in Table 7.1 but are not discussed in the accompanying text. The discussion in the text is limited to entries indicated in column 4, legislation passed by both houses of Congress. Actions included here are selected on the basis of several criteria: Legislation must involve monetary policy or the structure of the Federal Reserve. Routine oversight is excluded, but other oversight hearings are included, usually in column "0." Some legislation dealing with bank regulation is cited here, but only if it also included portions dealing with the structure of the Federal Reserve (e.g., the FINE hearings). Bank regulatory matters (e.g., electronic funds transfers, bank holding companies, interstate banking) are excluded despite the fact that financial innovation may have implications for monetary management. For this reason, many hearings in 1978–80 preparing the way for the eventual DIDMCA legislation are not reflected in this table. Despite the political importance of DIDMCA, as discussed in Chapter 4, it is excluded here. That decision could be debated, but given the legislative purposes this table is intended to represent (see the following text) it is consistent with the criteria governing other inclusions and exclusions. Legislation is excluded that involves routine reauthorization of status quo legislation (e.g., extending regulation Q), but proposals to alter the status quo are usually included. However, since the emphasis here is on legislation that is intended either to restrain the Federal Reserve, to guide its actions more closely, or to mitigate the problems of policy impact via credit allocation, some legislation altering the status quo is excluded that does not pursue one of these purposes. One example is S 2591 (1973), intended to do away with regulation Q. Also excluded are proposals dealing with other financial agencies.

Legislation is identified by year, by category of action (structure, credit, conduct) and by nature of action (i.e., 1 = hearings only; 2 = committee approval; 3 = approval of one house of Congress; 4 = approval by both houses of Congress.

1970

Conduct

1. Hearings requiring a rollback of interest rates, HCR 522 and HCR 523, March 1970.

1971

Structure

0. House Banking Committee, Subcommittee, oversight of the Federal Reserve System, September 1971.

Credit

1. Senate Banking Committee, Subcommittee, hearings on selective credit policies and wage–price stabilization, March–April 1981.
2. House Banking Committee, hearings on extending standby authority of the president, Federal Reserve Board, and Federal Home Loan Bank Board, HR 4246, February 1971.

Conduct

0. Senate Banking Committee, State of the National Economy 1971, March 1971.

1972

Structure

1. House Banking Committee, GAO audit proposed as part of legislation dealing with housing finance, HR 16704, H. Rept. 92–1429, September 1972.

1973

Structure

2. House Banking Committee, GAO audit, hearing, October 1973, HR 10265, H. Rept 93–585. (Tabled in Rules Committee.)

Conduct

0. House Banking Committee, hearings on credit crunch and reform of financial institutions, September 1973.
2. House Banking Committee, hearings and report on the Economic Stabilization Act of 1973, including proposals to freeze interest rates, HR 6168 (see the discussion in Chapter 8), H. Rept. 93–114, April 1973.

1974

Structure

3. House. Passed GAO audit, April 1974 (HR 10265, which had been reported to the House floor in October 1973).

Conduct

0. House Banking Committee, hearings on Federal Reserve policy and inflation and high interest rates, July and August, 1974.

0. Senate Banking Committee, Subcommittee, hearings on oversight of economic stabilization, January and February 1974.

1975

Structure

0. House Banking Committee, FINE hearings, November and December 1975.
1. Senate Banking Committee, hearings on legislation to require a GAO audit and to alter the conditions of appointment to Federal Reserve Board, S 2509, S 2285, October and November 1975.
2. House Banking Committee, voted legislation requiring GAO audit (subsequently killed in the Rules Committee), HR 7590, voted out in July 1975, H. Rept. 94–345.
1. House Banking Committee, hearings on the GAO audit, HR 4613, March–May 1975.

Credit

2. House Banking Committee, reported out a credit allocation bill, HR 6676, H. Rept. 94–225, subsequently defeated in the House, June 1975.
1. House Banking Committee, hearings on credit allocation, HR 212, February 1975.
1. House Banking Committee, hearings on credit allocation, HR 3161, February 1975.

Conduct

1. House Banking Committee, hearings on lowering interest rates, HR 212, February 1975.
1. House Banking Committee, hearing on lowering interest rates, HR 3160, February 24

1976

Structure

1. House Banking Committee, hearings on the Financial Reform Act of 1976, HR 10183, March 1976.
3. House approval of the Federal Reserve Reform Act, HR 12934, H. Rept. 94–1973, April 1976; Senate committee approval, S. Rept. 94–1151, but no floor action, August 1976.

Conduct

0. House Banking Committee, Subcommittee, hearings on the impact of the Federal Reserve's money policies on the economy, June 1976.

1977

Structure

3. House passed the GAO audit, HR 2176, October 1977; reported by the Government Operations Committee, H. Rept. 95–492, hearings in March 1977.
4. Dealing with oversight hearings, confirmation of chairman and vice-chairman of the Federal Reserve Board, and so on. Some portions of HR 6273 were included in HR 8094, which was reported as H. Rept. 95–559 in August 1977. These portions were incorporated as Title II of Regulation Q Extension Bill, HR 9710 (H. Rept. 95–775), which passed in October 1977 (PL 95–188).

Conduct

0. House Banking Committee, Subcommittee, hearings on tax rebates and the conduct of monetary policy, March 1977.

1978

Structure

1. House Banking Committee, Subcommittee, hearings on amendments of the Federal Reserve Act, including changes in the composition of boards of directors of Federal Reserve district banks, HR 13148, July 1978.

Credit

0. House Banking Committee, hearings on community credit needs, July, August, and September 1978.

Conduct

0. House Banking Committee, Subcommittee, hearings on a review of monetary policy in 1977, January 1978.

1979

Structure

2. House Banking Committee, consideration of legislation dealing with the publication of *FOMC Minutes,* HR 4998, H. Rept. 96–421, April 1979.
3. House approved amendments to the Federal Reserve Act dealing with chairman, HR 5037, H. Rept. 96–572; no action in the Senate, April 1979.

Credit

2. Senate Banking Committee, hearings on amending the Credit Control Act, S 35, S 389, May 1979.

Conduct

0. House Banking Committee, Subcommittee, hearings on employment and inflation goals of the Humphrey–Hawkins Act and the conduct of monetary policy, March 1979.
0. Senate Banking Committee, hearings on Federal Reserve policy action, October 1979.
0. House Banking Committee, Hearings on errors in money supply figures, October 1979.
1. Housing Banking Committee, Subcommittee, hearings on goals and conduct of monetary policy for the 1980s, HR 5476, November–December 1979.

1980

Structure

1. House Banking Committee, Subcommittee, hearings on legislation to modernize the Federal Reserve System, HR 7001, May 1980.

Credit

0. House Banking Committee, Subcommittee, hearings on credit controls and the effect on consumers and consumer lenders, May 1980.
0. Senate Banking Committee, hearings on implementation of the Credit Control Act, March 1980.

Conduct

0. House Banking Committee, Subcommittee, hearings on measurement and control of the money supply, March 1980.
0. Senate Banking Committee, Subcommittee, hearings on recent monetary policy developments, November 1980.

APPENDIX C

Academic Backgrounds and Career Experiences of Notable Monetarists

Name	Ph.D.	Chicago faculty	Other career experience
Andersen, Leonall	Minnesota (1962)	—	FRB, St. Louis, 1962–74
Brunner, Karl	LSE (1943)	—	Cowles Foundation Fellow (U. of Chicago), 1949–50; UCLA, 1951–66; Ohio S.U., 1966–71; Rochester, 1971–; SOMC
Cagan, Philip	Chicago (1950)	1955–8	NBER, 1953–5; Brown, 1958–65; Columbia, 1965–
Christ, Carl	Chicago (1952)	1955–61	Johns Hopkins, 1961–
Dewald, William	Minnesota (1963)	—	Ohio S.U., 1963–; editor, JMCB
Friedman, Milton	Columbia (1946)	1948–	Hoover Institute, 1977–; NBER, 1937–45, 1948–
Jordan, Jerry	UCLA (1969)	—	FRB, St. Louis, 1967–75; Pittsburgh National Bank, 1975–80; U. of New Mexico, 1980–1; CEA, 1981–
Jones, Homer	Chicago (1949)	—	FRB, St. Louis, 1958–71; SOMC
Laidler, David	Chicago (1964)	—	Manchester, 1969–75; W. Ontario, 73–
Lucas, Robert E.	Chicago (1964)	1975–	Carnegie-Mellon, 1964–75
Mayer, Thomas	Columbia (1953)	—	Mich. State, 1956–61; U. Cal. Davis, 1961–; SOMC
Meigs, A. James	Chicago (1960)	—	Argus Research; Claremont Men's College, 1975–; SOMC

Meiselman, David	Chicago (1961)	1958–62	NBER, 1955–8; government, 1962–6; Macalester College, 1966–71; VPI, 1971–; AEI adjunct scholar, 1976–
Meltzer, Allan	UCLA (1958)	1964–5	Carnegie-Mellon, 1957–; SOMC
Poole, William	Chicago (1966)	—	Johns Hopkins, 1963–9; BGFRS, 1969–73; Brown, 1974–; Brookings panel, 1970–7; FRB Boston, consultant
Rasche, Robert	Michigan (1966)	—	U. Penn, 1966–72, Mich. State, 1975–; FRB, St. Louis, 1976–7 SOMC
Sargent, Thomas	Harvard (1968)	—	Research assoc., Carnegie-Mellon, 1967–8; Minnesota, 1971–
Schmidt, Wilson	Virginia (1952)	—	George Washington U., 1950–66; Treasury, 1970–2; VPI, 1966–; SOMC
Schwartz, Anna J.	Columbia (1964)	—	NBER, 1950–; SOMC
Sprinkel, Beryl	Chicago (1952)	—	Harris Trust and Savings Bank, 1952–81; Treasury, 1981–; SOMC
Weintraub, Robert	Chicago (1954)	—	CUNY, 1956–65; U. Cal. Santa Barbara, 1965–76; Cong. staff, 1964, 1975–

Source: American Men and Woman of Science: Social and Behavioral Sciences, ed., Jacques Cattell Press (New York: Bowker, 1978); "Biographical Listing of Members," *American Economic Review* 68 (December 1978); and press accounts. Those who are not members of the SOMC are included primarily because of their publication of monetarist work. Lucas and Sargent represent the rational expectations variant of monetarism. Data as of 1981.

Notes

1. The Federal Reserve and the politics of monetary policy

1 Only recently have political scientists given any sustained attention to monetary policy and the Federal Reserve. Among the most important studies have been Michael D. Reagan, "The Political Structure of the Federal Reserve System," *American Political Science Review* 5 (March 1961): 64–76; Sanford F. Borins, "The Political Economy of 'The Fed,'" *Public Policy* 20 (Spring 1972): 175–98; Nathaniel Beck, "Presidential Influence on the Federal Reserve in the 1970s," *American Journal of Political Science*, 26 (August 1982):415–45.

2 Alan S. Blinder, *Economic Policy and the Great Stagflation* (New York: Academic Press, 1929), chap. 2.

3 See notes 28 and 29, this chapter.

4 There is further discussion of these questions in Chapter 5. The more curious or ambitious reader should consult one of the many economics textbooks addressed specifically to the topic of money and banking.

5 William Poole, "Optimal Choice of Monetary Policy Instruments in a Simple Stochastic Macro Model," *Quarterly Journal of Economics* 84 (May 1970): 197–216.

6 This is from Robert E. Cushman in *The Independent Regulatory Commissions* (New York: Oxford University Press, 1947), p. 3, a useful source on the legislation and debates preceding the creation of the early independent regulatory agencies. This and the other elements noted in the text can be found in more recent studies of regulatory commissions. See in particular, Marver H. Bernstein, *Regulating Business by Independent Commission* (Princeton, N.J.: Princeton University Press, 1955); and David M. Welborn, *The Governance of Federal Regulatory Agencies* (Knoxville: University of Tennessee Press, 1977). Contemporary analysis often focuses on "regulation" as the common denominator (rather than structure), and by the early 1980s this term had to cover a bewildering variety of agencies. See, for example, Congressional Quarterly, *The Federal Regulatory Directory 1979–1980* (Washington, D.C.: CQ, 1979).

7 In most cases, removal is "for cause" only. Except for the Federal Reserve Board, the boards created prior to 1934 chose their own chairman from anong their membership. Presidential designation of chairmen was extended to those boards in 1950.

8 As of 1982, the members of the Federal Reserve Board were appointed for fourteen-year terms, and there are no stipulations on the partisan composition of the board.

9 Assar Lindbeck, "Stabilization Policy in Open Economies with Endogenous Politicians," *American Economic Review* 66 (May 1976): 18; William D. Nordhaus, "The Political Business Cycle," *Review of Economic Studies* 42 (April 1975): 188.

10 Alan S. Blinder and Robert M. Solow, "Analytical Foundations of Fiscal Policy," in *The Economics of Public Finance* (Washington, D.C.: Brookings Institution, 1974).

11 I first proposed this definition in "Monetary Policy Instrumentation and the Relationship of Central Banks and Governments," *Annals of the American Academy of Political and Social Science* 434 (November 1977): 170. A similar definition and a useful discussion of independence are offered in Ralph Bryant, *Money and Monetary Policy in Interdependent Nations* (Washington, D.C.: Brookings Institution, 1980), parts of which I was privileged to read in draft form. Especially relevant here is Chapter 8.

12 A. Jerome Clifford, *The Independence of the Federal Reserve System* (Philadelphia: University of Pennsylvania Press, 1965), pp. 398–9.

13 G. L. Bach, *Making Monetary and Fiscal Policy* (Washington, D.C.: Brookings Institution, 1971).

14 Bach, *Making Monetary and Fiscal Policy,* pp. 163–4.

15 Edward J. Kane, "The Re-politicization of the Fed," *Journal of Financial and Quantitative Analysis* 9 (November 1974): 743–52; "New Congressional Restraints and Federal Reserve Independence," *Challenge* 18 (November 1975): 37–44; "Politics and Fed Policymaking: The More Things Change, the More They Remain the Same," *Journal of Monetary Economics* 6 (April 1980): 199–211; "External Pressures and the Operations of the Fed," in *Political Economy of International and Domestic Monetary Relations,* Raymond E. Lombra and Willard E. Witte, eds. (Ames: Iowa State University Press, 1982), pp. 211–32.

16 This is especially developed in Kane, "External Pressures and the Fed."

17 In exception to my general argument, a principal might try education alone, without coercion, supervision, or prescriptive rule. This applies, of course, only if the reason for failure is lack of competence.

18 See R. H. Timberlake, "Monetization Practices and the Political Structure of the Federal Reserve System," Cato Policy Analysis #2 (Washington, D.C., Cato Institute).

19 Mancur Olson, *The Logic of Collective Action: Public Goods and the Theory of Groups* (Cambridge, Mass.: Harvard University Press, 1971).

20 For example, see Sherman J. Maisel, "The Effects of Monetary Policy on Expenditures in Specific Sectors of the Economy," *Journal of Political Economy* 76 (July–August 1968): 796–814; Federal Reserve Bank of Boston, *Housing and Monetary Policy,* Conference Series No. 4, October 1970; Lawrence S. Ritter and William L. Silber, *Money,* 2nd ed. (New York: Basic Books, 1973), p. 229; Lyle E. Gramley, "Short-Term Cycles in Housing Production: An Overview of the Problem and Possible Solutions," in Board of Governors of the Federal Reserve System, *Ways to Moderate Fluctuations in Housing Construction: A Federal Reserve Staff Study* (Washington, D.C.: 1972); Herbert M. Kaufman, "A Study in Conflicting Goals: Federal Stabilization and Mortgage Market Policies," in *The Politics of Economic Policy-Making,* Michael P. Dooley, Herbert M. Kaufman, and Raymond E. Lombra, eds. (Beverly Hills: Sage, 1979), pp. 129–48. Also see Frank de Leeuw and Edward M. Gramlich, "The Channels of Monetary Policy: A Further Report on the Federal Reserve–MIT Econometric Model," *Federal Reserve Bulletin* 55 (June 1969): 472–91.

21 See Thomas Mayer, *Monetary Policy in the United States* (New York: Random House, 1968), p. 171; George Leland Bach and C. J. Huizenga, "The Differential Effects of Tight Money," *American Economic Review* 51 (March 1961): 52–80; Deane Carson, "The Differential Effects of Tight Money: Comment," *American Economic Review* 51 (December 1961): 1039–42; Dale Tussing, "The Differential Effects of Tight Money: Comment," *American Economic Review* 53 (September 1963): 740–3; Donald D. Hester, "An Empirical Examination of a Commercial Bank Loan Offer Function," *Yale Economic Essays* (Spring 1962): 3–57; William L. Silber and Murray E. Polakoff, "The Differential Effects of Tight Money: An Econometric Study," *Journal of Finance* 25 (March 1970): 83–97; Jonas Prager and Jacob Paroush, "On the Differential Effects of Tight Money: A Comment," *Journal of Finance* 26 (1971): 951–4; Manak C. Gupta, "Differential Effects of Tight Money: An Economic Rationale," *Journal of Finance* 27 (June 1972): 825–38; D. C. Rao, "Selective Credit Policy: Is It Justified and Can It Work?" *Journal of Finance* 27 (May 1972): 423–80; Dwight M. Jaffee, *Credit Rationing in the Commercial Loan Market* (New York: Wiley, 1971).

22 See Paul F. McGouldrick and John E. Petersen, "Monetary Restraint and Borrowing and Capital Spending by Large State and Local Governments in 1966," *Federal Reserve Bulletin* 54 (July 1968): 552–81; John F. Petersen and Paul F. McGouldrick, "Monetary Restraint, Borrowing, and Capital Spending by Small Local Governments and State Colleges in 1966," *Federal Reserve Bulletin* 54 (December 1968):

953–82; John E. Petersen, "Response of State and Local Governments to Varying Credit Conditions," *Federal Reserve Bulletin* 57 (March 1971): 209–32; also, for 1969, see Andrew F. Brimmer, "Multi-National Banks and the Management of Monetary Policy in the United States," *Journal of Finance* 28 (May 1973): 439–54.

23 Jeffrey D. Sachs, "Wages, Profits and Macroeconomic Adjustment: A Comparative Study," *Brookings Papers on Economic Activity* #2, 1979, pp. 269–332; Maurice D. Levi, "Money and Corporate Earnings," *Journal of Money Credit and Banking,* 12 (February 1980): 84–93.

24 See Henry J. Aaron, *Politics and the Professors: The Great Society in Perspective* (Washington, D.C.: Brookings Institution, 1979), p. 119; Edward M. Gramlich, "The Distributional Effects of Higher Unemployment," *Brookings Papers on Economic Activity,* #2, 1974, pp. 293–336.

25 See the interesting discussion of Charles S. Maier, "The Politics of Inflation in the Twentieth Century," in *The Political Economy of Inflation,* Fred Hirsch and John H. Goldthorpe, eds. (Cambridge, Mass.: Harvard University Press, 1978), pp. 37–72. Maier usefully stresses that it is easier to link the impact of inflation to roles than to actual persons.

26 Reuben A. Kessel, "Inflation-Caused Wealth Redistribution: A Test of a Hypothesis," *American Economic Review* 46 (March 1956): 128–41; Louis De Alessi, "Do Business Firms Gain from Inflation?" *Journal of Business* 37 (April 1964): 162–66.

27 G. L. Bach, *The New Inflation: Causes, Effects, Cures,* (Englewood Cliffs, N.J.: Prentice-Hall, 1973). For an attempt to disentangle the financial consequences of inflation, see Phillip Cagan and Robert E. Lipsey, *The Financial Effects of Inflation,* National Bureau of Economic Research General Series #103 (Cambridge, Mass.: Ballinger, 1978).

28 For example, see Samuel Kernell, "Explaining Presidential Popularity," *American Political Science Review* 72 (June 1978): 506–22; Kristen R. Monroe, "Economic Influences on Presidential Popularity," *Public Opinion Quarterly* 42 (Fall 1978): 360–9; Bruno S. Frey and Friedrich Schneider, "An Empirical Study of Politico-Economic Interactions in the United States," *Review of Economics and Statistics* 60 (May 1978): 174–83; Douglas Hibbs, "Why Are U.S. Policy-Makers So Tolerant of Unemployment and So Intolerant of Inflation?" Processed, May 1978, Brookings Project on the Politics and Sociology of Global Inflation (Washington, D.C.: Brookings Institution); Edward R. Tufte, *Political Control of the Economy* (Princeton, N.J.: Princeton University Press, 1978). Research using survey data on voting is somewhat less supportive of the notion that macroeconomic conditions have a substantial *direct* influence on the voting decision. See Morris P. Fiorina, "Economic Retrospective Voting in

American National Elections: A Micro-Analysis," *American Journal of Political Science* 22 (May 1978): 426–443; and idem., "Short- and Long-Term Effects of Economic Conditions on Individual Voting Decisions," California Institute of Technology Social Science Working Paper 244, December 1978.

29 Gerald H. Kramer, "Short-Term Fluctuations in U.S. Voting Behavior," *American Political Science Review* 65 (March 1971): 131–43; George J. Stigler, "General Economic Conditions and National Elections," *American Economic Association Papers and Proceedings: American Economic Review* 63 (May 1973): 160–7; Edward R. Tufte, "Determinants of the Outcomes of Midterm Congressional Elections," *American Political Science Review* 69 (September 1975): 812–26; Francisco Arcelus and Allan Meltzer, "The Effects of Aggregate Economic Variables on Congressional Elections," *American Political Science Review* 69 (December 1975): 1232–8; Howard S. Bloom and H. Douglas Price, "Voter Response to Short-Run Economic Conditions: The Asymmetric Effect of Prosperity and Recession," *American Political Science Review* 69 (December 1975): 1240–54; Saul Goodman and Gerald H. Kramer, "Comment on Arcelus and Meltzer; The Effects of Aggregate Economic Conditions on Congressional Elections," *American Political Science Review* 69 (December 1975): 1255–65.

30 Observers should not be confused on this fact by headlines in the financial press referring to "pressures." For example, see Tom Herman, "Pressures on Fed to Tighten Credit Further Is Expected to Push Up Interest Rates Soon," *Wall Street Journal*, July 30, 1979, p. 16; Edward F. Foldessy, "Pressure Mounts for Further Tightening of Credit, But Analysts See Fed Resisting," *Wall Street Journal*, July 10, 1979, p. 8. These references to pressure should be understood as indicating observed changes in variables believed to be monitored by the System. In contrast to direct pressure, an inescapable fact of the policy environment is indirect pressure from many sources. A useful discussion of indirect pressure in a related context is found in Jonathan David Aronson, *Money and Power* (Beverly Hills: Sage, 1977).

2. A capsule history of the Federal Reserve System

1 Banks were prohibited in Texas, Iowa, Arkansas, California, and Oregon; banks were restricted in Wisconsin, Florida, and Illinois. Banks were state monopolies in Indiana and Missouri. Bray Hammond, *Banks and Politics in America from the Revolution to the Civil War* (Princeton, N.J.: Princeton University Press, 1957), pp. 605, 617.

2 Friedman and Schwartz say that the currency was to be guaranteed by the government. Milton Friedman and Anna Jacobson Schwartz, *A Monetary History of the United States, 1867–1960* (Princeton, N.J.: Princeton University Press, 1963), p. 117. Robert Craig West, *Banking Reform and the Federal Reserve 1863–1923* (Ithaca, N.Y.: Cornell University Press, 1977), pp. 43–44; Gabriel Kolko, *Triumph of Conservatism: A Reinterpretation of American History 1900–1916* (Chicago: Quadrangle Books, 1967), pp. 147–48; Margaret G. Myers, *A Financial History of the United States* (New York: Columbia University Press, 1970), pp. 147–8.

3 Weibe notes that the division, one that continued to mark the debate over bank reform, was between large banks, including midwestern city banks, and smaller rural banks, referred to as country banks. Robert H. Weibe, *Businessmen and Reform: A Study of the Progressive Movement* (Cambridge, Mass: Harvard University Press, 1962), p. 62; Kolko, *Triumph of Conservatism,* pp. 147–9; Myers, *Financial History,* p. 220.

4 Kolko, *Triumph of Conservatism,* pp. 153–6; Friedman and Schwartz, *Monetary History,* pp. 156–61; Weibe, *Businessmen and Reform,* pp. 70–2.

5 Aldrich's bill would have provided an emergency currency that could be issued by bank associations in times of crisis. The currency would be backed by long-term bonds issued by the banks. The Fowler bill permitted banks to issue notes based on short-term commercial loans.

6 Aldrich-Vreeland allowed currency associations to issue emergency currency based either on bonds or on commercial loans. Kolko, *Triumph of Conservatism,* pp. 156–8; West, *Bank Reform* pp. 50–1; Friedman and Schwartz, *Monetary History,* pp. 169–70.

7 Weibe, *Businessmen and Reform,* pp. 75–6.

8 Kolko, *Triumph of Conservatism,* p. 184; West, *Banking Reform,* pp. 71–2.

9 Arthur S. Link, *Wilson: The New Freedom* (Princeton, N.J.: Princeton University Press), p. 201.

10 To present-day economists, the fact that this second issue arose is evidence of a lack of understanding of economics on the part of some reformers. The answer today is that yes, high-powered money is high-powered money. At the time, many were not sure. West discusses this at some length in *Banking Reform,* especially pp. 76–7, 84–5. The issue cropped up in later Federal Reserve debate in Congress. See Richard H. Timberlake, Jr., *The Origins of Central Banking in the United States* (Cambridge, Mass.: Harvard University Press, 1978), pp. 201–3.

11 West, *Banking Reform,* pp. 74–5, 81, 86–7; On an executive board (nine members), government appointees would have been outnumbered five to four. Also see Kolko, *Triumph of Conservatism,* p. 184.

12 For example, in contrast to the relative obscurity in which monetary policy now operates, the issue of control managed to find its way into the Democratic platform in 1912. See Link, *Wilson,* pp. 201–2. On the attitudes of bankers and public attitudes toward bankers, see West, *Banking Reform,* p. 87.

13 Partly because support waned for this particular banking reform in light of Pujo committee revelations, which are discussed in this chapter.

14 Kolko, *Triumph of Conservatism,* pp. 185–9; West, *Banking Reform,* pp. 79–82; Weibe, *Businessmen and Reform,* p. 77.

15 West, *Banking Reform,* pp. 77–8; Kolko, *Triumph of Conservatism,* p. 186.

16 Kolko, *Triumph of Conservatism,* p. 227; West, *Banking Reform,* pp. 120–1.

17 Wilson acted partly at the urging of the famous populist and former presidential candidate William Jennings Bryan, then serving as Wilson's secretary of state. The first months of 1913 were marked by continued negotiation and maneuvering within the administration and between the administration and Glass. This account is far too brief to capture the drama. See Link, *Wilson,* pp. 206–13; West, *Banking Reform,* p. 122.

18 See the discussion in Link, *Wilson,* pp. 215–17; Weibe, *Businessmen and Reform,* p. 131–6; Kolko, *Triumph of Conservatism,* p. 234.

19 Kolko, *Triumph of Conservatism,* pp. 234–5.

20 Richard Hofstadter, *The Age of Reform: From Bryan to FDR* (New York: Vintage, 1955), p. 232. "The mind reeled in horror at the thought of such a vast power, unchecked by any comparable or equal power responsible to the public, moving quietly and relentlessly toward the achievement of its political goals." Ibid., p. 233.

21 Link, *Wilson,* pp. 218–22; Kolko, *Triumph of Conservatism,* pp. 220–1, 239.

22 Timberlake, *Origins of Central Banking,* pp. 202–3. For instance, Congress decided on the following during floor action: the level of required reserves (40 percent against notes, 35 percent against deposits), a tax on reserve deficiencies, and prohibition of the use of reserve notes as legal reserves for member banks.

23 Timberland, *Origins of Central Banking,* p. 205.

24 Ibid., pp. 194, 196, 198.

25 Ibid., p. 199. Timberlake sees in retrospect the unself-conscious creation of a potential central bank, that is, an institution capable of generating inflation, vulnerable to political pressure, without "scientific objectivity to determine the system's money supply" (p. 133). His ultimate objection is to the creation of a central bank with discretion (p. 226 and throughout Chapter 14).

26 Although there were many similarities, the System did not fully conform to the independence formula in 1913. The primary func-

tions were to be performed in regional reserve banks, not by the central board. The central board included as ex officio members two Treasury officials, whereas the independence formula calls for no ex officio members. Also, the original version of the Federal Reserve was more ambiguous about the role of public authority in making policy than is the independence formula.

It is quite clear that the independent commission model had been fairly well defined by 1913. This can be seen in the 1914 debates concerning the establishment of the Federal Trade Commission. Robert E. Cushman, *The Independent Regulatory Commissions* (New York: Oxford University Press, 1947), pp. 188–96.

27 Marver H. Bernstein, *Regulating Business by Independent Commission* (Princeton, N.J.: Princeton University Press, 1955), pp. 45–6. Not surprisingly, reformers had to feel their way in developing the independence formula. The timidity of early regulators is understandable, given the confrontation between their activities and the dominant ideology. See Bernstein, *Regulating Business*, pp. 13–14, 21–4; and Cushman, *Regulatory Commissions,* pp. 54–8, 61–2, 64–105. What is striking is that the progressive reformers repeatedly turned to this organizational form to house new state activities. In this period, many activities deviating from the standards of laissez-faire were located in this kind of commission. All of the early independent commissions involved exactly such activities. Politics was acceptable in the management of the minimal state but not of the interventionist state.

The independence formula should be understood as a set solution to a general problem reformers confronted at the turn of the century. It defined an appropriate organizational structure for intervening in the economy in ways needed by the emergent industrial order. Such special forms were required partly because the intervention was not fully legitimate under the dominant laissez-faire ideology. The independent commission provided a way to guarantee that critical economic functions would be performed and that key constituencies would be assured that their interests would be given preferential treatment.

28 Friedman and Schwartz, *Monetary History,* pp. 191–5.

29 The real bills theory in fact provided "no effective limit to the quantity of money." Friedman and Schwartz, *Monetary History,* pp. 191–3.

30 Friedman and Schwartz, *Monetary History,* pp. 190, 223–39, 254–66.

31 A. Jerome Clifford, *The Independence of the Federal Reserve System* (Philadelphia: University of Pennsylvania Press, 1965), pp. 94–5.

32 Ibid., p. 106; Friedman and Schwartz, *Monetary History,* fn. 15, p. 251.

33 Clifford, *Independence,* pp. 11, 108–10; Friedman and Schwartz, *Monetary History,* pp. 256, 362 (fn. 26), 368.

34 The Federal Deposit Insurance Corporation (FDIC) was also established under the Banking Act of 1933 to insure bank deposits. The Securities and Exchange Commission was formed in 1934 to regulate the stock market. The Federal Home Loan Bank Board, a 1932 creation, provided for a regional system similar to the Federal Reserve to make advances to savings and loan associations secured by the associations' first mortgages. These agencies remind us that the modern Federal Reserve was a part of New Deal reforms aimed at revitalizing American capitalism and nurturing consumer and investor confidence.

The FDIC should be especially noted. It was perhaps the most important reform in banking regulation since the National Bank Act because it provided an effective way of guaranteeing that the vast majority of bank depositors could have high levels of confidence in the safety of their bank deposits. Its inspection procedures subject all insured banks to uniform national banking standards. See Raymond P. Kent, "Dual Banking Between the Two World Wars," in *Banking and Monetary Studies*, Deane Carson, ed., (Homewood, Ill.: Irwin, 1963), pp. 60–3; Friedman and Schwartz, *Monetary History,* pp. 434–42.

35 The issue of how to prevent both bankers and politicians from dominating the board was prominent in 1935, as it had been in 1913. The bankers again argued for the concept of a "Supreme Court of finance." Cushman, *Regulatory Commissions,* pp. 172–6.

36 Marriner Eccles proposed that the System be charged to "promote conditions conducive to business stability and to mitigate by its influence unstabilizing fluctuations in the general level of production, trade, prices, and employment so far as may be possible within the scope of monetary action and credit administration." Marriner S. Eccles, *Beckoning Frontiers: Public and Personal Recollections* (New York: Alfred A. Knopf, 1951), p. 228.

37 Eccles, *Beckoning Frontiers,* p. 205.

38 Ibid., pp. 222–6. The entire account, upon which this section has been based, is found in pp. 165–229.

39 Friedman and Schwartz, *Monetary History,* p. 520. Three factors figured in this result. The Treasury was able to execute its own open market policy using segregated gold in its Stabilization Fund. The president supported the Treasury's position. A blunt warning was given that if the Federal Reserve failed to produce the desired policy, the government would intervene directly in monetary policy. Clifford, *Independence of the Federal Reserve,* pp. 152–159. This is not to overlook the important role of Chairman Marriner Eccles in economic policy during this period.

40 Clifford, *Independence,* p. 167 and chap. 6; Friedman and Schwartz, *Monetary History,* chap. 10.

41 The preceding three paragraphs are based on Clifford, *Independence,* chap. 8; see also Henry C. Wallich and Peter M. Keir, "The Role of Operating Guides in U.S. Monetary Policy: A Historical Review," *Kredit and Kapital* 11 (1978): 3–29.

42 Friedman and Schwartz, *Monetary History,* pp. 613–23. Also see James Tobin, "Discussion 3," in "Proceedings of a 50th Anniversary Symposium," Federal Reserve Bank of Boston *Annual Report,* 1964, pp. 30–3; Herbert Stein, *The Fiscal Revolution in America* (Chicago: University of Chicago Press, 1969), esp. chap. 10.

43 Friedman and Schwartz, *Monetary History,* pp. 627–32.

44 Benjamin Haggott Beckhart, *The Federal Reserve System* (Washington, D.C.: American Institute of Banking, 1972), p. 511.

45 91 Stat 1387 (PL 95–188).

3. Recruitment and selection of Federal Reserve personnel

1 For example, E. Ray Canterbery, "A New Look at Federal Open Market Voting," *Western Economic Journal* 6 (December 1967): 25–38.

2 Marver Bernstein, *Regulating Business by Independent Commission* (Princeton, N.J.: Princeton University Press, 1955), p. 106. See also the analysis in Committee on Government Operations, *The Regulatory Appointments Process,* 95th Cong., 1st sess., 1977, pp. 153–6, stressing that although White House "political" appointments are not rare, a more frequent factor is the need to respond to congressional support for candidates. See further discussion in this chapter.

3 Hugh Heclo, "Issue Networks and the Executive Establishment," in *The New American Political System,* Anthony King, ed. (Washington, D.C.: American Enterprise Institute, 1978), pp. 87–124.

4 Interview, December 14, 1978.

5 It should be clear that this characterization was offered well before Sherrill's consideration for a board appointment, when he was being promoted inside the White House for other possible appointments. His promoter is now well known for his own enthusiastically partisan memoranda to the president. See Memo, Jack Valenti to President, May 18, 1965, EX PE 2, WHCF, LBJ Library; also idem., July 13, 1965, EX PE 2, WHCF, LBJ Library and other relevant memoranda in the William Sherrill name file.

6 Memo, Walter W. Heller to President, January 26, 1966, EX PE 2, WHCF, LBJ Library.

7 G. Calvin MacKinzie, *The Politics of Presidential Appointments* (New York: Free Press, 1981).

8 Including all of the Ph.D. economists: Daane, Mitchell, Maisel, Brimmer, Wallich, Holland, Partee, Teeters, Gramley, and P. Martin.

9 Memo, Valenti to President, March 31, 1965, EX FG 233, WHCF, LBJ Library.
10 Interview, June 21, 1978.
11 Letters in Sherman Maisel name file, WHCF, LBJ Library, most dated January 18, 1965. Also, Maisel interview, February 1, 1978.
12 These from Letter, W. M. Martin to President, February 2, 1966, EX FG 233/A, WHCF, LBJ Library.
13 Ibid. See also idem., January 26, 1966, EX PE 2, WHCF LBJ Library; idem., January 26, 1966 (filed February 5, 1966), EX PE 2, WHCF, LBJ Library. In late February, Martin passed word to the White House that "the appointment of Mr. Brimmer has worked out well at the Federal Reserve System." Memo, Marvin Watson to President, February 28, 1966, EX FG 233, WHCF, LBJ Library. A generally accurate account of Brimmer's selection is in "President Orders Aides to Seek Out New Methods to Fight Inflation Short of Tax Increases, Stiff Controls," *Wall Street Journal,* February 28, 1966, p. 3.
14 Memo, Walter Heller to President, February 8, 1966, EX PE 2, WHCF, LBJ Library.
15 Memo, Marvin Watson to President, February 24, 1966, Brimmer name file, WHCF, LBJ Library.
16 Mackenzie, *Politics of Presidential Appointments,* p. xx.
17 Brimmer and other candidates were quizzed closely about how they would have voted. Brimmer recalls that Johnson complained bitterly to him about the board's action during a preappointment interview at the White House on February 24, 1966. See also Memo, Walter Heller to President, January 26, 1966, EX PE 2 WHCF, LBJ Library.
18 Sherrill was then serving as a director of the FDIC. See Cross-reference, Memo, John W. Macy to President, April 19, 1967, William W. Sherrill name file (originally filed EX FG 223/A) and attachments. Also Cross-reference, Memo, Macy to President, April 21, 1967, William W. Sherrill name file (originally filed EX FG 223, but not available in open files). Both WHCF, LBJ Library.
19 B. Drummond Ayers, Jr., "Texan Will Serve on Reserve Board," *New York Times,* April 23, 1967, p. 1; Letter, David Rockefeller to President, May 8, 1967, William W. Sherrill name file, WHCF, LBJ Library. The Rockefeller letter praising Sherrill's appointment was forwarded by LBJ to an aide with the marginal note to "show this to two or three people."
20 Memo, Gardner Ackley to President, April 13, 1967, EX FG 233, WHCF, LBJ Library.
21 This is, of course, true of all regulatory appointments. As Senate staff wrote, "his or her positions will be somewhere in the mainstream of popular thinking." Senate Committee on Government Operations, *Study on Federal Regulation,* p. 159.

22 However, the senatorial role is probably substantially less important than it is in many other kinds of appointments. Doris Kearns recounts an anecdote illustrating the point. The story, attributed to LBJ himself, involves the president telling Senator Russell Long that Long's candidate for the Federal Reserve (J. W. Adcock) would not be the appointee. Long realizes that not only is his man not going to be chosen, but that LBJ is about to nominate Andrew Brimmer, a black. Long asks for another drink. "My God, do you realize what this means? . . . When they all jump on me because I couldn't get one Louisianan on the Federal Reserve Board, I can say I did get one – a nigger." Doris Kearns, *Lyndon Johnson and the American Dream* (New York: Harper & Row, 1976), p. 185.

23 Heller, oral history interview, Vanderbilt University Institute of Public Policy Studies (Knoxville: University of Tennessee Press, forthcoming).

24 This appointment is discussed further in Chapter 6. Memo, John W. Macy to President, February 20, 1967, EX FG 233, WHCF, LBJ Library; Memo, Joseph Califano to President, February 20, 1967, EX FG 233, WHCF, LBJ Library.

25 Edwin L. Dale, "Johnson Renames Martin as Federal Reserve Head," *New York Times,* March 30, 1967, p. 1.

26 See, for example, Charls Walker, "The Economic Case for Reappointing Burns," *Washington Post,* November 10, 1977, p. A23; Ira R. Allen, "Key Group in Senate Urges Carter to Reappoint Burns as Fed Chief," *Washington Post,* November 5, 1977, p. A5; William Safire, "While Burns Roams," *New York Times,* December 1, 1977, p. 39; "After Burns the Fed Will Lean to the Left," *Business Week,* November 21, 1977, pp. 108–16; Leonard Silk, "The Fed Chairmanship: Courses Open to President," *New York Times,* December 20, 1977, p. 59.

27 "The Dollar Chooses a Chairman," *Business Week,* August 6, 1979, p. 20, emphasis added. Also note similar evaluations in "Paul Volcker: A Big Man for a Tough Job," *St. Louis Post-Dispatch* July 26, 1979, p. 4B (*New York Times* News Service story), and Richard F. Janssen, "Surveying the Thoughts of Chairman Volcker," *Wall Street Journal,* July 31, 1979, p. 9.

28 Those familiar with the battles over the regulation of financial institutions realize that there are many issues that divide these subgroups. The assumption here is that they are guided by more agreement than division on fundamental questions of economic outlook and values.

29 Henry C. Wallich, "Some Uses of Economics," *Banca Nazionale del Lavoro Quarterly Review* 141 (June 1982): 119–46.

30 Consider the following figures from various sources:

Prior employment in a regulated industry[a]

Commission	Percentage of appointees with prior employment	Number of appointees with prior employment
Federal Communications Commission	50.0	24
Federal Power Commission	5.6	18
Federal Trade Commission	40.0	20
Interstate Commerce Commission	14.3	21
Securities and Exchange Commission	47.4	19
Federal Reserve Board	25.8	31
District bank president	27.3	44
Nuclear Regulatory Commission	65	N.A.
U.S. Food and Drug Administration	44	N.A.

Note: These data are deliberately selected to give the least favorable comparison possible for the Federal Reserve. This is partly to ensure the most conservative interpretation possible is advanced and partly because there are some ambiguities about the definitions used in the congressional study. For instance, in classifying appointees with different prior occupations, the congressional staff used a weighting process that put more emphasis on the appointee's most recent occupation. The figures I use for comparison are the "longest employment" category, which is higher than the "immediately prior" category for board members and bank presidents. Also, my definition of "private financial" is a very broad definition of "banking." See House, Committee on Interstate and Foreign Commerce, Subcommittee on Oversight and Investigation, and Senate, Committees on Commerce and Government Operations, *Joint Hearings on Regulatory Reform, Volume I: Quality of Regulators,* 94th Cong., 1st sess., 1975, p. 47. The Common Cause study showed that "more than half" of commissioners appointed during fiscal year 1971–5 were from regulated industries as previously defined. A cursory inspection of the Carter nominees suggests that the Common Cause finding may be more typical of a Republican than a Democratic administration. It is not clear whether the finding refers to more than half of the appointees at each agency or to the total of all appointees at all agencies.

[a]For all except the Federal Reserve, includes employment in law firms primarily specializing in the relevant area of the law that is, indirect employment.

Sources: For all except Federal Reserve Board and district bank presidents, Nuclear Regulatory Commission, and Food and Drug Administration, House, Committee on Interstate and Foreign Commerce, Subcommittee on Oversight and Investigation, and Senate, Committees on Commerce and Government Operations, *Joint Hearings on Regulatory Reform, Volume I: Quality of Regulators,* 94th Cong., 1st sess., 1975, p. 47. Includes years 1960–75. Data on Federal Reserve officials cover the years 1955–82 and are from various sources, especially the *Federal Reserve Bulletin* and *Who's Who in America.* The Nuclear Regulatory Commission estimate concerns appointees for fiscal years 1971–5 who were from industry or enterprises under contract to the agency. "Common Cause Says U.S. Agencies Are Hurt by Conflicts of Interest," *New York Times,* October 21, 1976, p. 22. The Food and Drug Administration estimate is from "FDA Pursued Historic Role Amid Public, Industry Pressure," *National Journal,* February 15, 1975, p. 254; data attributed to the Center for Science for the Public Interest.

31 Senate, Committee on Government Operations, *A Study on Federal Regulation, Volume I: The Regulatory Appointments Process* (prepared persuant to S. Res 71), 95th Cong., 1st sess., Committee Print (January 1977), p. 157. Also see *Joint Hearings on Regulatory Reform,* p. 51, exhibit. 6.

32 The factor would increase to five or more if top staff were included in the calculation. David T. Stanley, Dean E. Mann, and Jamison W. Doig, *Men Who Govern: A Biographical Profile of Federal Political Executives* (Washington, D.C.: Brookings Institution, 1967), Table D7, pp. 120–1.

33 Employment in private financial posts included six officers of banks (the lowest being a senior vice president) and one president of the New York Stock Exchange. Employment in public financial posts included former chairmen of the CEA and the Federal Home Loan Bank Board, a director of the FDIC, an official in the office of the Comptroller of the Currency, and the comptroller of the city of Chicago.

34 Stanley, Mann, and Doig, *Men Who Govern,* p. 128.

35 Thomas R. Dye, *Who's Running America?* 2nd and 3rd eds. (Englewood Cliffs, N.J.: Prentice Hall, 1979, 1983), pp. 172 (2nd), 196 (3rd). "Prestigious" schools include Harvard, Yale, Chicago, Stanford, Columbia, MIT, Cornell, Northwestern, Princeton, Johns Hopkins, Pennsylvania, and Dartmouth.

36 Lawrence Ingrassia, "Volcker's Right Hand Man, Corrigan, May Be Next Minneapolis Fed President," *Wall Street Journal,* July 15, 1980, p. 4.

37 Of course, the Board of Governors also approves or disapproves this appointment. When it appeared that J. L. Robertson would not be reappointed to the board, Malcolm Bryan offered him a post at

the Atlanta bank with the understanding that he would be the leading candidate to succeed Bryan when he retired. Letter, Malcolm Bryan to J. L. Robertson, October 30, 1963, Box 12, James Louis Robertson Collection, Library of Congress.

38 The following table shows the source of presidents for each Federal Reserve Bank during the period 1955–82.

All FRS,[a] all home-grown	All FRS, mixed-origin (share home-grown)	Mostly FRS (ratio FRS)	Mostly not FRS (ratio FRS)
Philadelphia	Dallas (3/4)	Atlanta (3/4)	Boston (1/3)
Richmond	San Fran. (2/3)	St. Louis (3/4)	Chicago (1/4)
Kansas City	Minneapolis (4/5)	Cleveland (3/4)	New York (0)

[a]FRS = Federal Reserve System.

39 The Wharton School at the University of Pennsylvania. Other positions included undersecretary of the Treasury; director, U.S. Bureau of the Budget; four bank vice-presidents; and two officials of corporations, each of whom had previously been vice-presidents in large banks.

40 Martin Greenberger, Matthew A. Crenson, and Brian L. Crissey, *Models in the Policy Process: Public Decision Making in the Computer Era* (New York: Russell Sage Foundation, 1976), pp. 210–11.

41 By "very highest staff," I mean all members of the Office of the Staff Director for Research and Economic Policy (sometimes known by other names) and the director and deputy directors of the Division of Research and Statistics. For department rankings, I constructed an average based on reports in A. M. Cartter, *An Assessment of Quality in Graduate Education* (Washington, D.C.: American Council on Education, 1966); Kenneth D. Roose and Charles J. Andersen, *A Rating of Graduate Programs* (Washington, D.C.: American Council on Education, 1970); W. J. Moore, "The Relative Quality of Graduate Programs in Economics, 1958–72," *Western Economic Journal* 11 (March 1973): 1–23; John J. Siegfried and Thomas A. Zak, "Predicting Graduate Faculty Ratings for the 1970's," *Economic Inquiry* 14 (June 1976): 291–3; James W. Dean, "An Alternate Rating System for University Economics Departments," *Economic Inquiry* 14 (March 1976): 146–53.

42 Robert V. Eagly, "Contemporary Profile of Conventional Economists," *History of Political Economy* 6 (Spring 1974): 81.

43 James Tobin, *The New Economics One Decade Older* (Princeton, N.J.: Princeton University Press, 1972), p. 13.

44 In comparison to other small voting bodies, the FOMC appears to be remarkably cohesive. See data in Bradley C. Canon, "Voting Behavior on the FCC," *Midwest Journal of Political Science* 13 (Novem-

ber 1969): 591. Discussions of FOMC voting that stress other reasons for unanimity are found in William P. Yohe, "A Study of Federal Open Market Committee Voting, 1955–64," *Southern Economic Journal* 33 (April 1966): 396–405; and E. Ray Canterbery, "A New Look at Federal Open Market Voting," *Western Economic Journal* 6 (December 1967): 25–38. This question is examined at more length in my Ph.D. dissertation, "The Federal Reserve and the Political Economy of Monetary Policy," (University of Wisconsin–Madison, 1980), chap. 8. Data cited above are drawn from the period 1965–81.

45 Canterbery, "A New Look," esp. pp. 28, 30–32.

46 Jonathan Aranson, *Money and Power: Banks and the World Monetary System* (Beverly Hills: Sage, 1977), p. 59.

47 John Sheehan in Edwin L. Dale, Jr., "Insider Views the Fed," *The New York Times,* May 14, 1975, p. 63.

48 38 Stat 251, Section 10 (2).

49 Dewey Daane became an official of the Commerce Union Bank in Nashville, Tennessee. William Sherrill for a time headed a financial subsidiary of Gulf & Western Corp., Associates Corporation, N.A. Arthur Burns, Philip Coldwell, and William McChesney Martin included financial institutions among their directorships after leaving the board chairmanship. Burns, of course, was later named ambassador to West Germany.

50 I excluded from the survey two governors who died in office. Private industry: Lilly, Sheehan, King. Law: Bucher. Consultants: Mitchell, Shepardson, Brimmer, Szymczak, Coldwell. University: Maisel, Balderston. Research: Burns. Interest group: Holland. Several of these also hold or held additional directorships. W. Miller was involved with managing his own investments.

51 The Federal Reserve Board percentage is 9.1 The Federal Power Commission is closest, with a rate of subsequent appointment of 15.4 percent. Percentages for other commissions were: Interstate Commerce Commission, 20.0; Federal Communications Commission, 21.1; Federal Trade Commission, 46.2; Securities and Exchange Commission, 65.0. See the discussion of sources in note 30, this chapter.

52 It is difficult to assemble accurate lists of staff and particularly difficult to follow their careers after they leave the System. The problem is especially great with respect to district bank staff. Despite the fact that most are economists, for example, many are not members of the American Economic Association (AEA) and thus cannot be traced through the AEA biographical directory. On the demand for the expertise of former Federal Reserve staff, see "Fed Watching Grows in the Markets, Spurring Frenzied, Anxious Trading," *Wall Street Journal*, November 8, 1982, p. 25.

4. Bankers and the Federal Reserve

1 A recent collection of essays claims to thoroughly debunk the capture theory. See James Q. Wilson, ed., *The Politics of Regulation* (New York: Basic Books, 1980).

2 See, for example, statements by the late Rep. Wright Patman in "The Federal Reserve System: A Brief for Legal Reform," *St. Louis University School of Law Journal* 10 (Spring 1969): 299–326, reproduced in JEC, *The Federal Reserve System,* by Wright Patman, Joint Committee Print, 94th Cong., 2nd sess. (1976), pp. 143–61, esp. pp. 156–7. Also see Rep. Henry Reuss, in House, Committee on Banking, Currency, and Housing, *Federal Reserve Directors: A Study of Corporate and Banking Influence,* Staff Study, Committee Print, 94th Cong., 2nd sess., 1976, p. iv. Representative comments by labor officials appear in, for example, JEC, *The 1975 Economic Report of the President, Hearings Before the Joint Economic Committee,* 91st Cong., 1st sess. 1975, pp. 1220–1 and JEC, *The 1969 Economic Report of the President, Hearings Before the Joint Economic Committee,* 91st Cong., 1st Sess., 1969, p. 877. Ralph Nader's sentiments are in House, Committee on Banking, Currency, and Housing, *Audit of the Federal Reserve, Hearings Before the Subcommittee on Domestic Monetary Policy of the Committee on Banking, Currency, and Housing,* 94th Cong., 1st sess., 1975, p. 228. Also, see Morton Mintz and Jerry S. Cohen, *Power Inc.: Public and Private Rulers and How to Make Them Accountable* (New York: Bantam Books, 1977), p. 177, chap. 12.

3 See, for example, J. David Greenstone, *Labor in American Politics* (New York: Vintage Books, 1969), chap. 1; Jonathan R. T. Hughes, *The Governmental Habit: Economic Controls from Colonial Times to the Present* (New York: Basic Books, 1977), pp. 85–7, 124.

4 Member banks retain some privileges that are not available to nonmember banks, in particular, the right to participate in the election of six of the nine district bank directors and a guaranteed 6 percent return on stock owned (since member banks are technically stockholders in the district banks).

5 An interesting overview of developments by various firms that challenge the banks may be found in Julie Salamon, "Bankers Getting Increasingly Upset about Unregulated Status of Rivals," *Wall Street Journal*, October 5, 1981, p. 29.

6 Edward J. Kane, "External Pressures and the Operations of the Fed," in *Political Economy of International and Domestic Monetary Relations,* Raymond E. Lombra and Willard E. Witte, eds. (Ames: Iowa State University Press, 1982) p. 223.

7 Stuart I. Greenbaum, Mukhtar M. Ali, and Randall C. Merris, "Monetary Policy and Banking Profits," *Journal of Finance* 31 (March

1976): 89–101. They assert (p. 89) that no prior econometric studies of the relationship between bank profits and monetary policy have been published. For a noneconometric and rather unconvincing statement, see Guy Noyes, "Monetary Policy and Banking," in *The Changing World of Banking,* Herbert V. Prochnow and Herbert V. Prochnow, Jr., eds. (New York: Harper & Row, 1974), esp. p. 337.

8 The argument is plainly stated in Armen A. Alchian and Reuben A. Kessel, "Redistribution of Wealth through Inflation," *Science* 130 (September 1959): 535–9.

9 William Poole, "Benefits and Costs of Stable Monetary Growth," in *Institutional Arrangements and the Inflation Problem,* Allan H. Meltzer and Karl Brunner, eds., Carnegie Rochester Conference Series on Public Policy, vol. 3, (Amsterdam: North Holland, 1976), pp. 15–50.

10 In the February 1969 FAC meeting, the council advised the board: "the principal thesis of the Council's thinking was that bankers would accommodate to almost any policy of restraint when it was applied gradually, but that sudden twists caused serious dislocations." *FAC Minutes,* p. 26.

An example of financial sector anger over unpredictable Federal Reserve action can be found in the period October–November 1977. The Federal Reserve abruptly raised the federal funds rate in the middle of a Treasury financing operation – traditionally an "even keel" period for monetary policy. Many cries of confusion were reported in the financial press, and the event seemed almost to precipitate a minor crisis between the board and the Carter administration over the direction of monetary policy. See, for example, *New York Times* articles of November 1, 1977, p. 53; November 2, 1977, pp. A1, A56; November 3, 1977, p. 52; and November 7, 1977, p. 55. Also see "The Bond Market Falls into a Fed Trap," *Business Week,* November 14, 1977, pp. 187, 190. There, an "exasperated banker" is quoted as saying, "Our industry spends millions of dollars on brains to follow what the Fed is doing. If it's going to be capricious and irrational, then our ability to assume risk as government bond dealers is diminished. What's especially irritating here is their timing."

11 This happened widely in 1980. See "Why Banks Keep the Prime So High," *Business Week,* January 19, 1981, p. 92; John M. Geddes, "Most Banks in West Germany Were Hurt By a Jump in Interest Rates during 1980," *Wall Street Journal,* April 8, 1981, p. 30. For the related academic arguments, see Edward J. Kane, "The Three Faces of Commercial Bank Liability Management," in *The Political Economy of Policy Making,* Michael P. Dooley, Herbert M. Kaufman, and Raymond E. Lombra, eds. (Beverly Hills: Sage, 1979), pp. 149–74. Also see Hyman P. Minsky, "Private Sector Asset Management and the Effectiveness of Monetary Policy: Theory and Practice," *Journal*

of Finance 24 (May 1969): 233–8. An interesting nontechnical introduction to the development of liability management is found in Martin Mayer, *The Bankers* (New York: Ballantine Books, 1974).

12 Evidence of harm done to these banks is reported in Tom Herman, "Many Banks Gripe, but Higher Prime Rate May Help Some Become More Profitable," *Wall Street Journal,* December 17, 1980, p. 27.

13 Milton Friedman, "Should There Be an Independent Monetary Authority?" in *In Search of a Monetary Constitution,* Leland B. Yeager, ed. (Cambridge, Mass.: Harvard University Press, 1962), pp. 236–8.

14 William Jackson, "Depository Institutions, Financial Innovations, and Economic Activity: Cycles and Trends Since the Accord," in JEC, *The Business Cycle and Public Policy 1929–80,* 96th Cong., 2nd sess., 1980, pp. 282–98. The quotation is from p. 291.

15 Donald D. Hester, "The Effects of Eurodollar and Domestic Money Market Innovations on the Interpretation and Control of Monetary Aggregates," in *The Political Economy of International and Domestic Monetary Relations,* R. Lombra and W. Witte, eds. (Ames: Iowa State University Press, 1982), pp. 303–24.

16 Examples of ABA lobbyists with such broad experience have included Matthew Hale, John W. Holton, James B. Cash, Jr., John F. Rolph III, Charles O. Zuver, Ronald L. Leymeister, and Fred Mutz. Two top ABA lobbyists later took government jobs: Charls Walker and James E. Smith. I have drawn information from several sources: John F. Berry, "Influential Bank Lobby Is Hard at Work on Hill," *Washington Post,* June 25, 1978, p. M1; David Burnham, "Banks' Lobby Called Strongest in Capital," *New York Times,* December 23, 1977, p. 1; Frank V. Fowlkes, "Washington Pressures: The Big-Bank Lobby," *National Journal,* December 6, 1969, pp. 295–9. I have also traced Banking Committee staff departures from staff listings in the *Congressional Directory* and have learned about their subsequent activities from various sources, including Craig Colgate, Jr., ed., and John M. Berry, asst. ed., *Directory of Washington Representatives of American Associations and Industry* (Washington, D.C.: Columbia Books, 1978), and *Martindale and Hubble Law Directory, 1979* (Summit, N.J.: M&H, 1979).

17 See accounts in Berry, "Influential Bank Lobby," and in Burnham, "Banks' Lobby Called Strongest in Capital."

18 The groups include The Association of Bank Holding Companies, the Association of Reserve City Bankers, the Bankers Association for Foreign Trade, the Consumer Bankers Association, the Dealer Bankers Association, the Electronic Funds Transfer Association, the Independent Bankers Association, the Mortgage Bankers Association, the National Association of Mutual Savings Banks, the National Bankers Association, and the National Savings and Loan

League. There has been very little systematic study of these organizations. Some lobbyists with extensive experience in government include John H. Yingling, Lewis G. Odom, Donald L. Rogers, Carl A. S. Coan, Ken Guenther, and John S. Rippey.

19 In 1978 five of the top ten banks; fourteen of the top one hundred. Bank rankings are drawn from "How the Top 200 Banks Performed in 1978," *Business Week,* April 23, 1979, pp. 93 ff.; lobby listings are from Colgate and Berry, eds., *Directory of Washington Representatives.*

20 See, for example, Fowlkes, "The Big-Bank Lobby," 297; Burnham, "Banks' Lobby Called Strongest in Congress," D3; and Berry, "Influential Bank Lobby," M1; Jonathan Aranson, *Money and Power: Banks and the World Monetary System* (Beverly Hills: Sage, 1977), p. 57.

21 "Banking Bill Is Approved by Conferees," *Wall Street Journal,* March 6, 1980, p. 2; "House Approves Compromise Bill on Banks, S&Ls," *Wall Street Journal,* March 28, 1980; G. Christian Hill, "S&Ls See Tough Times in Vying with Banks as Regulations Wane," *Wall Street Journal,* December 11, 1980, p. 1.

22 "S&Ls Show Their Political Punch," *Business Week,* November 23, 1981, p. 113; "The DIDC: Walking an Economic and Political Tightrope," *National Journal,* September 4, 1982.

23 See Donald D. Hester, "Special Interests: The FINE Situation," *Journal of Money, Credit, and Banking* 9 (November 1977): 652–61.

24 Charles Hoffman interview, June 7, 1978.

25 Stewart Lewis telephone interview, June 6, 1978.

26 On the biasing influence of bank regulatory policy see James L. Pierce, "The FINE Study," *Journal of Money, Credit, and Banking* 9 (November 1977): 612. In congressional hearings, Federal Reserve Board Chairman Arthur Burns once noted that he met often with many financial industry groups. House, Banking, Currency, and Housing Committee, Subcommittee on Domestic Monetary Policy, *Hearings on An Act to Lower Interest Rates and Allocate Credit (HR 212),* 94th Cong., 1st sess., 1975, p. 218.

27 The board has an informal rule prohibiting contact with the particular parties to a given decision. Competing positions are presented to the board entirely through the staff – who may be lobbied. By all evidence, this rule is taken very seriously. One former governor described contacts he initiated in specific cases in violation of this principle because he believed that information banks should be aware of was not being communicated to them. Former Governor George Mitchell is reported to have voted against a bank on a regulatory question, despite the fact that on the merits of the case he supported the bank's position, because he had been contacted by a representative of the bank in question.

28 Although it is not known how many banks use economists for this purpose, an ABA survey of the largest 100 U.S. commercial banks

revealed that 92 employed financial economists – that is, economists with a Ph.D. or equivalent work experience. American Bankers Association, *Directory of Bank Economists* (Washington, D.C.: ABA, 1976).

29 Robert Holland interview, June 6, 1978. Holland's characterization of the role of the FAC under Burns has been confirmed in my reading of the *Minutes* of the FAC meetings for the first three Burns years, 1970–2.

30 Others concur in judging the FAC to be relatively unimportant. See, for instance, G. L. Bach, *Making Monetary and Fiscal Policy* (Washington, D.C.: Brookings Institution, 1971). On the history of the FAC, see James Thomas Lindley, "An Analysis of the Federal Advisory Council of the Federal Reserve System, 1914–1938," Ph.D. dissertation, University of Georgia, 1977; Benjamin Haggott Beckhart, *The Federal Reserve System* (Washington, D.C.: American Institute of Banking, 1972), pp. 38–9. The 1974 FAC statement can be found in the *Federal Reserve Bulletin,* September 1974, pp. 679–80. Burns later said that the statement was drafted independently by the FAC and that the board distributed it because it was "constructive in spirit." *Hearings on an Act to Lower Interest Rates,* p. 279.

31 For example, one unidentified board member warned that "if the Federal Reserve accepted the premise that it would bail banks out of their difficulties, banks tacitly accepted a responsibility to watch their commitments." *FAC Minutes,* December 3, 1972, p. 20. Subsequent events certainly do not show that the board's warning was sufficient to overcome other incentives to banks to continue to extend such commitments.

32 Thomas M. Havrilesky, William P. Yohe, and David Schirm, "The Economic Affiliations of Federal Reserve District Banks," *Social Science Quarterly* 54 (December 1973), esp. 611–15; House, Committee on Banking, Currency, and Housing, *Federal Reserve Directors: A Study of Corporate and Banking Influence,* A Staff Study, Committee Print; 94th Cong., 2nd sess., 1976. Also on the same issues, see Andrew F. Brimmer, "Characteristics of Federal Reserve Bank Directors," *Federal Reserve Bulletin* 58 (June 1972): 550–9.

33 *Federal Reserve Directors,* p. 58.

34 One report indicated that Chairman Martin regularly held dinner meetings with major New York bankers and suggested that this practice continued under Burns. *National Journal* October 31, 1970, p. 2392. Martin, of course, had been head of the New York Stock Exchange prior to his appointment to the Federal Reserve, and Burns had been a consultant to at least one New York bank, Thus, it is quite reasonable that bankers should have been among their acquaintances.

35 At one point in this research, I undertook a rudimentary content analysis of the *FOMC Minutes.* The enterprise was eventually aban-

doned as far too time-consuming compared to the benefits it seemed to be yielding. For five meetings examined from 1969, I found five to six members on average making some kind of reference to bankers (very broadly defined) as opposed, for example, to three members on average making some kind of reference to business, two to three to unemployment, and none to one to unions. I also noted that in no meeting following the FAC meetings during this period was any explicit reference to those meetings recorded in the *FOMC Minutes*. Whether such references are edited out of the *Minutes* is not known.

36 Markley Roberts, "Monetary Policy – the Fed's Grip," *The American Federationist,* February 1975 (reprinted by the AFL–CIO). Of course, the Consumer Advisory Council now meets quarterly with the board, but it does not discuss monetary policy issues. Some (possibly five) labor representatives serve on district bank boards of directors or the boards of branch banks.

37 Sherman J. Maisel, *Managing the Dollar* (New York: Norton, 1973), p. 166.

38 Kane, "External Pressures and . . . the Fed," 223.

39 This is mentioned in Richard F. Janssen, "Bill Griggs, Second-Guessing the Fed, Fears It Will Slacken Credit Too Soon," *Wall Street Journal,* May 13, 1980, p. 6.

40 Stewart Lewis, June 6, 1978.

41 "The Role of Private Organizations in Changing Public Policy," a speech to the Second National Governmental Affairs Conference of the ABA, Washington D.C., July 19, 1972. On file at the Federal Reserve Research Library, Washington, D.C.

42 JEC, *Hearings on the Economic Report of the President,* various years, various Congresses.

43 Ibid., 1967, p. 1010.

44 Ibid., 1974, pp. 979–80; 1975, p. 1217.

45 See note 12, this chapter.

46 Kenneth H. Bacon, "Can U.S. Control Money Stock Better by Changing Rules?," *Wall Street Journal,* November 5, 1981, p. 18; "Fed Decreases to 2 Days the Lag For Banks' Reserve Accounting," *International Herald Tribune,* June 30, 1982, p. 11. "At Volcker's Fed, Yawns and Mumbles and Monetary Moves," *National Journal,* July 3, 1982, p. 1169. "Fed's New Practice on Reserve Deposits Starts February 2, 1984," *Wall Street Journal,* September 30, 1982, p. 10.

47 Senator Proxmire, *Congressional Record,* October 23, 1979, p. S14938.

48 "The DIDC," *National Journal,* September 4, 1982, p. 1501. Another conflict between banks and savings and loans emerged in the late 1970s over the payment of interest on demand deposits. In particular, the banks were concerned about their losses to savings and loans offering NOW (Negotiable Order of Withdrawal) accounts. These accounts let savings and loans offer what were for all intents and

purposes interest-bearing checking accounts. The Federal Reserve's response was to allow banks to offer Automatic Funds Transfer accounts, which allowed banks to shift money automatically from interest-bearing savings accounts to demand deposits. This meant, in effect, that customers could have interest-bearing demand deposits at banks, despite the fact that these were not permitted by law. See Judith Miller, "Fed Moving to Let Banks Pay Interest on Check Accounts," *New York Times,* February 3, 1978, p. 1.

49 See Volcker's testimony in House, Committee on Banking, Finance, and Urban Affairs, Subcommittee on Domestic Monetary Policy, *Hearings on Extension of Reserve Requirements to Include Other Transactions Accounts and Mechanisms (Money Market Mutual Funds)* (HR 2591), 97th Cong. 1st sess., 1981, p. 242. "An Itchy Congress Moves on Bank Reform," *Business Week,* July 13, 1981, p. 24; "Money Funds' Assets Grew 2.7% in Week, Intensifying Concern of Lawmakers, Fed," *Wall Street Journal,* February 20, 1981, p. 32; "Bank Board Considers Allowing Thrifts Edge on Savings Certificates," *Wall Street Journal,* December 4, 1979, p. 6.

50 Tom Herman, "Measures to Restrict Money-Market Funds Are Rapidly Losing Support in Congress," *Wall Street Journal,* May 14, 1981, p. 14.

51 "Volcker Opposes Banks' Offering Money Funds," *Wall Street Journal,* October 30, 1981, p. 4.

52 Passed October 1, 1982; the contents are described in "Savings and Loan Aid Package Boosts Powers of Banks, Thrifts," *Congressional Quarterly Weekly Report,* October 2, 1982, pp. 2423–4.

53 The dual tasks of fighting inflation and preventing crises are discussed in Hyman P. Minsky, "The Federal Reserve: Between a Rock and a Hard Place," *Challenge,* May–June 1980, pp. 30–6.

5. Economists and the Federal Reserve

1 The classic statement of this idea is found in Thomas S. Kuhn, *The Structure of Scientific Revolutions,* 2nd. ed. (Chicago: University of Chicago Press, 1970).

2 See Duncan MacRae, Jr., *The Social Function of Social Science* (New Haven, Conn.: Yale University Press, 1976), particularly the discussions in chaps. 1, 3, and 5.

3 This argument, not surprisingly, is made most forcefully by clearly identified political liberals. The most sophisticated discussion is in Benjamin Ward, *What's Wrong with Economics* (New York: Basic Books, 1972), especially parts 1, 4, and 5. Less rigorous, but interesting, are accounts in Robert Lekachman, *Economists at Bay: Why the Experts Will Never Solve Your Problems* (New York: McGraw-Hill, 1976), especially chaps. 1–3; John Kenneth Galbraith, *Economics and the Public*

Purpose (Boston: Houghton Mifflin, 1973), especially parts 1 and 2; and Robert A. Solo, "The Economist and Economic Roles of the Political Authority in Advanced Industrial Societies," in *Stress and Contradiction in Modern Capitalism,* Leon N. Lindberg et. al., eds. (Lexington, Mass.: Lexington Books, 1977). A kind of response to Ward was issued by Walter W. Heller in his AEA presidential address: "What's Right with Economics," *American Economic Review* 65 (March 1975): 1–26. Also of interest are George Stigler, "The Politics of Political Economists," in *Essays in the History of Economics* (Chicago: University of Chicago Press, 1965); Robert Aaron Gordon, "Rigor and Relevance in a Changing Institutional Setting," *American Economic Review* 66 (March 1976): 1–14; Barbara R. Bergmann, "Economists and the Real World," *Challenge,* March–April 1978, pp. 9–10; and Fred Hirsch, *Social Limits to Growth* (Cambridge, Mass.: Harvard University Press, 1976).

4 See, for example, the interesting discussion by George Stigler in which he puzzles over the failure of the "public" to agree with the economists' diagnoses. "Do Economists Matter?" *Southern Economic Journal* 42 (January 1976): 347–54. Stigler writes, "My central thesis is that economists exert a minor and scarcely detectable influence on the societies in which they live" (p. 351). He argues instead that developments in economic ideas follow the emergence of major economic interests. A response came from Martin Bronfenbrenner, "Mutterings About Mattering," *Southern Economic Journal* 42 (January 1976): 355–63. For additional recent views on the influence of economists, see articles by Kenneth E. Boulding and Robert L. Heilbroner in *Challenge,* March–April 1978, pp. 11–13, 16–17. On the political compromises required of economists in governmental service, see William R. Allen, "Economics, Economists, and Economic Policy: Modern American Experience," *History of Political Economy* 9 Spring (1977): 48–88.

5 This portrait, it might be objected, attributes to mainstream economists a position that might better be ascribed primarily to *Chicago* economists. Indeed, considerable theoretical research during the 1970s has clarified the ways in which informational asymmetries (e.g., between buyers and sellers) lead to undesirable market performance. See, for example, George A. Akerlof, "The Market for 'Lemons': Quality Uncertainty and the Market Mechanism," *Quarterly Journal of Economics* 84 (August 1970): 488–500. Nonetheless, in recent years it has been argued and empirically demonstrated that it is precisely on normative microeconomic issues that economists have the most agreement. See the general argument in Heller, "What's Right with Economics," 5. The empirical work is reported in J. R. Kearl, Clayne L. Pope, Gordon C. Whiting, and Larry T. Wimmer, "A Confusion of Economists?" *American Economic Review: American Economic As-*

sociation Papers and Proceedings 69 (May 1979): 28–37. It is precisely these microtheoretical agreements and welfare assumptions underlying them that have concerned the critics previously cited.

6 Skeptics on this point may wish to contrast the findings reported subsequently for monetarists to the analysis of public interest groups presented by Jeffrey M. Berry in *Lobbying for the People: The Political Behavior of Public Interest Groups* (Princeton, N.J.: Princeton University Press, 1977). Berry's definition of a public interest group may be found on p. 7. On organizational structure, see Tables III-5 (on employees) and II-5 (on local chapters) and related text. On finances, see Tables III-5 and III-7 and related text. On origins and maintenance, see chaps. 1 and 2, especially Tables II-1 and II-2. On strategies and tactics, see chaps. 8 and 9. Especially note the discussion of the strategy of "embarrassment and confrontation" (pp. 268–9). The objective is to create controversy, place the adversary on the defensive, and, if possible, provoke a response that lends legitimacy to the attacker. The monetarists have successfully adopted this strategy.

7 Carl F. Christ, "A Simple Macroeconomic Model with a Government Budget Restraint," *Journal of Political Economy* 76 (January–February 1968): 53–67; Bent Hansen, "On the Effects of Fiscal and Monetary Policy: A Taxonomic Discussion," *American Economic Review* 63 (September 1973): 546–71; Alan S. Blinder and Robert M. Solow, "Analytical Foundations of Fiscal Policy," in Blinder and others, *The Economics of Public Finance* (Washington, D.C.: Brookings Institution, 1974); Ralph C. Bryant, *Money and Monetary Policy in Interdependent Nations* (Washington, D.C.: Brookings Institution, 1980), chapter 14.

8 General outlines of this debate can be found in Robert J. Gordon, ed., *Milton Friedman's Monetary Framework: A Debate with His Critics* (Chicago: University of Chicago Press, 1974); Jerome Stein, ed., *Monetarism* (New York: North Holland, 1976); Alan S. Blinder and Robert M. Solow "Analytical Foundations of Fiscal Policy." Also see the view expressed by David Fand in his "Comments" in the *Brookings Papers on Economic Activity, #2*, 1972, pp. 336–8; and Richard E. Davis, "Implementing Open Market Policy with Monetary Aggregates Targets," in *Monetary Aggregates and Monetary Policy,* (New York: Federal Reserve Bank of New York, 1974), pp. 7–19.

A congressional staff study may capture the sense of conflict as well as any. See House, Subcommittee on Domestic Monetary Policy, Committee on Banking Currency and Housing, *The Impact of the Federal Reserve System's Monetary Policies on the Nation's Economy,* a Staff Study, 94th Cong., 2nd sess., December 1976.

9 A. Robert Nobay and Harry G. Johnson, "Monetarism: A Historic-Theoretic Perspective," *Journal of Economic Literature* 15 (June 1977):

470–85. Another useful introduction to the disagreements between monetarists is found in the articles assembled in *The Structure of Monetarism,* Thomas Mayer, ed (New York: Norton, 1978).

10 This is drawn largely from Thomas Mayer, "The Structure of Monetarism (I)," in *The Structure of Monetarism,* p. 2. These propositions are also easily discovered in the writings of leading monetarists.

11 See the discussion by Anthony M. Solomon, president of the Federal Reserve Bank of New York, in "New Strategies for the Federal Reserve?" *Challenge*, March–April 1982, pp. 18–24.

12 There are problems with interpretation of the published results, but they are the only available indicator of the extent of agreement among economists with two monetarist principles. The results are based on a rather modest 33 percent return in a stratified sample of economists. The research is reported in Kearl, Pope, Whiting, and Wimmer, "A Confusion of Economists?"

The original sample included 100 economists in the top seven graduate programs, 200 other academic economists, 150 economists in government positions, and 150 economists in private nonacademic employment. The aggregated results (e.g., Table 5.1 of this book) appear not to be weighted by the relative proportions of economists in each group.

One question relevant to the monetarist position is not reported in Table 5.1 because the published results for responses contain an apparent typographical error that makes them uninterpretable (see proposition 21, p. 30).

13 Despite the argument of some observers that monetarism is not necessarily politically conservative, nowhere do we observe left-of-center political parties embracing monetarist propositions as fundamental precepts. The neutrality argument is found in David Cobham, "The Politics of the Economics of Inflation," *Lloyds Bank Review* 128 (April 1978): 19–32; Joseph Aschheim and George S. Tavlas, "On Monetarism and Ideology," *Banca Nazionale del Lavoro Quarterly Review* 129 (June 1979): 167–86.

14 Walter Heller, *New Dimensions of Political Economy* (New York: Norton, 1967); Arthur Okun, *The Political Economy of Prosperity* (Washington, D.C.: Brookings Institution, 1970).

15 Known today as the MPS or the FMP model, for MIT–University of Pennsylvania–Social Science Research Council, or Federal Reserve–MIT–University of Pennsylvania model. A description of the early version of the model is found in Frank de Leeuw and Edward M. Gramlich, "The Federal Reserve–MIT Econometric Model," *Federal Reserve Bulletin* 54 (January 1968): 11–40.

16 Memo, Ackley to President, February 20, 1967, copy in Miller alphabetical file (original, CF FG 233, not open to the public), WHCF, LBJ Library. Further evidence of independent CEA contacts with

the Federal Reserve staff is in Memo, Heller to President, March 2, 1964, CF FI 8, WHCF, LBJ Library.

17 Memo, Heller to President, February 8, 1966, EX PE 2, WHCF, LBJ Library. Emphasis added.

18 Raymond Lombra and Michael Moran, "Policy Advice and Policymaking at the Federal Reserve," in *Monetary Institutons and the Policy Process,* Karl Brunner and Allan H. Meltzer, eds., vol. 13, Carnegie-Rochester Conference Series on Public Policy (Amsterdam: North-Holland, 1980), pp. 9–68.

19 Henry C. Wallich, "Policy Research, Policy Advice, and Policymaking," in *Political Economy of International and Domestic Monetary Relations,* Raymond E. Lombra and Willard E. Witte, eds. (Ames: Iowa State University Press, 1982).

20 William G. Dewald, editor of *Journal of Money, Credit, and Banking,* in his discussion of Wallich's paper in Lombra and Witte, *Political Economy of International and Domestic Monetary Policy.*

21 Particularly useful historical anecdotes are found in the *Journal of Monetary Economics,* vol. 2, no. 4 (November 1976), symposium dedicated to Homer Jones, who was a major force in the development of monetarist analysis at the Federal Reserve Bank of St. Louis. Also see A. James Meigs, "The Nixon Administration and the Federal Reserve: A Flawed Experiment in Monetary Policy," in *Issues in Monetary Economics,* H. G. Johnson and A. R. Nolay, eds. (Oxford: Oxford University Press, 1974). On media attention, see John T. Woolley, "Monetarists and the Politics of Monetary Policy," *Annals of the American Academy of Political and Social Science* 459 (January 1982): 148–60. The monetarists have received excellent media coverage thanks to their allies in major media posts: William Wolman, *Business Week,* Lindley H. Clark, Jr., *Wall Street Journal,* and H. Erich Heineman, *New York Times.*

22 Karl Brunner and Allan Meltzer, *The Federal Reserve's Attachment to the Free Reserve Concept,* prepared for the Subcommittee on Domestic Finance of the House Committee on Banking and Currency, 88th Cong., 2nd sess., 1964.

23 See various accounts, including much of the narrative in Sherman J. Maisel, *Managing the Dollar* (New York: Norton, 1973); Andrew F. Brimmer, "The Political Economy of Money: Evolution and Impact of Monetarism in the Federal Reserve System," *American Economic Review Papers and Proceedings* 62 (May 1972): 344–52; Sanford F. Borins, "The Political Economy of the Fed," *Public Policy* 20 (Spring 1962): 175–98; Benjamin M. Friedman, "The Inefficiency of Short-Run Monetary Targets for Monetary Policy," *Brookings Papers on Economic Activity* 2 (1977): 297–301; Richard G. Davis, "Implementing Open Market Policy with Monetary Aggregate Objectives," in *Monetary Aggregates and Monetary Policy* (Federal Reserve Bank of New York, 1974), pp. 7–10; Henry C. Wallich and Peter M. Keir,

"The Role of Operating Guides in U.S. Monetary Policy: A Historical Review," *Kredit und Kapital* 11 (1978): 30–52.

24 Maisel, *Managing the Dollar,* p. 177. Also see Partee's account of the period in *FOMC Minutes,* February 14, 1972, p. 120 and Daane's comments in ibid., January 11, 1972, p. 83.

25 Henry C. Wallich and Peter M. Keir, "The Role of Operating Guides in U.S. Monetary Policy: A Historical Review," *Kredit und Kapital* 11 (1978): 41. In a spoof of FOMC vagueness in the 1960s, Malcolm Bryan, President of the Federal Reserve Bank of Atlanta composed the following:

> It is the current policy of the Committee to prevent an excessive degree of credit and monetary expansion but to permit an adequate degree of expansion, so as to encourage but at the same time to limit (to a degree not inconsistent with the Directive) the fuller utilization, or if possible the full utilization of the economy's resources provided balance of payment considerations are not inconsistent with the above defined degree of expansion, or if inconsistent therewith provided an appropriate degree (but not an excessive degree) of expansion can be achieved within the framework of this directive.
>
> To implement this policy, operations of the Open Market Account shall be conducted with a view to providing reserves for the above defined degree of credit and monetary expansion with full allowance for seasonal requirements but without the necessity of offsetting all temporary factors if this is inconsistent with this directive, provided the rate of increase of total reserves shall be somewhat slower than would otherwise be necessary to provide an excessive degree of monetary expansion. Operations shall place emphasis on an increase or a decrease of the three months Treasury bill rate provided it does not remain unchanged within the framework of the above defined objectives. No overt action shall be taken.

From the James Louis Robertson Collection, Library of Congress, Box 58, "Open Market Committee" file.

26 The external critique included, from the monetarist side, Brunner and Meltzer, previously cited, and James Meigs, *Free Reserves and the Money Supply* (Chicago: University of Chicago Press, 1962). A critique originating from within the System was by J. M. Guttentag, "The Strategy of Open Market Operations," *Quarterly Journal of Economics* 80 (February 1966): 1–38. The staff was quite hostile to much of this critique, however. See accounts in Borins, "Political Economy of the Fed," and in Maisel, *Managing the Dollar.* The tone is well captured in Daniel Brill, "Criteria for Conduct of Monetary Policy: Implications of Recent Research," in *Monetary Process and Policy,* George Horwich, ed. (Homewood, Ill.: Irwin, 1967). On the

recognition of policy failures within the System, see Maisel, *Managing the Dollar,* pp. 77–86; Brimmer, "The Political Economy of Money," 348.

27 See Maisel's account in *Managing the Dollar,* 221–31, 251–4.

28 See Brimmer, "The Political Economy of Money," 350.

29 See Davis, "Implementing Open Market Policy," and William Poole, "The Making of Monetary Policy: Description and Analysis," *Economic Inquiry* 13 (June 1975): 253–65.

30 See Davis, "Implementing Open Market Policy," 7.

31 Federal Reserve Bank of Boston, *Monetary Aggregates and Monetary Policy,* Conference Series No. 4 (1969); Board of Governors of the Federal Reserve System, *Open Market Policies and Operating Procedures – Staff Studies* (July 1971); many issues of the Federal Reserve Bank of St. Louis *Review;* Federal Reserve Bank of New York, *Monetary Aggregates and Monetary Policy* (October 1974). Bearing on the question of the Federal Reserve behavior, see Paul De Rosa and Gary H. Stern, "Monetary Control and the Federal Funds Rate," *Journal of Monetary Economics* 3 (April 1977): 217–30.

32 Lists published in 1973, 1974, and 1975 included the following individuals (for more information on them, see Appendix C): Brunner, Meltzer, Schwartz, Rasche, Jones, Meigs, Schmidt, Mayer, and Sprinkel. Not included in Appendix C because of lack of information, but members of the SOMC during that period, were James Ford (then of the Ford Motor Co.), William Wolman (now of *Business Week*), and Erich Heinemann (of Morgan Stanley & Co).

On the SOMC, see John H. Allan, "Economists Back Growth Rate of 5% to 5.5% in Money," *New York Times,* March 11, 1974, p. 43; John H. Allen, "Monetarists Huddle, Send Central Bankers a Play," *New York Times,* September 17, 1973, p. 49; Allen, "Shadow Panel Warns That Deficits Peril U.S. Economy," *New York Times,* September 13, 1975, p. 31; and Paul Lewis, "Monetarists Meet and Critique Carter," *New York Times,* March 8, 1977, p. 43; "Shadow Committee Calls to Extend Money Growth," *New York Times,* September 14, 1976, p. 51; "Reduction Is Urged in Money Supply," *New York Times,* September 20, 1977, p. 59; "Shadow Market Warns on Dollar Upswing," *New York Times,* March 14, 1978, p. 59; "Economists Warn on Interest Rates," *New York Times,* September 18, 1979, p. D11. The *Wall Street Journal* has typically treated the SOMC as less important news, leaving references primarily in the columns of Lindley H. Clark, Jr. See, for example, the tiny space devoted to the SOMC's founding: "Open-Market Committee Rapped by 'Shadow' Panel," *Wall Street Journal,* September 17, 1973, p. 2.

33 See the biographical and intellectual sketch in Leonard Silk, *The Economists* (New York: Avon Books; originally published by Basic Books, 1976), chap. 2. Also, Karl Brunner, "The 1976 Nobel Prize in Economics," *Science* 194 (5 November 1976): 594 ff.

34 In general on Brunner, see the various biographical sketches collected in *Journal of Money, Credit, and Banking* 9, no. 1, pt. 2 (February 1977): 243–58. Since 1977 the Shadow European Economic Policy Committee (SEEPC) has shadowed the Organization for Economic Cooperation and Development (OECD), which it views as being far too Keynesian and activist. Articles on SEEPC include "Watchdog Economic Unit Assails Europe's Pay-Price Curb Policy," *Wall Street Journal,* May 30, 1977, p. 23; Philip Revzin, "Dissident Group of European Economists Urges Tax Cuts, Slower Growth of Money," *Wall Street Journal,* June 1, 1978, p. 13.

35 *Journal of Money, Credit, and Banking* founded in 1969 (at Ohio State University) and the *Journal of Monetary Economics* (at Rochester University) in 1974.

36 Thus, in editing the series, Brunner and Meltzer are advised by a committee composed of monetarists Carl Christ, Jacob Frenkel, Pieter Korteweg (also a member of the SEEPC), David Laidler, and William Poole. All except Korteweg are Chicago Ph.D.s. An examination of volumes 1–2, and 4–12 of the series shows that of sixteen individuals who made contributions to more than one volume, ten were either monetarists or rational expectations theorists.

37 C. R. Whittlesey, "Power and Influence in the Federal Reserve System," *Economica* 30 (February 1963): 33–44; Borins, "Political Economy of the Fed;" Maisel, *Managing the Dollar;* Wallich, "Policy Research, Policy Advice."

38 DeRosa and Stern, "Monetary Control and the Federal Funds Rate," 217–30; Ira Kaminow, "Fed Policy Under Resolution 133 (1975–1978): Is What They Said What They Did?" Working paper (Washington, D.C.: Government Research Corporation, 1979).

39 Wallich, "Policy Research, Policy Advice," 238–9. Criticism is noted in Lombra and Moran, "Policy Advice and Policymaking."

40 This hostility is reported in Borins, "Political Economy of the Fed." Several board members were vocal opponents, but the views of Maisel and Brimmer were particularly well known.

41 Wallich, "Some Uses of Economics," 142.

42 Wallich, "Policy Research, Policy Advice," 243.

43 Lombra and Moran, "Policy Advice and Policymaking," 44. I have also discussed this in my doctoral dissertation, "The Political Economy of Monetary Policy in the United States," University of Wisconsin-Madison, 1980, chap. 9.

44 Solomon, "New Strategies for the Federal Reserve?" 24.

45 Lindley H. Clark, Jr., "Speaking of Business: The Elderly Economist," *The Wall Street Journal,* February 12, 1980, p. 20.

46 This is based on interviews with staff and with Governors Teeters, Wallich, Partee, and Schultz in January 1981.

47 Calculations based on figures published in Federal Reserve Bank of St. Louis, "Monetary Trends." Comparison with cyclical conditions

similar to those of the post-1979 period (i.e., 1973–6) also shows the growth rates of the recent period to be much more volatile.

48 Ralph C. Bryant, "Federal Reserve Control of the Money Stock," and John D. Paulus, "Comment," in *Journal of Money, Credit, and Banking* 14 (November 1982): 597–633.

49 Henry Aaron, *Politics and the Professors: The Great Society in Perspective* (Washington, D.C.: Brookings Institution, 1979), especially chap. 5.

50 Hugh Heclo, "Issue Networks and the Executive Establishment," in *The New American Political System,* Anthony King, ed. (Washington, D.C.: American Enterprise Institute, 1978), especially pp. 102–7.

51 One consequence, certainly, has been to reinforce other pressures for unanimous voting in the FOMC. Some reflection of increased uncertainty can be found in Stephen M. Goldfeld and Alan S. Blinder, "Some Implications of Endogenous Stabilization Policy," *Brookings Papers on Economic Activity,* vol. 3, 1972, pp. 585–644; Stephen M. Goldfeld, "The Case of the Missing Money," *Brookings Papers on Economic Activity,* vol. 3, 1976, pp. 683–730; and Friedman, "The Inefficiency of Short-Run Monetary Targets." On ways policy makers deal with dissonance and uncertainty, see John D. Steinbruner, *The Cybernetic Theory of Decision* (Princeton, N.J.: Princeton University Press, 1974).

52 Note the tone of Karl Brunner in "The Commitment to Permanent Inflation," in Center for the Study of American Business, *Alternate Policies to Combat Inflation* Conference Proceedings, Working Paper No. 40 (Washington University, St. Louis, Missouri: CSAB, January 1979).

6. The President and the Federal Reserve

1 Thomas E. Cronin, *The State of the Presidency,* 2nd ed. (Boston: Little, Brown, 1980), chap. 5.

2 See the following discussion on the political business cycle.

3 Robert E. Weintraub, "Congressional Supervision of Monetary Policy," *Journal of Monetary Economics* 4 (April 1978): 356. See also William Poole, "Discussion of the Levy and Meltzer Papers," in *Stabilization Policies: Lessons from the 70s and Implications for the 80s,* Conference Proceedings, Working Paper No. 53 (St. Louis: Center for the Study of American Business, April 1980), p. 189.

4 Nathanial Beck "Presidential Influence on the Federal Reserve in the 1970s," *American Journal of Political Science* 26 (August 1982): 443.

5 Edward J. Kane, "External Pressure and the Operations of the Fed," in *Political Economy of International and Domestic Monetary Relations,* Raymond E. Lombra and Willard E. Witte, eds. (Ames: Iowa State University Press, 1982), p. 217.

6 John T. Woolley, "Central Banks and Inflation: Influence and Independence," in *The Political Economy of Global Inflation and Recession,* Leon N. Lindberg and Charles S. Maier, eds. (Washington, D.C.: Brookings Institution, 1984). Sources include G. L. Bach, *Making Monetary and Fiscal Policy* Washington, D.C.: Brookings Institution, 1971); Okun, *The Political Economy of Prosperity;* Walter W. Heller, *New Dimensions of Political Economy* (Cambridge, Mass.: Harvard University Press, 1966); Sherman J. Maisel, *Managing the Dollar* (New York: Norton, 1973); documentary evidence in the files of the Lyndon Baines Johnson Library at Austin, Texas; personal interviews with various participants; and newspaper accounts.

7 The quotations from Stein and McCracken and the references to them again below are drawn from transcripts of oral history interviews with all CEA chairmen prior to Charles Schultze prepared by the Vanderbilt University Institute of Public Policy. These transcripts, together with analytical essays by several authors, are to be published by the University of Tennessee Press. Okun's views may be found in the same place and also in his book, *The Political Economy of Prosperity* (Washington, D.C.: Brookings Institution, 1970).

8 Richard E. Neustadt, *Presidential Power: The Politics of Presidential Leadership,* rev. ed. (New York: Wiley, 1976). Also see Cronin, *State of the Presidency.*

9 The classic example is the State Department. For an account of a refusal to cooperate by the Navy, see the account in Graham Allison, *Essence of Decision: Explaining the Cuban Missile Crisis* (Boston: Little, Brown, 1971), pp. 127–32. Kelman argues that there were *no* instances of presidential involvement in OSHA rule making prior to 1978 – which surely must make that agency more independent in any sense of the word than the Federal Reserve. Steven Kelman, "Occupational Safety and Health Administration," in *The Politics of Regulation,* James Q. Wilson, ed. (New York: Basic Books, 1980).

10 Cronin, *State of the Presidency,* p. 138. John Brigham and Kenneth M. Dolbeare conclude that the Federal Reserve is unusually independent and largely autonomous. See "Agency and Advice: The Determinants of National Economic Policy," in *Making Public Policy: Studies in American Politics* John Brigham, ed. (Lexington, Mass.: Heath, 1977).

11 Arthur Okun, *The Political Economy of Prosperity* (Washington, D.C.: Brookings Institution, 1970), p. 71. Congressional refusal to provide flexible tax instruments for the president is another source of criticism. The problem is outlined in Joseph A. Pechman, *Federal Tax Policy* (Washington, D.C.; Brookings Institution, 1977), pp. 49–50. The various indictments are reviewed in James L. Sundquist, "Congress and the President: Enemies or Partners," in *Setting National Priorities,* Henry Owen and Charles L. Schultze, eds. (Washington, D.C.: Brookings Institution, 1976), pp. 583–618.

12 Note that this is not support for greater independence from *presidential* oversight. Two prominent instances are: statement by Treasury Secretary Douglas Dillon, in *The Federal Reserve After Fifty Years,* hearings before the Subcommittee on Domestic Finance of the House Committee on Banking and Currency, 88th Cong., 2nd sess., 1964, pp. 1231–2; statement of Deputy Treasury Secretary Stephen Gardner, in *Financial Institutions and the Nation's Economy "Discussion Principles,"* hearings before the Subcommittee on Financial Institutions Supervision, Regulation and Insurance of the House Committee on Banking, Currency, and Housing, 94th Cong. 1st and 2nd sess., 1975–6, p. 604.

13 In addition to the individuals cited in the text, the following have served in both the Federal Reserve and the Treasury: FOMC: Dewey Daane, Henry Wallich, Bruce MacLaury, Stephen Gardner, Frank Morris, Robert Mayo, and Paul Volcker; top professional staff: Sidney Jones, Samuel Chase, and Peter Sternlight.

14 See, for example, Lawrence Pierce, *The Politics of Fiscal Policy Formation* (Pacific Palisades, Calif.: Goodyear, 1971); and G. L. Bach, *Making Monetary and Fiscal Policy* (Washington, D.C.: Brookings Institution, 1971). Subsequent to the periods examined by these authors, administrations have used very samiliar mechanisms, often under different names. Sidney Jones interview, June 14, 1977.

15 From oral history interviews, Vanderbilt University Institute of Public Policy, University of Tennessee Press, forthcoming.

16 Louis Kohlmeier, "The Growing Role of Arthur Burns in Carter Economic Policy," *The Financier,* May 1977, pp. 6–10.

17 "In this episode, the Federal Reserve's independence proved to be a valuable national asset. It permitted the President and his administration to assume a passive role, tolerating an unpopular tight money policy silently without explicitly approving or endorsing it. The Council's job was to make sure that the administration did not impede the Fed in execution of its unpleasant assignment." Okun, *The Political Economy of Prosperity,* p. 79.

18 "The New Activism at the Fed," *Business Week,* September 17, 1979, p. 30.

19 See Murray Edelman, *The Symbolic Uses of Politics* (Urbana: University of Illinois Press, 1964), especially chap. 4.

20 This was calculated for the membership at the start of each calendar year. The decline was apparently due, in part, to policy and personality clashes during the Burns years that led to relatively early resignations. However, there is also a more general phenomenon at work here as well, which can be seen throughout government: the difficulty of recruiting top-notch private sector officials to take relatively modest-paying positions in the government.

21 Walter W. Heller, "Open Letter to G. William Miller," *Challenge,* March–April 1978, p. 19.

22 Memo, Walter W. Heller to President, February 25, 1967, CF FG 233 WHCF, LBJ Library.

23 Cross-reference, Memo, Gardner Ackley to President, February 20, 1967, Confidential Alphabetic Files ("Miller"); the original is filed CF FG 233 and was not open to the public at the time of this research. WHCF, LBJ Library.

Victor Navasky has reported another example involving Robert Kennedy, attorney general for John F. Kennedy: ". . . we were talking about the executive order on housing as it related to the Federal Reserve Board and somebody raised the political science question about the independence of the Federal Reserve Board, which would preclude the President from telling it what to do. Bobby said bring me a list of the Federal Reserve Board members and when their terms expire. He received the list looked it over and said, 'I see they're only independent until June of 1963. doesn't ——— [sic] have a son who works for the federal government?'" Victor S. Navasky, *Kennedy Justice* (New York: Atheneum, 1971), p. 171. The reference to June 1963 could possibly be to the term of G. H. King, who did resign in September 1963.

24 Interview, July 24, 1978. It is likely that these differences were characteristic of differences in the Johnson and Nixon styles of handling appointments. See G. Calvin MacKenzie, *The Politics of Presidential Appointments* (New York: Free Press, 1981). Also see Senate, Committee on Government Operations, *Study on Federal Regulation,* vol. I, *The Regulatory Appointments Process,* 95th Cong. 1st sess., January 1977, chap. 9, dealing especially with the Nixon and Ford processes.

25 Most notable in recent years have been the Commission on Money and Credit, sponsored by the Committee for Economic Development in the early 1960s, the Hunt Commission assembled by Nixon in the early 1970s, and the FINE study by the House Banking Committee in 1975.

26 For instance, in spring 1965 Treasury Secretary Dillon, in commenting on congressional agitation for interest rate ceilings, complained that the action tended to distract attention from "appropriate and useful reforms" such as making the term of the chairman more coterminus with that of the president, realigning board terms to ensure a president an appointment soon after taking office, shortening the terms of board members, reducing the size of the board, and eliminating the private ownership of district Federal Reserve Banks. Johnson did not encourage Dillon. Nor did he seize the opportunity to make this an issue in early 1966. See Memo, Douglas Dillon to President, EX FI 8, March 31, 1965, and Cross-reference Memo, Gardner Ackley to President, EX FG 233 (orig. at SP 2–2, EX), January 31, 1966, WHCF, LBJ Library.

27 Memo, Joe Califano to President, EX FG 233, March 25, 1967, WHCF, LBJ Library.

28 *Economic Report of the President, 1969* (Washington, D.C.: USGPO, 1969), p13.

29 Memo, Arthur Okun to President, August 31, 1968 EX FI 8, WHCF, LBJ Library. "Some of the district banks were clearly dragging their heels. . . . The present attitude of the district banks is worrisome, because the recent discount rate cut was only the first of many steps we will need to ease credit adequately."

30 For example, abolishing the FOMC and concentrating authority in the board. Memo, Warren L. Smith to Larry Levinson, November 4, 1968, CF FI 9-1, WHCF, LBJ Library.

31 See the account in chap. 8. Good "insider" sources on the events are William Safire, *Before the Fall: An Inside View of the Pre-Watergate White House* (New York: Doubleday, 1975); and Charles Colson, *Born Again* (Old Tappan, N.J.: Chosen Books, 1976).

32 "Dollar at 12-Year Peak as U.S. Reviews Policies," *Financial Times,* June 22, 1982, p. 1.

33 Vartanig G. Vartan, "Independent Fed Is Supported," *New York Times,* June 28, 1982, p. D7.

34 Forecasts have differed somewhat. For example, from 1968 to 1972, Federal Reserve forecasts as reported in the *FOMC Minutes* were marginally less optimistic than were the administration's. That is, the Federal Reserve forecast lower real GNP growth, higher unemployment, and higher inflation than did the administration.

35 I have presented this analysis in "Central Banks and Inflation: Influence and Independence," in *The Politics and Sociology of Global Inflation and Recession,* Leon N. Lindberg and Charles Maier, eds. (Washington, D.C.: Brookings Institution, 1984).

36 See Cross-reference, Memo, Gardner Ackley to President, February 15, 1965, "Martin" Name File (orig. in EX FG 11-3); and Henry Fowler to President, April 24, 1965, EX FI, WHCF, LBJ Library.

37 See Memo to President from Douglas Dillon, Kermit Gordon, and Gardner Ackley, March 31, 1965, EX BE-5, WHCF, LBJ Library.

38 For an example of this kind of thinking, see Memo, Gardner Ackley to President, May 5, 1965, EX BE 5, WHCF, LBJ Library.

39 The meeting was prompted partly by a speech Martin gave on June 1 in which he appeared to liken the current economic environment to that of 1929. Among the relevant documents are Memo, Henry Fowler to President, June 2, 1965, Diary Backup; Cross-reference, Memo, Gardner Ackley to President, June 3, 1965, EX FG-233 (orig. at EX SP/FG-233); and Memo, Gardner Ackley to President, June 9, 1965, Diary Backup; WHCF, LBJ Library. Following the Quadriad meeting, there was a joint press conference intended to demonstrate unanimity, at which it was clear that Martin was skeptical about the chances for continued economic expansion. See Press Briefing Transcript, June 19, 1965, EX FI, WHCF, LBJ Library.

40 Memo, Gardner Ackley to President, July 16, 1966, EX FI-8, WHCF, LBJ Library.

41 Memo, Gardner Ackley to President, September 16, 1965, EX FI-8, WHCF, LBJ Library. The president dispatched Fowler to have a talk with Martin. White House tension is evident in two subsequent Ackley memos on September 29 – EX FI-8 and CF BE-5 – and another memo on October 1, 1965: EX FI-8, WHCF, LBJ Library.

42 This must surely have aroused suspicions at the board. Cross-reference, Memo, Charles Schultze to President, October 4, 1965, EX FI-4 (orig. at EX FI-9), WHCF, LBJ Library.

43 Memo, Gardner Ackley to President, October 17, 1965, EX FI-8, WHCF, LBJ Library.

44 Memo, Henry Fowler to President, November 3, 1965, CF FI, WHCF, LBJ Library.

45 Memo, Gardner Ackley to President, November 13, 1965, EX FI, WHCF, LBJ Library.

46 Memo, Henry Fowler, Gardner Ackley, and Charles Schultze to President, December 1, 1965, CF FI 9, WHCF, LBJ Library.

47 In oral history interview, Vanderbilt University, Institute of Public Policy, University of Tennessee Press, forthcoming.

48 A report of lobbying allies is found in Memo, Gardner Ackley to President, July 16, 1966, EX FI 8, WHCF, LBJ Library.

49 Memo, Jake Jacobson to President, November 30, 1965, EX FG 233, LBJ Library; "Secretary Fowler reports that he had breakfast this morning in Florida with Mr. Daane of the Federal Reserve. He states that he got his point across and that Daane was sympathetic; however, he is still uncertain as to how Daane will vote." Careful readers will have found the handwritten notation at the top of Exhibit 6.1 reading, "Talked to Sec. Fowler, 11–29–65 3 p., JJ." Daane reported that this episode was the only one in which he ever felt any pressure from the White House about monetary policy. Interview, January 23, 1978.

50 Califano attached a note to the memo from Fowler et al. cited in note 46, this chapter. This account is limited to the current public record and is almost certainly not complete. Many contacts may not have produced sufficient information to warrant sharing with the president.

51 Arthur Okun indicated his awareness of White House–Federal Reserve friction in late 1974 and early 1975, but Ford CEA member William Fellner insisted that he was not aware of any such friction. If conflict occurred at cyclical turning points, one would expect conflict at exactly those times. Carter CEA member Lyle Gramley indicated that there was some disagreement on targets at the outset of 1978 but minimized it, saying that it was due to the "cyclical phase." Arthur Okun interview, February 7, 1978; Herbert Stein interview,

July 27, 1978; William Fellner interview, July 12, 1978; Lyle Gramley interview, June 16, 1978.

52 Greenspan interview, in oral history interview, Vanderbilt University, Institute of Public Policy, University of Tennessee Press, forthcoming.

53 Lyle Gramley interview, June 16, 1978. The press accounts can be found in the *New York Times* in John H. Allen, "White House Warns Fed Against Lifting of Interest Rates," October 21, 1977, p. 1; Thomas E. Mullaney, "The White House Attack on the Fed's Monetary Policy," October 25, 1977, p. 63; John H. Allan, "Fed Lifts Discount Rate to 6% Despite Pressures from Carter," October 26, 1977, p. 53; James L. Rowe, Jr., "Burns Criticizes Carter," October 27, 1977, p. 1; "Transcript of Presidential News Conference," October 28, 1977, p. 14; Clyde H. Farnsworth, "Moves by Fed Spur Burns–Carter Fight," November 2, 1977. p. A1; Clyde H. Farnsworth, "Burns Says Reserve Plans to Keep Brake on Growth in Money," November 10, 1977, p. 1; Charles Mohr, "President Says He's Not a Critic of Burns Policy," November 11, 1977, p. A1. Also see Art Pine, "When Is Attack on Fed Not an Attack on Fed?" *Washington Post,* October 23, 1977, p. F3.

54 Thus, what *Business Week* proclaimed as "The New Miller–Carter Economic Accord" on May 29, 1978, became "A Strained Accord with the Fed" by July 10, although the evidence of a serious disagreement was not very convincing.

55 "World Turned Upside Down," April 2, 1979; also see the very interesting account in Richard J. Levine, "Efforts to Persuade Fed to Tighten Credit Are Abandoned by Carter Administration," *Wall Street Journal,* April 17, 1979, p. 3.

56 Bach, *Making Monetary and Fiscal Policy,* p. 94.

57 Edward R. Tufte's *Political Control of the Economy* (Princeton, N.J.: Princeton University Press, 1978) is probably the best-known contribution to this literature, although serious writing on the topic clearly originated with Nordhaus, an economist, who claims a heritage from Kalecki's recently discovered 1943 article. William D. Nordhaus, "The Political Business Cycle," *Review of Economic Studies* 42 (April 1975): 169–90; M. Kalecki, "Political Aspects of Full Employment," *Political Quarterly* 14 (October–December 1943): 322–31. Also, Assar Lindbeck, "Stabilization Policy in Open Economies with Endogenous Politicians," *American Economic Review Papers and Procedings,* 66 (May 1976): 1–19; C. Duncan MacRae, "A Political Model of the Business Cycle," *Journal of Political Economy* 85 (April 1977): 239–63; Bruno S. Frey and Friedrich Schneider, "A Politico-Economic Model of the United Kingdom," *The Economic Journal* 88 (June 1978): 243–53; James Alt and Alec Chrystal, *Political Economics* (Berkeley: University of California Press, 1983), chap. 5; Bruno S. Frey, *Modern Political Economy* (New York: Wiley, 1978).

58 See especially the exchange filed together as Letter, President to Seymour E. Harris, January 23, 1964, EX FI, WHCF, LBJ Library; Memo, Ackley to President, March 27, 1964, and attached memo of March 27, 1964, EX FI 9, WHCF, LBJ Library. Also bearing on this matter is Letter, George Reedy to President, August 30, 1966, CF BE 5, WHCF, LBJ Library.

59 This view almost certainly stemmed from the perception that in the election of 1960 a recession partly provoked by Federal Reserve policy had been blamed for Nixon's defeat. This case will figure again in the account of Chapter 9, this book.

60 See the excellent review and analysis in Alt and Chrystal, *Political Economics*.

61 Nordhaus, "The Political Business Cycle," 182.

62 Perhaps this is intended as irony. Perhaps it reflects Nordhaus's unstated belief that the central banks in those countries are not in fact independent, or perhaps he would point out that central banks can be political *and* independent.

63 Tufte does not report actual growth rates, so the size – and importance – of the observed differences is unclear. Tufte, *Political Control of the Economy,* pp. 50–1. In an unpublished work, David Cameron examined the patterns in rates of growth of M1 for annual periods ending *a full year* prior to the election. His research also supported the PBC concept. David R. Cameron, "Taxes, Deficits, and Inflation," unpublished paper prepared for the Brookings Institution Project on the Politics and Sociology of Global Inflation and Recession, December 1978.

64 The rate of growth of the detrended monetary base increased in five of seven pre-election biennial periods and also increased in five of eight post-election biennial periods. The rate of growth was calculated from the first quarter of an odd-numbered year to the last quarter of the subsequent even-numbered year. I also compared the growth rates of the monetary base (both detrended and not) averaged over even and odd years and presidential and congressional election years. There is a difference. For example, in *presidential* election years, the detrended monetary base grew on average by 2.2 percent, whereas in all odd years, it grew on average by only 1.7 percent. The difference, calculated with a difference of means test, is not statistically significant (even at the 0.10 level), although it is in the expected direction. When *all* even years are compared to odd years, the difference is even smaller. Tufte's measures are not detrended. Using quarterly figures for the monetary base without detrending produces results marginally less supportive of Tufte's position.

The monetary base consists of member bank deposits at Federal Reserve Banks, vault cash held by member and nonmember banks, and currency held by the public. The measure used here includes an adjustment for changes in reserve requirement ratios and is seasonally adjusted. See Albert E. Burger and Robert H. Rasche, "Revision of the Monetary Base," Federal Reserve Bank of St. Louis *Review* 59 (July 1977): 13–28. Research attempting to produce an accurate measure of monetary policy impact indicates that the detrended monetary base is a substantially better indicator of monetary policy impact than is the detrended change in M1. See Alan S. Blinder and Stephen M. Goldfeld, "New Measures of Fiscal and Monetary Policy," *American Economic Review* 66 (December 1976): 780–96.

65 David G. Golden and James M. Poterba, "The Price of Popularity: The Political Business Cycle Reexamined," *American Journal of Political Science* 24 (November 1980): 696–714.

66 This may reflect the fact that policy effects involve lags. The findings are reported in Woolley, "The Political Economy of Monetary Policy in the United States," Ph.D. dissertation, University of Wisconsin-Madison, 1980, chap. 5.

67 Beck, "Presidential Influence on the Federal Reserve."

68 Maisel, *Managing the Dollar,* p. 117.

69 The categories of liabilities against which reserves have been required have varied considerably through the years. The figures used here reflect changes in reserves required for demand deposits at the largest category of banks as officially defined at a given time.

70 If observations for 1980 and previous years are excluded on the grounds that the Federal Reserve was following a new operating regimen, the difference would be greater: 0.415 in presidential years versus 0.814 in odd-numbered years. But then, what reason is there for excluding those years? Doesn't the PBC explicitly hold that political considerations will override these kinds of technical considerations?

71 Okun interview, February 7, 1978; and in Vanderbilt transcripts, forthcoming, University of Tennessee Press. Bargaining is reflected in CEA memoranda to the president. See, for example, Memo, Gardner Ackley to President, November 25, 1966, CF FI 9 (also filed as EX FG 233, dated November 26, 1966), WHCF, LBJ Library; and idem., June 19, 1967, EX BE 5, WHCF, LBJ Library.

7. Congress and the Federal Reserve

1 A. Jerome Clifford, *The Independence of the Federal Reserve System,* (Phladelphia: University of Pennsylvania Press, 1965), p. 330.

2 David R. Mayhew, *Congress: The Electoral Connection* (New Haven, Conn.: Yale University Press, 1974); Morris P. Fiorina, *Congress: Keystone of the Washington Establishment* (New Haven, Conn.: Yale University Press, 1977); Richard F. Fenno, *Home Style: House Members in their Districts* (New York: Little, Brown, 1978).

3 Lawrence C. Dodd, "Congress and the Quest for Power," in *Con-*

gress Reconsidered, Lawrence C. Dodd and Bruce I. Oppenheimer, eds. (New York: Praeger, 1977). Also see Christopher J. Deering, "Congress: The Dual Incentive System," paper prepared for delivery at the 1979 annual meeting of the American Political Science Association.

4 They have tended to appeal to urban legislators or those with a background in banking. Kenneth A. Shepsle, *The Giant Jigsaw Puzzle: Democratic Committee Assignments in the Modern House* (Chicago: University of Chicago Press, 1978), p. 46; The Ralph Nader Congress Project, Lester M. Salamon, director, *The Money Committees: A Study of the House Banking and Currency Committee and the Senate Banking, Housing and Urban Affairs Committee* (New York: Grossman, 1975) [hereafter cited by reference to Salamon], p. 47. Examination of the backgrounds of Senate Committee members in the 93rd Congress and the nature of their constituencies does not confirm this association in the Senate. It is true that a higher proportion of committee members than nonmembers represent districts in which finance, insurance, or real estate is the primary industry measured in terms of employment. However, knowing the nature of state's industry does not aid in predicting the likelihood of the state's being represented on the committee.

Data on state industry rankings are from Michael Barone, Grant Ujifusa, and Douglas Matthews, *The Almanac of American Politics, 1974* (Boston: Gambit, 1973).

5 As in the case of similar committees studied by Fenno, some members probably are attracted to the Banking Committees primarily because of interest in the issues they consider. Fenno suggests in a footnote (p. 9) that the Banking Committees fit quite closely his characterization of the House Education and Labor and Foreign Affairs committees. Richard F. Fenno, Jr., *Congressmen in Committees* (Boston: Little, Brown, 1973).

Average rates of turnover for the House Banking Committee, measured as the percentage of new members at the start of each session, 88–94th Congresses, was 25.7 percent for Democrats and 36.0 percent for Republicans. For the Senate Banking Committee, the figures were 20.9 percent for Democrats and 37.2 percent for Republicans.

Various studies place the House Banking Committee in the lower half of all committees by various measures of attractiveness. See Charles S. Bullock III, "Committee Transfers in the United States House of Representatives," *Journal of Politics* 35 (February 1973): 94; James W. Dyson and John W. Soule, "Congressional Committee Behavior on Roll Call Votes: The U.S. House of Representatives, 1955–64," *Midwest Journal of Political Science* 14 (November 1970): 634; Charles Bullock and John Sprague, "A Research Note on the Committee Reassignments of Southern Democratic Congressmen," *Jour-*

nal of Politics 31 (May 1969): 499; George Goodwin, *The Little Legislatures: Committees of Congress* (Amherst: University of Massachusetts Press, 1970); Shepsle, *The Giant Jigsaw Puzzle,* pp. 54–7.

On the lack of attractiveness of the Senate Banking Committee, see John F. Bibby and Roger Davidson, *On Capitol Hill: Studies in the Legislative Process* (New York: Holt, Rinehart & Winston, 1967), especially chap. 5; Goodwin, *The Little Legislatures.*

6 For example, Salamon, *The Money Committees,* pp. 47, 76.

7 See the discussion in Chapter 2 of this book.

8 Again, this generally follows the logic of Fenno's *Congressmen in Committees,* especially pp. 30–3.

9 Salamon stresses this point with respect both to the House and Senate Banking Committees in *The Money Committees,* pp. 52–5, 74–5. On the House Banking Committee, for instance, members acting in this fashion in recent years would include Thomas L. Ashley (D., Ohio), William Moorehead (D., Pa.), Richard Hanna (D., Calif.), and Thomas Rees (D., Calif.). These men all received ratings of 100 percent support for the voting position of the AFL–CIO's Committee on Political Education in 1970, 1971, or 1972, but were strong banking supporters on the committee.

10 These links were detailed in Chapter 4 of this book.

11 Since Congress began requiring public financial disclosures from its members in 1968, the proportion of members of the House Banking Committee who own stocks in banks, savings and loan associations, or bank holding companies has dropped from a high of 38 percent in 1968 to only 5 percent (or two members) in 1976. (In 1977, the proportion rose again to 14 percent.) At the peak in 1968, most of the members with such potential conflicts of interest were Democrats – by an eight-to-four margin. In 1977, when senators first revealed their financial holdings in any detail, only two members of the Senate Banking Committee, Sparkman (D. Ala.) and Morgan (D., N.C.), reported ownership of stocks in financial institutions.

Summary and analysis of the annual reports by House members have been reported in *Congressional Quarterly Weekly Reports* as follows: May 23, 1969, p. 762; May 29, 1970, pp. 1390–1; May 28, 1971, p. 1183; June 17, 1972, pp. 1383–4; June 30, 1973, pp. 1640–1; August 30, 1974, pp. 2133–4; July 12, 1975, p. 1468; July 31, 1976, pp. 2055–6; July 23, 1977, pp. 1513–14; September 2, 1978, pp. 2301–2412. Senate figures are in the September 2, 1978, issue.

12 In 1976, banking PACs were not among the top nine largest corporate PACs. Forty-five bank and savings and loan PACs accounted for only about 6.5 percent of the total campaign contributions by the top 450 PACs. Michael C. Jensen, "9 Corporate Political Action' Units Gave 20% of Aid in 76 Campaigns," *New York Times,* September 14, 1977, p. D1.

In the 1978 elections, the ABA's "BANK PAC" made contributions of $232,180 – less than 1 percent of the total contributions made by PACs to federal election candidates and well out of the top ten largest PACs (the AMA's PAC led the way with $1.645 million, 4.7 percent of all PAC contributions). *Congressional Quarterly Weekly Report,* June 2, 1979, pp. 1044–5.

Other information on contributions is found in Warren Weaver, Jr., "Special Interests Donated $325,000 to Campaigns of 15 House Leaders," *New York Times,* February 5, 1977, p. 1; idem, "Interest Groups Gave Vital Help to Key Senators," *New York Times,* January 16, 1977. Also of interest on PACs are Edwin M. Epstein, "An Irony of Electoral Reform," and Michael J. Malbin, "Neither a Mountain Nor a Molehill," both in *Regulation,* May–June 1979, pp. 35–43.

13 David Burnham, "Banks' Lobby Called Strongest in Capital," *New York Times,* December 23, 1977, p. A1.

14 See the *Congressional Quarterly* issues cited in note 11, this chapter.

15 Burnham, "Banks' Lobby Called Strongest in Capita" p. A1.

16 See note 5, this chapter.

17 Based on Conservative Coalition support scores for the 87th through 94th Congresses, the Banking Committees in both houses have been more liberal than the house as a whole. The Senate committee's average support score is 5.6 percent lower than that of the Senate as a whole. The House committee's is 10.2 percent lower. Conservative Coalition scores calculated from data in various issues of *Congressional Quarterly Almanac.* Precise figures are available on request. Confirming findings for the 80th through 90th Congresses are in Goodwin, *The Little Legislatures,* pp. 108–9.

Of the House committee, Salamon observed that "it bristles with antagonisms and tensions, which frequently erupt into brawls." Salamon, *The Money Committees,* p. 55. Bibby and Davidson characterize the Senate Banking Committee as one in which partisanship is frequently strong. Bibby and Davidson, *On Capitol Hill,* p. 192.

Ideological divisiveness, as measured by the difference between the Republican and Democratic Conservative Coalition support scores show the respective committees to be more divided than the House for five out of eight Congresses (87th – 94th Congresses; the exceptions are the 91st and 92nd) and more so than the Senate in six out of eight Congresses (the exceptions are the 91st and 93rd).

Overall, Dyson and Soule's findings show that the Banking Committee's success on the floor is in the lower half of congressional committees – thirteenth out of twenty. Their explanation of floor success is compatible with Fenno's – that higher degrees of committee integration result in higher levels of floor success. Dyson and Soule's figures show a moderate relationship between committee integration and floor success; $r = 0.65$. Dyson and Soule, "Congressional Committee Behavior on Roll Call Votes," 636.

18 See Seymour Scher, "Conditions for Legislative Control," *Journal of Politics* 25 (August 1963): 526–51; Morris S. Ogul, *Congress Oversees*

the Bureaucracy: Studies in Legislative Supervision (Pittsburgh: University of Pittsburgh Press, 1976). Aberbach's findings of a very strong association between growth of committee staff and growth of oversight activity can be interpreted as meaning that the cost of oversight has been declining for members of Congress, and thus its frequency should increase even if benefits stay constant. In a post–Watergate world of suspicion of the executive branch, the benefits for members of Congress from oversight may have increased, too. Joel D. Aberbach, "The Development of Oversight in the United States Congress: Concepts and Analysis," paper prepared for delivery at the 1977 annual meeting of the American Political Science Association (also, University of Michigan, Institute for Public Policy Studies Discussion Paper #100).

19 Scher, "Conditions for Legislative Control," 530. Scher's study included the Education and Labor Committee, which, as I have noted, is similar to the Banking Committee in several respects.

20 John F. Bibby, "Committee Characteristics and Legislative Oversight of Administration," *Midwest Journal of Political Science* 10 (February 1966), 94. Bibby concluded of the Senate Banking Committee that "most members, . . . feel that investment of their valuable time, staff, and good will to oversee agencies under the committee's jurisdiction is not worthwhile." See Bibby and Davidson, *On Capitol Hill*, p. 189.

21 A good description of such visits may be found in Jonathan Alter, "Defrocking the Fed," *Washington Monthly*, June 1982, pp. 12–21.

22 Frequency of testimony is based on my tallies of testimony included in the card file of the Research Library of the Federal Reserve Board. Exact figures are available on request to the author.

23 The late 1960s were marked by some hearings but by no successful laws. In 1964 Wright Patman's Subcommittee on Domestic Finance of the House Banking Committee produced a searching examination of the Federal Reserve that today retains its interest for researchers and that identified many types of criticism of the Federal Reserve of continuing importance.

Shortly after the completion of the 1964 hearings, Patman drew up legislation that he subsequently introduced in every session through 1973 – HR 11. It was an ambitious piece of legislation that would have required a GAO audit, subjected the Federal Reserve to the congressional budget process, vested all open market authority in the board (removing the district bank presidents), shortened the term of board members, made the term of the chairman coterminus with that of the president, and required the president to set out monetary guidelines necessary to achieving the goals of the 1946 Employment Act. HR 11 functioned primarily to pave the way for later legislation. In the mid-1970s, acts were passed that, at least nominally, enacted many of these reforms.

House, Subcommittee on Domestic Finance, Committee on

Banking and Currency, *The Federal Reserve After Fifty Years, Hearings Before the Subcommittee on Domestic Finance of the House Committee on Banking and Currency,* 88th Cong., 2nd sess., 1964.

24 See John T. Woolley, "Central Banks and Inflation: Influence and Independence" in *The Political Economy of Inflation and Recession,* Leon N. Lindberg and Charles Maier, eds. (Washington, D.C.: Brookings Institution, 1984).

25 I have included in Appendix B a brief summary of the legislation (and legislative activity) reflected by the entries in Table 7.1 not discussed in the text.

26 *Congressional Quarterly Almanac, 1971,* p. 470. See also the excellent discussion in Salamon, *The Money Committees,* chap. 5.

27 PL 95–188 (HR 9710); 91 Stat 1387. See *Congressional Quarterly Almanac 1977,* p. 152. See also Daniel J. Balz, "For Arthur Burns and the Fed, the Year May Never End," *National Journal,* June 19, 1976, pp. 846–52; and Henry S. Reuss, "Federal Reserve: A Private Club for Public Policy," *The Nation,* October 16, 1976, p. 372.

28 This account is discussed in more detail in John T. Woolley, "The Political Economy of Monetary Policy in the United States," Ph.D. dissertation University of Wisconsin-Madison, 1980. The relevant documentary sources are *Congressional Record,* May 29, 1974, pp. 16812–14; Henry Reuss, "What the Secret Minutes of Federal Reserve Banks Meetings Disclose," May 24, 1977 (processed), *Congressional Record,* February 11, 1976, p. H949; *Congressional Record,* November 17, 1975, p. H11297; and *Congressional Record,* February 23, 1976, p. H1227.

29 *The Conference on Inflation: Economists,* vol. I, September 5 and 23, 1974 (Superintendent of Documents). Arthur Okun, summarizing the conference, stated that "the overwhelming majority of the economists on this panel would recommend a course of Federal Reserve policy that should be consistent with gradually declining interest rates in the months ahead" (p. 253). The tone was rather different in the conference of financial sector participants. See summary in *The Financial Conference on Inflation: Report,* September 20, 1974, p. 5 (Superintendent of Documents).

30 Burns told the assembled group that "I have received a good deal of advice this morning, all of which suggested that the monetary spigot should be opened up. I was told to let the money supply expand more rapidly so that interest rates could come down. If that advice were followed, the inflation would become much more intense and interest rates, as they always do in such circumstances, would go higher and higher and soon be a good deal above their present level." The statement is reproduced in Arthur F. Burns, *Reflections of an Economic Policy Maker* (Washington, D.C.: American Enterprise Institute, 1978), pp. 182–3.

31 Based on conservative coalition support scores; see note 16, this chapter.

32 Especially Sanford Rose, "The Agony of the Federal Reserve," *Fortune,* July 1974, pp. 90ff.

33 Federal Reserve Governor Phillip Coldwell joked about this: "Wright Patman was the best friend we ever had because he refused to compromise. He wanted to run monetary policy himself." This view was seconded by former Patman staffers Robert Weintraub and Jane d'Arista. Coldwell interview, July 17, 1978.

34 Aberbach, "The Development of Oversight."

35 The increase was from twenty-two (permanent and investigatory) in 1960 to fifty-five in 1975 (an increase of 150 percent). Figures are from Senate, Government Operations Committee, *Study on Federal Regulation,* vol. II, *Congressional Oversight of Regulatory Agencies,* Appendixes E and F, pp. 155–9. During the period, permanent staff remained almost constant, increasing from nine to twelve. The big jump in investigatory staff came between 1970 and 1975, jumping from thirteen in 1971 to twenty-four in 1972 and finally reaching forty-three in 1975.

36 Except for the Housing Subcommittee, Bibby concluded that "there is no specialized staff within the Banking and Currency Committee available to oversee the work of the other agencies under the Committee jurisdiction. As a result, Committee review of these agencies has been severely restricted." Bibby, "Committee Characteristics," p. 88.

37 In the case of voluntary credit allocation, Burns offered to have the Federal Reserve staff assist in drafting legislation. The result was Reuss's HR 6676; the cooperative stance taken by Burns in this matter reportedly angered other board members who preferred more of a stonewall. House, Committee on Banking, Currency, and Housing, *To Lower Interest Rates; The Credit Allocation Act of 1975, Hearings before the Committee on Banking, Currency, and Housing, on HR 3160 and HR 3161,* 94th Cong., 1st sess., February 19, 1975. On the proposal for voluntary credit allocation, see the exchange with Representative Moorhead, pp. 27–28 and with Representatives Grassley and Blanchard, pp. 49–51.

38 On the events in general, see House Report 94–20; Senate Report 94–38; and House Report 94–91 (the conference committee report), all 94th Cong., 1st sess; *Congressional Quarterly Almanac, 1975,* pp. 167–9; Robert E. Weintraub, "Congressional Supervision of Monetary Policy," *Journal of Monetary Economics* 4 (April 1978): 341–7; and Edward J. Kane, "New Congressional Restraints and Federal Reserve Independence," *Challenge,* November–December 1975, pp. 37–44.

39 This emphasis can clearly be credited to staffer Robert Weintraub, a very active advocate of monetarist analysis in Congress. Burns was still not a pushover. During a private negotiating session with Burns in Proxmire's offices, a staff member is credited by another person present with making an error of economic analysis that Burns suc-

cessfully pounced on, moving Proxmire to assume a more compromising stance.

40 Burns himself has received considerable credit from close observers for derailing the legislation being considered in the House Banking Committee and for softening the tone of the Senate legislation. It also seems likely that very strong action, in the form of a regular bill rather than a resolution, would have been vetoed by the president.

41 "Nothing in this resolution shall be interpreted to require that such ranges of growth or diminution be achieved if the Board of Governors and the Federal Open Market Committee determine that they cannot or should not be achieved because of changing conditions." House Report 94–91.

42 House Report 94–20; *Congressional Record, House,* 1975, pp. 5085–5101. Reuss's description of the Conference Report is in ibid., pp. 8414–17. Recall, too, that one of the House Banking Committee bills preceding HCR 133 was entitled "A Bill to Lower Interest Rates."

43 "Congress and the Federal Reserve," *Newsweek,* June 2, 1975, p. 62.

44 For example, Steven M. Roberts, "Congressional Oversight of Monetary Policy," *Journal of Monetary Economics* 4 (August 1978): 543–56. This was also expressed in interviews with staffers Roberts, Robert Weintraub, Howard Lee, and Lamar Smith.

45 Data for the period 1975–7 are drawn from Roberts, ibid. The percentages for the full period are as follows: in the Senate, 36.1 percent (S.D. 11.87) of members attended hearings when the chairman appeared (twelve appearances, excluding one day when a hearing was held during a blizzard); 15.6 percent (S.D. 7.93) attended when others appeared to testify (eighteen days). In the House, 62.4 percent (S.D. 13.21) of members attended when the chairman appeared (fourteen appearances, also excluding one day following a blizzard); and 44.9 percent (S.D. 17.96) attended when others appeared (fourteen days).

46 At the comparison hearings, Burns's presence attracted 66 percent of the membership (two to three more than the regular oversight hearings). When Burns was not testifying, attendance averaged about 55 percent, well above the 38 percent attending oversight hearings. Hearings involved HR 12934 in 1976, HR 6676 in 1975, and informational hearings on Federal Reserve policy in 1974. The timing of these other hearings may be sufficient to account for the higher levels of attendance. Several were held during periods of economic crisis that had apparently passed during much of the routine oversight period. If so, attendance at oversight hearings should have risen during subsequent economic downturns – which did not happen.

47 There were earlier monetarist efforts associated with 1964 hearings observing the Federal Reserve's fiftieth anniversary. Brunner and Meltzer then presented as a staff study for the House Banking Committee a classic monetarist critique of Federal Reserve procedures.

See *The Federal Reserve's Attachment to the Free Reserve Concept,* prepared for the Subcommittee on Domestic Finance of the House Committee on Banking and Currency, 88th Cong., 2nd sess., 1964. This developed a critique published earlier by another prominent monetarist: James Meigs, *Free Reserves and the Money Supply* (Chicago: University of Chicago Press, 1962).

48 See the discussion of the monetarists in Chapter 5 of this book.

49 See Committee on Banking, Finance, and Urban Affairs, *Report on Monetary Policy for 1979,* House Report 96–32, 96th Cong., 1st sess.; *Second Report on Monetary Policy for 1979,* House Report 96–396, 96th Cong., 1st sess.; and *Monetary Policy for 1980,* House Report 96–881, 96th Cong., 2nd sess.

50 See, by contrast, the language used in House of Representatives, *Monetary Policy Report for 1982, Eighth Report,* H. Rept. 97–786, 97th Cong., 2nd sess., August 29, 1982.

51 Both reports for 1982 are instructive in this regard. See Senate, Committee on Banking, Housing, and Urban Affairs, *First Monetary Policy Report for 1982,* S. Rept. 97–383, April 13, 1982, and *Second Monetary Policy Report for 1982,* S. Rept. 97–663, October 18, 1982; both 97th Cong., 2nd sess.

52 JEC, *Report on the Economy, 1978,* 95th Cong., 2nd sess., H. Rept. 95–995, p. 34. The most "monetarist" JEC comments were in 1979 (S. Rept. 96–44) 1974 (H. Rept. 93–927). The stress on interest rates is dominant in other years (1977: H. Rept. 95–75; 1976: S. Rept. 94–690; 1975: S. Rept. 94–61; 1973: H. Rept. 93–90; 1972: S. Rept. 92–708; 1971: S. Rept. 92–49; and 1970: H. Rept. 91–972).

53 See, for example, James Pierce, "A Difference of Opinion: An Interview," *Fortune,* March 27, 1978, p. 151. Also see Roger S. White, "Description and Critique of the System Used for Quarterly Federal Reserve System Announcements to the Congress of Projected Ranges of Growth for Monetary Aggregates," a Congressional Reference Service Study included in Senate, Committee on Banking, Housing, and Urban Affairs, *First Meeting on the Conduct of Monetary Policy, Hearings before the Senate Committee on Banking Housing and Urban Affairs,* 95th Cong., 1st sess., November 1977. Also see Kane, "New Congressional Restraints," pp. 42–3.

54 *FOMC Minutes,* 1975, pp. 434–65 (April meeting).

55 That concern was implicit in the suggestion by Bruce MacLaury, president of the Federal Reserve Bank of Minneapolis, and others that the single announced target should be nonborrowed reserves. This suggestion did receive some discussion, but it would be straining a great deal to conclude that the ensuing debate was over the prospect of reorienting Federal Reserve monetary policy procedures.

56 This wider range was favored by several members because it would be easier to hit than would a narrower range.

Minutes, 1975, p. 698 (June meeting).
aminow, "Politics, Economics, and Procedures in U.S. Money Dynamics," in *Political Economy of International and Domestic Relations,* Raymond E. Lombra and Willard E. Witte, eds. owa State University Press, 1982), pp. 181–196.

59 In May 1977 the FOMC narrowed its intermeeting target range for the Federal funds rate to only 0.5 percentage points. See FOMC policy actions summarized in Board of Governors of the Federal Reserve System, *64th Annual Report, 1977* (Washington, D.C., 1978).

60 Ira P. Kaminow, "Fed Policy in the Era of Resolution 133 (1975–1978): Is What they Said What they Did?" (Washington, D.C.: Government Research Corporation, 1979.). Similar findings for the pre-HCR 133 period are given in Paul DeRosa and Gary H. Stern, "Monetary Control and the Federal Funds Rate," *Journal of Monetary Economics* 3 (April 1977): 217–30. Also see Nathaniel Beck, "Time-Varying Parameter Regression Models," *American Journal of Political Science* 27 (August 1983), esp. 576–93.

8. Making monetary policy in a political environment: the election of 1972

1 Sanford Rose, "The Agony of the Federal Reserve," *Fortune,* January 1974, p. 91.

2 Ibid., pp. 186, 188.

3 Edward R. Tufte, *Political Control of the Economy* (Princeton, N.J.: Princeton University Press, 1978) p. 50; in general, see pp. 45–55.

4 For example by Alan S. Blinder, *Economic Policy and the Great Stagflation* (New York: Academic Press, 1979), p. 143.

5 Alan S. Blinder and Stephen M. Goldfeld, "New Measures of Fiscal and Monetary Policy, 1958–73," *American Economic Review* 66 (December 1976): 780–96.

6 See, for example, the discussion in Blinder, *Economic Policy,* p. 91; Otto Eckstein, *The Great Recession* (Amsterdam: North-Holland, 1978), chaps. 6–9.

7 Some evidence on this was reviewed in Chapter 6 of this book. Also see G. L. Bach, *Making Monetary and Fiscal Policy* (Washington, D.C.: Brookings Institution, 1971), p. 267; Memo, Gardner Ackley to President, March 26, 1964, and attached memo of March 27, 1964, Ex FI 9, WHCF, LBJ Library; Walter W. Heller, *New Dimensions of Political Economy* (Cambridge, Mass.: Harvard University Press, 1966), p. 12; Letter, George Reedy to President, August 30, 1966, CF BE 5, WHCF, LBJ Library; Tufte, *Political Control,* pp. 5–9.

8 Richard M. Nixon, *Six Crises* (Garden City, N.Y.: Doubleday, 1962), pp. 309–10; Rowland Evans, Jr., and Robert D. Novak, *Nixon in*

the White House: The Frustration of Power (New York: Random House, 1971), p. 180.

9 Milton Viorst, "The Burns Kind of Liberal Conservatism," *New York Times Magazine,* November 9, 1969, p. 30. Harley H. Hinrichs, "Burns Appointment Spells Policy Change at the Fed," *National Journal,* December 6, 1969, pp. 283, 285.

10 Evans and Novak, *Nixon in the White House,* p. 308. The political vulnerability of the Federal Reserve had been, interestingly enough, noted in a scholarly publication at about the same time. The author quoted an unnamed board staffer as recounting a conversation that was apparently prophetic:

> I asked some members of the staff who attend FOMC meetings whether the FOMC members are concerned about the Administration's predicted 1971 GNP of $1065 billion. They replied, "The room is full of it." I asked if it entered into their discussions, or affected their decisions. They replied, "Not at all." I asked what would happen if President Nixon were to phone the Governors to ask them to "go along" with him by permitting a faster rate of growth of the money supply. They replied, "Though there would be a small minority which would vote against, *the FOMC would go along.*"

Sanford F. Borins, "The Political Economy of 'The Fed,'" *Public Policy* 20 (Spring 1972): 196. Emphasis added.

11 "Nixon's Go-Go Economic Policy for '72," *Business Week,* January 29, 1972, p. 52.

12 It is easy to discover references to this in early 1972. See, for example, Thomas E. Mullaney, "Economy on an Express Track," *New York Times,* January 9, 1972, section III, p. 1; "Pullout on Controls," *New York Times,* January 16, 1972, section IV, p. 14.

13 Speech to the ABA, Hot Springs, Virginia, Arthur F. Burns, "Inflation: The Fundamental Challenge to Stabilization Policies," in *Reflections of an Economic Policy Maker: Speeches and Congressional Statements, 1969–1978* (Washington, D.C.: American Enterprise Institute, 1978), pp. 91–102. Also, on this general period, see Neal de Marchi, "The First Nixon Administration: Prelude to Controls," in *Exhortation and Controls: The Search for a Wage–Price Policy, 1945–1971,* Craufurd D. Goodwin, ed. (Washington, D.C.: Brookings Institution, 1975), especially pp. 316–48.

14 Richard F. Janssen, "Some Nixonites Fret as Their Man at Fed Shows an Independence," *Wall Street Journal,* August 31, 1970, p. 1.

15 Burns especially irritated the White House in his speech at Pepperdine College. Burns, "The Basis for Lasting Prosperity," in *Reflections,* pp. 113–14. The speech was reprinted in full, to the consternation of the White House, in the *New York Times,* December 8, 1970, p. 34. In an interview, Burns reported White House pressure

to alter the tone of the speech. Interview, February 17, 1979. Paul McCracken, then CEA chairman, has recalled that the president was scheduled to give a major economic speech only a week later and that Burns's address seemed to put the president on the spot. (Vanderbilt transcript, forthcoming. See Chapter 6, note 7.) Also see Evans and Novak, *Nixon in the White House,* p. 370. Nixon's comments are found in his speech to the National Association of Manufacturers, December 4, 1970; from Richard Nixon, *Public Papers of the President of the United States, 1970* (Washington, D.C.: National Archives, 1971), p. 1090.

16 JEC, *The 1971 Economic Report of the President, Hearings Before the Joint Economic Committee,* 92nd Cong., 1st sess., 1971, p. 245.

17 Ibid., p. 247. Arthur Laffer, then a staff economist at the CEA, had recently come to notoriety among Washington economists. He was a major author of an econometric model showing that a GNP of $1,065 billion (rather than about $1,050 billion, which most forecasters predicted) was possible in fiscal year 1972, and linking achievement of that level to adequate monetary policy. The implication of these projections, that monetary policy should be strongly expansionary, had not been lost on members of the Federal Reserve Board. See Sherman J. Maisel, *Managing the Dollar* (New York: Norton, 1973), pp. 268, 278.

18 Burns interview, February 17, 1979.

19 The *Wall Street Journal* reported that at the end of June Nixon had "called Arthur on the carpet" and "read the riot act to him" about urging wage and price controls. Richard F. Janssen, "Rift Between Nixon, Burns Widens; Consumer Price Rate Up 6% in June," *Wall Street Journal,* July 28, 1971, p. 2.

20 Colson's attack included proposals to reform the Federal Reserve by changing the size of the board and by bringing it under the umbrella of the White House. He also alleged (falsely) that Burns was lobbying for an increase in his own salary at the same time that he was calling publicly for an incomes policy.

21 Burns interview, February 17, 1979. Burns contacted both Safire and Shultz to say that he "expected reparations." See the accounts in William Safire, *Before the Fall: An Inside View of the Pre-Watergate White House* (New York: Doubleday, 1975), pp. 491–6; Charles Colson, *Born Again* (Old Tappan, N.J.: Chosen Books, 1976), pp. 62–3, 160–3, 185–7. Had Nixon not apologized, Burns had planned to write his good friend, Senator John Sparkman, asking for hearings on the matter. It never came to that. "But I was determined that I was going to clear my name."

22 This interpretation enjoys very wide oral circulation among economists but it is more difficult to track down in print. Blinder suggests in *Economic Policy* (p. 184) that this interpretation is due to William Poole. Poole's highly condensed argument is rather similar to my

own. "Burnsian Monetary Policy: Eight Years of Progress," *The Journal of Finance* 34 (May 1979): 480–1; On this period, also see James L. Pierce, "The Political Economy of Arthur Burns," *Journal of Finance* 34 (May 1972): 488–90; Nathaniel Beck, "Presidential Influence on the Federal Reserve in the 1970s," *American Journal of Political Science* 26 (August 1982): 415–45; Gerald Rosen, "Arthur Burns: How Good a Job?" *Duns Review,* December 1977, pp. 68 ff.; Sanford Rose, "Agony," op. cit.; Raymond Lombra and Michael Moran, "Policy Advice and Policymaking at the Federal Reserve," in *Monetary Institutions and the Policy Process,* Karl Brunner and Allan H. Meltzer, eds. (Amsterdam: North-Holland, 1980).

23 Maisel, *Managing the Dollar,* p. 146.

24 An interesting account of the Camp David meeting is found in Safire, *Before the Fall,* chap. 5.

25 Each exceeded $23 billion on a unified budget basis. *Economic Report of the President, 1979,* table B-69. Herbert Stein reports that Nixon lectured the cabinet for the first time ever in 1972 on the need "to get out there and spend their budgets." Oral history interview, Vanderbilt University.

26 Estimates of full employment deficit are to be found in Eckstein, *Great Recession,* p. 41, and in Keith M. Carlson, "The Mix of Monetary and Fiscal Policies: Conventional Wisdom vs. Empirical Reality," *Review* of the Federal Reserve Bank of St. Louis 64 (October 1982): 7–21; Blinder, *Economic Policy,* p. 145.

27 Measured in current dollars. In 1971, 35.5 percent; in 1972, 25.1 percent. U.S. Department of Commerce, Bureau of Economic Analysis, *National Income and Product Accounts of the United States, 1929–1974* (Washington, D.C.: USGPO, n.d.).

28 In 1971, 10.6 percent; in 1972, 20.7 percent. *Federal Reserve Bulletin,* Statistical Tables, various issues.

29 JEC, Subcommittee on Priorities and Economy in Government, *Federal Subsidy Programs: A Staff Study,* 93rd Cong., 2nd sess., October 1974, pp. 13, 88.

30 To a substantial degree, it appears that the housing boom was initially sustained by various inflows from the private sector to savings institutions – no doubt underwritten indirectly by stimulative monetary and fiscal policy. There was only one major piece of legislation with respect to housing in this period; this increased the Department of Housing and Urban Development (HUD) appropriation by $2.9 billion (PL 91–609). *Congressional Quarterly Annual, 1970,* p. 726. During 1971, Federal Home Loan Bank net advances to savings and loans actually declined by $2,678 million, and in 1972 the increase was only $42 million. By contrast, when interest rates shot up in 1973, net advances shot up to $7,168 million for the year. Federal Home Loan Bank Board *Journal,* December 1974, table S.2.4.

31 See, for example, "Mortgage, Construction, and Real Estate Mar-

kets," *Federal Reserve Bulletin* 58 (March 1972): 201–15, and another article with the same title in *Federal Reserve Bulletin* 59 (July 1973): 481–92.

32 The party line had, of course, been articulated long before my interviews occurred. At the time the Rose article was initially published, a sheaf of letters was shot back from within the Federal Reserve in protest. Letters from Brimmer and Burns were published in *Fortune,* but Brimmer's was heavily edited, excluding a strong statement by Brimmer that he had reviewed the FOMC minutes and his own notes for 1972 and could not recall such an incident. *Fortune* chose not to publish the letter from Robert Holland, then secretary of the FOMC and charged with preparing the *Minutes.* He too flatly denied that such an episode occurred. See *Fortune,* August 1974, p. 113. The full correspondence was later reproduced in the *Congressional Record* on August 20, 1974, and again in House, Committee on Banking and Currency, *Federal Reserve Policy and Inflation and High Interest Rates, Hearings Before the Committee on Banking and Currency,* 93rd Cong., 2nd sess., 1974, pp. 416–22.

33 Rose telephone interview, April 28, 1980. Rose recounted a conversation with Andrew Brimmer following publication of the *Fortune* article. But see Brimmer's correspondence with *Fortune* referred to in note 32.

34 Holland interview, June 19, 1978; Mitchell intreview, December 14, 1978; Coldwell interview, July 13, 1978. As Mitchell put it, "I know Burns was mad as hell and went and adjourned the meeting. But I don't think he went and called the President."

35 *FOMC Minutes,* 1972, p. 820. I will quote, sometimes at length, from the detailed "Memorandum of Discussion," commonly referred to, and cited here, as the *FOMC Minutes.*

36 *FOMC Minutes,* p. 855. The concern for "expectations" was not merely within the Federal Reserve. De Marchi writes that then Treasury Secretary Connally "was receiving advice from [assistant Treasury secretaries] Murray Weidenbaum and Paul Volcker that a freeze might be a useful way of jolting inflationary expectations and effecting a recovery." De Marchi, "The First Nixon Administration," p. 339.

37 Partee relates the story of going to talk to White House officials, only to find John D. Ehrlichman sitting in. As the Federal Reserve contingent departed, Ehrlichman admonished them: "Every night before you get up from your desk to go home, stop and think, 'what have you done for the money supply today?'" Partee interview, August 3, 1978.

38 See Burns's statement, *FOMC Minutes,* 1971, p. 1175.

39 Ibid., pp. 1233–4.

40 On the Europeans' anger see H. Erich Heinemann, "U.S. Monetary Policy Vexes Europeans," *New York Times,* February 8, 1972, p. 41;

"Burns Defends Easy Money Policy," *New York Times,* February 10, 1972, p. 63; Edwin L. Dale, Jr., "Reserve Resents Censure on Rates," *New York Times,* February 28, 1972, p. 47.

41 *FOMC Minutes,* 1972, p. 339.

42 Brimmer did in fact cast a dissenting FOMC vote in January, but that dissent related not to the direction of policy but to the adoption of reserve targets.

43 No doubt this kind of behavior underlay the suspicion expressed in a mid-1973 *Wall Street Journal* article that Sheehan was "nothing but a Burns lackey" – an assertion that stung Sheehan badly. May 7, 1973, p. 1.

44 Mitchell interview, December 14, 1978.

45 For further discussion on this point, see John T. Woolley, "The Federal Reserve and the Political Economy of Monetary Policy," Ph.D. dissertation, University of Wisconsin-Madison, 1980, chap. 8.

46 Edwin L. Dale, Jr., "More Stimulus Is Urged for Economy," *New York Times,* February 19, 1972, p. 41.

47 H. Erich Heinemann, "Reserve Rebuff on Rates Is Told," *New York Times,* March 6, 1972, p. 49; idem., "Most Business Analysts Discern Upturn But Economy Is Still Key Election Issue," *New York Times,* April 2, 1972, p. 1; idem., "Funds are Added to Money Market," *New York Times,* June 2, 1972; Lindley H. Clark, Jr., "Some Critics Call Fed Too Free-Handed, Some Just Opposite," *Wall Street Journal,* September 15, 1972, p. 1; *Argus Weekly Staff Report,* December 19, 1972. For related criticisms and commentary, see Lindley H. Clark, "Speaking of Business," *Wall Street Journal,* September 15, 1972, p. 12; and Edward P. Foldessy, "Federal Reserve Gets Misleading Signals from Key Indicators," *Wall Street Journal,* October 31, 1972, p. 14.

48 Federal Reserve figures show that the rate of growth of M1 from the third to the fourth quarters of 1972 (using quarterly averages of money outstanding) was 7.1 percent – a figure close to the October recommendation of Wallich and Samuelson.

49 Blinder, *Economic Policy,* p. 35. Specifically, the GNP gap estimated at the time for 1972 was $46 billion; the subsequent data show a gap of only $15 billion.

50 JEC, *The 1972 Midyear Review of the Economy,* 92nd Cong., 2nd sess., 1972, pp. 143, 153.

51 In Edwin L. Dale, "Budget Outlook – After the Election," *New York Times,* November 12, 1972, Section III, p. 4; and "Economist and His Crystal Ball," *New York Times,* November 15, 1972, p. 70.

52 *FOMC Minutes,* 1972, p. 292.

53 Memo, Lyle E. Gramley to James Louis Robertson, "The RPD Experiment," December 26, 1972, JLR Collection, Box 58, FOMC File, Library of Congress.

54 Edward Cowan, "Outlook Cheers Business Council," *New York Times,* May 13, 1972, p. 39; idem., "Continued Growth in '73 Seen by Business Council," *New York Times,* October 21, 1972, p. 43.
55 Burns interview, February 17, 1979.
56 *FOMC Minutes,* 1971, p. 810.
57 "White House Summons Executives of Six Firms That Boosted Dividends," *Wall Street Journal,* September 7, 1971, p. 3.
58 "Reserve Board's Open Market Committee to Buy, Sell Federal Agencies – Issues," *Wall Street Journal,* September 17, 1971, p. 16.
59 "Mutual Savings Banks – Pledge," *Wall Street Journal,* September 27, 1971, p. 5.
60 "Level Interest Rates for Freeze Thus Far Are Observed by Burns," *Wall Street Journal,* September 28, 1971, p. 7.
61 *FOMC Minutes,* 1971, p. 983.
62 Despite Burns's extensive involvement in the design and implementation of much of the controls program, he apparently was not included in this particular meeting. The meeting was held on October 5, 1971. See John Osborne, *The Third Year of the Nixon Watch* (New York: Liveright, 1972), pp. 152–5. Present at the meeting were Connally, McCracken, Stein, and Shultz. Burns's role in planning the work of the Price Commission is discussed in Robert F. Lanzillotti, Mary T. Hamilton, and R. Blaine Roberts, *Phase II in Review: The Price Commission Experience* (Washington, D.C.: Brookings Institution, 1975), pp. 18, 30.
63 The only official source I have been able to locate on the CID is the statements included in the series *Economic Stabilization Program Quarterly Report,* published by the Cost of Living Council in the Executive Office of the President. Horvitz cites a CID *Report* that seems not to be indexed separately with the Superintendent of Documents. Paul M. Horvitz, "The Committee on Interest and Dividends: An Assessment," *Policy Analysis* 3 (Winter 1977): 85–105. On the October meeting, see *Economic Stabilization Program Quarterly Report* (August 15–December 31, 1971): 86.
64 Horvitz, "The Committee on Interest and Dividends," 90.
65 Action taken on December 22, 1971. *Economic Stabilization Program Quarterly Report,* ibid., p. 88.
66 So, for example, in the April 1972 FOMC meeting, Burns warned that "the key question was whether increases in short-term rates would spread to the long term market – particularly to rates on mortgages. There already were signs of such a tendency in the secondary mortgage market. If that tendency continued, the Committee on Interest and Dividends would undoubtedly come under mounting pressure to stabilize such rates at existing levels." Ibid., pp. 416–17, 445.
67 Robert D. Hershey, "Direct U.S. Controls?" *New York Times,* July 9, 1972, section III, p. 9.

68 *FOMC Minutes,* 1972, p. 826.

69 Rinfret also said that recommendations had already been made to the president that interest rates should be controlled. "Most Large Banks Raise Prime Loan Rate to 5¾%," *New York Times,* October 3, 1972, p. 61.

70 H. Erich Heinemann, "Bankers Warned on High Interest," *New York Times,* October 9, 1972, p. 47.

71 *Economic Stabilization Program Quarterly Report,* October 1, 1972 through January 10, 1973, p. 31. Also see Horvitz, "The Committee on Interest and Dividends," pp. 91–2.

72 "Rate Rises Spur Closer Scrutiny of Bank Earnings," *Wall Street Journal,* October 13, 1972, p. 3. Also see H. Erich Heinemann, "Walker Cautions Bankers on Rates," *New York Times,* October 11, 1972, p. 57; Edward Cowan, "Burns Warns on Climbing Rates," *New York Times,* October 13, 1972, p. 55; John H. Allen, "Traders Fear U.S. Will Limit Rates," *New York Times,* October 16, 1972, p. 57.

73 This idea also suggested itself to some observers at the time. See H. Erich Heinemann, "The Hobgloblin of Higher Rates," *New York Times,* October 22, 1972, section III, p. 1.

74 H. Erich Heinemann, "No Ceiling Seen on Cost of Money," *New York Times,* December 4, 1972, p. 63.

75 Senate hearings began on January 29; the CID confrontation with major banks about increases in the prime rate began on February 3. Ernest Hollingsworth, "4 Banks Asked to Justify Increase in Loan Rates," *New York Times,* February 5, 1973, p. 1.

76 On April 16, the House concluded its actions on Phase III authorizations, and the CID enunciated its "dual prime rate" scheme.

77 The vote was forty-five to forty-one. The measure would have passed except for the opposition of southern Democrats.

78 *Congressional Quarterly Almanac,* 1973, pp. 205–18.

79 Burns interview, February 17, 1979.

80 *FOMC Minutes,* 1972, p. 914.

81 There are some scattered suggestions that Burns, and perhaps the FOMC, believed that negotiations could be pursued with congressional committees about the level of budget deficits. The bargain, it is clear, was to involve interest rates – yet another possible incentive to keep interest rates down. In early February, Burns testified in executive session before the Ways and Means Committee in a meeting concerned with a pending debt ceiling bill. Burns was promoting legislation setting a budget ceiling, and this presumably was his reason for meeting with Ways and Means. Although it was not entirely clear to observers in February, by September Burns believed he was using interest rates as a bargaining chip to induce the Ways and Means Committee to pass a budget ceiling.

Also in September, JEC members questioned Burns about the

possibility of a credit squeeze, which they feared. Burns suggested that a squeeze could probably be avoided. The questioning of members of Congress may have reinforced Burns's sense of the hazards of tighter money at that time. Burns, in turn, had again mentioned his support for imposing a ceiling on government spending. Implying that a bargain could be struck, he noted that a ceiling "will have a very reassuring influence on the market. . . . It would be our best insurance against rising interest rates."

The February meeting was reported in Fred L. Zimmerman, "Clear Report Lacking on What Burns Said About Interest Rates," *Wall Street Journal,* February 3, 1972, p. 28. Also see *FOMC Minutes,* 1972, p. 914; Edward L. Dale, "A Credit Squeeze Doubted By Burns," *New York Times,* September 16, 1972, p. 1.

82 During JEC hearings in April 1972 to review the Phase II controls, little attention was given to interest rates or the CID. In the JEC *Report* on those hearings, released in May, there was similarly no discussion of interest rates or the CID. In the first half of July, Congress was in recess for the Democratic Convention. Congress recessed again in August for the Republican Convention.

83 *FOMC Minutes,* 1972, pp. 9–10.

84 JEC, *The 1972 Economic Report of the President: Hearings Before the Joint Economic Committee,* 92nd Cong., 2nd sess., 1972, p. 194.

85 Burns read this statement to the subsequent FOMC meeting to impress members with the commitment the Federal Reserve had made to support the recovery. *FOMC Minutes,* 1972, pp. 204–5. Original in JEC, *The 1972 Economic Report,* p. 121.

86 JEC, *Report of the Joint Economic Committee on the 1972 Economic Report of the President* (JEC printing), 92nd Cong., 2nd sess., 1972, p. 18.

87 JEC, *The 1972 Midyear Review of the Economy: Hearings Before the Joint Economic Committee,* 92nd Cong., 2nd sess., 1972, pp. 105–6. Proxmire's concept of making monetary policy "without regard to politics" is a stunningly narrow concept of politics.

88 Ibid.

89 Ibid., p. 107.

90 Ibid., p. 123. The full exchange occupies pp. 117–23.

91 JEC, *Report of the Joint Economic Committee on the 1972 Midyear Review of the Economy* (JEC printing), 92nd Cong., 2nd sess., 1972, August 28, 1972.

92 Wright Patman, "What's Wrong with the Federal Reserve and What to Do About It," *American Bar Association Journal* 61 (February 1975): 179–84; reprinted in JEC, *The Federal Reserve System: A Study Prepared for the Joint Economic Committee* by Wright Patman (JEC printing), 94th Cong., 2nd sess., 1976, dated January 3, 1977.

93 Senate Banking Committee, *Economic Stabilization Legislation: Hear-*

ings Before the Senate Committee on Banking, Housing, and Urban Affairs, 93rd Cong., 1st sess., 1973, p. 494; emphasis added.

94 Instead, questions focused on the balance of payments, the weaknesses of Phase III controls, the possibility for an international central bank, ways to soak up the unusually high level of tax refunds that were anticipated, the problem of the Eurodollar market, and "jawboning" by the CID to lower the prime rate. JEC, *The 1973 Economic Report,* pp. 407–40.

95 Ibid., p. 416; emphasis added.

96 Senate, Proxmire speaking, *Congressional Record,* 1973, p. 36533.

97 House, Committee on Banking, Currency, and Housing, *Hearings to Lower Interest Rates, the Credit Allocation Act of 1975 in H.R. 3160 and H.R. 3161 before the Committee on Banking, Currency, and Housing,* 94th Cong., 1st sess., 1975, pp. 8, 20–1.

98 Correspondence between Burns and Proxmire, in Proxmire speaking, *Congressional Record,* 1973, p. 36536.

9. Monetary politics: a summary

1 Lasswell has drawn our attention to "who gets what, when, and how." Easton emphasizes "authoritative allocations of value." Key speculates on the kinds of political systems benefiting the have-nots. Schattschneider emphasizes how "biases" in "pressure systems" shaped political outcomes. Dahl's work has repeatedly been concerned with the nature of access to policy makers. Lowi calls attention to the ways in which the coercive powers of the state are used in distributing benefits among groups and classes.

2 This is true as well for Pareto optimal choices (non-zero-sum), which make some better off while making none worse off; that is, they are not redistributive. A policy making some people relatively better off is politically important not only because it implies unequal benefits but because it involves creating resources relevant for influencing future policy decisions.

3 Douglas A. Hibbs, Jr., "Political Parties and Macroeconomic Policy," *American Political Science Review* 71 (December 1977): 1467–87.

4 Nathaniel Beck, "Parties, Administrations, and American Macroeconomic Outcomes," *American Political Science Review* 76 (March 1982): 83–93.

5 The relevant literature is very large, and the language is sometimes maddeningly opaque. Most of the following sources are quite accessible and pose the basic issues: Nicos Poulantzas, "The Problem of the Capitalist State," *New Left Review* 58 (November–December 1969): 67–78; idem., "The Capitalist State: A Reply to Miliband and Laclau," *New Left Review* 95 (January 1976): 63–83; Ralph Miliband, *The State in Capitalist Society* (New York: Basic Books, 1969); idem.,

Marxism and Politics (Oxford: Oxford University Press, 1977); idem., "Poulantzas and the Capitalist State," *New Left Review* 82 (November–December 1973): 83–92; idem., "The Capitalist State: Reply to Nicos Poulantzas," *New Left Review* 59 (January–February 1970): 53–6; James O'Connor, *The Fiscal Crisis of the State* (New York: St. Martin's Press, 1973); David A. Gold, Clarence Y. H. Lo, and Eric Olin Wright, "Recent Developments in Marxist Theories of the Capitalist State, Part I," *Monthly Review* 27 (October 1975): 29–43; David Vogel, "Why Businessmen Distrust Their State: The Political Consciousness of American Corporate Executives," *British Journal of Political Science* 8 (January 1978): 45–78; Fred Block, "The Ruling Class Does Not Rule: Notes on the Marxist Theory of the State," *Socialist Revolution* no. 33 (May–June 1977): 6–28.

6 Nathaniel Beck, "Presidential Influence on the Federal Reserve in the 1970s," *American Journal of Political Science* 26 (August 1982): 415–45; David G. Golden and James M. Poterba, "The Price of Popularity: The Political Business Cycle Re-examined," *American Journal of Political Science* 24 (November 1980): 696–714.

7 This is the same hypothesis referred to previously at various points. See Edward J. Kane, "External Pressure and the Operation of the Fed," in *Political Economy of International and Domestic Monetary Relations,* Raymond E. Lombra and Willard E. Witte, eds. (Ames: Iowa State University Press, 1982), pp. 211–32.

8 Influence is regularly attributed to the chairman of the Federal Reserve in the *U.S. News and World Report* annual surveys of top leaders to identify "the most influential individuals" in the United States generally and in particular fields. April 22, 1974, p. 30; April 21, 1975, p. 28; April 19, 1976, p. 24; April 18, 1977, p. 28; April 17, 1978, p. 30.

9 James L. Pierce, "Making Reserve Targets Work," in *Controlling Monetary Aggregates III,* Federal Reserve Bank of Boston Conference Series No. 23 (Boston: FRBB, 1980), especially pp. 261–2.

Appendix A

1 These issues are discussed in Richard D. Erb., ed., *Federal Reserve Policies and Public Disclosure* (Washington, D.C.: American Enterprise Institute, 1978), and in House, Subcommittee on Domestic Monetary Policy of the Committee on Banking, Finance, and Urban Affairs, *Maintaining and Making Public Minutes of Federal Reserve Meetings, Hearings Before the Subcommittee on Domestic Monetary Policy,* 95th Cong., 1st sess., 1977. The latter includes reproductions of quite interesting letters received from prominent economists and former System officials surveyed for their reaction to the System's decision.

2 *FOMC Minutes,* 1972, p. 108.

3 Maisel describes the meeting as "the most bitter debate I experienced in my entire service on the FOMC." Sherman J. Maisel, *Managing the Dollar* (New York: Norton, 1973), p. 250; Andrew Brimmer also discussed this meeting, but not the nature of the record, in an interview.

4 Useful discussions of the problems of this sort of interviewing are found in Joel D. Aberbach, James D. Chesney, and Bert A. Rockman, "Exploring Elite Political Attitudes: Some Methodological Lessons," in *Political Methodology* 2 (1975): 1–27, and Louis A. Dexter, *Elite and Specialized Interviewing,* (Evanston, Ill.: Northwestern University Press, 1970).

5 Sanford Rose, phone conversation, April 21, 1980.

Bibliographic Note

When I began the research for this book, there were almost no published writings by political scientists dealing with the Federal Reserve or monetary policy. Since then, the number has increased severalfold, but the total number is still very small. Here I wish to refer exclusively to published analyses that would be good introductory materials for scholars interested in the Federal Reserve. Other citations for more specialized points may be found in the notes to relevant passages of the text. My emphasis is on works dealing with the relationships between the Federal Reserve and other actors, and of necessity references to the large number of journalistic sources are excluded. A great deal about the Federal Reserve and its relationships with other political actors can be learned from a diligent reading of sources such as the *Wall Street Journal,* the *New York Times,* the *National Journal,* and any of the major business magazines. For a discussion of data sources for further research, see Appendix A. Certain scholarly journals in economics often contain articles of considerable interest to students of monetary politics. See especially the *Journal of Money, Credit, and Banking* and the *Journal of Monetary Economics.*

As a general rule, the bulk of the scholarly work examining the political relationships of the Federal Reserve has been produced by economists, not political scientists. More important, most of the economists producing that work are monetarists. Why monetarists advance political analyses of the Federal Reserve more frequently than their academic opponents – who are also often very critical of the Federal Reserve's performance – is an interesting question for sociologists of knowledge. Nonetheless, scholars new to the field should be alert to the fact that much of the political analysis is advanced in the context of a larger monetarist critique. Appendix C lists the names of many prominent monetarists, and many of their names appear subsequently in this essay as well. Much of the balance of the writing by economists of political interest is by former Federal Reserve insiders. Many of them are *former* insiders because of policy disputes that precipitated their departure. Readers should be alert for the possibility that these authors also have an old score to settle.

In terms of a historical overview from the early days of the System through the 1950s, the most strongly political account is found in A. Jerome Clifford, *The Independence of the Federal Reserve System* (Philadelphia: University of Pennsylvania Press, 1965). Clifford refers to most of the standard sources, and his bibliography will be useful. Readers should not fail to look into Milton Friedman and Anna Jacobson Schwartz, *A Monetary History of the United States, 1867–1960* (Princeton, N.J.: Princeton University Press, 1963), a rich account of monetary developments in the United States from a monetarist perspective. This necessarily involves a great deal of information about the Federal Reserve. The most interesting passages from a political standpoint are usually in the footnotes; your diligence will be rewarded. Also of interest are two books by George Leland Bach: *Federal Reserve Policy-Making: A Study in Government Economic Policy Formation* (New York: Knopf, 1950) and *Making Monetary and Fiscal Policy* (Washington, D.C.: Brookings Institution, 1971). Bach's long association with the Federal Reserve has included organizing the meetings of the Economic Consultants Group for many years. A general discussion of the political implications of the monetarist debate and the relationship of that debate to the issue of independence can be found in Ralph C. Bryant, *Money and Monetary Policy in Interdependent Nations* (Washington, D.C.: Brookings Institution, 1980), chap. 18.

All of the prior works will help introduce the question of the relationship between the president and the Federal Reserve. A recent work by a political scientist that includes a bibiography with useful references to other works is Nathaniel Beck, "Presidential Influence on the Federal Reserve in the 1970s," *American Journal of Political Science* 26 (August 1982): 415–45. I have found quite valuable the overview of the Federal Reserve's relationships with several other actors by Edward J. Kane, "External Pressures and the Operation of the Fed," in *Political Economy of International and Domestic Monetary Relations,* Raymond E. Lombra and Willard E. Witte, eds. (Ames: Iowa State University Press, 1982). Kane's work is a synthesis and distillation of many years of watching the Fed, and it is both witty and very stimulating. His previous work, listed in the bibliography of "External Pressure," is also well worth reading. Kane is clearly sympathetic to the monetarist position. Another monetarist whose overview and critique of the Federal Reserve I found to be a good introduction is Thomas Mayer, "The Structure and Operation of the Federal Reserve System: Some Needed Reforms," in *Financial Institutions and the Nation's Economy,* essays prepared for the FINE study, Book II, House, Committee on Banking, Currency, and Housing, 94th Cong., 2nd sess., 1976.

Valuable writings that focus somewhat more on Congress (but not exclusively) are also primarily by monetarists. Two by Robert Weintraub, a congressional economist, are "Congressional Supervision of Monetary Policy," *Journal of Monetary Economics* 4 (April 1978): 341–62, and "Some Neglected Monetary Contributions: Congressman Wright Patman (1893–1976)," *Journal of Money Credit and Banking* 9 (November 1977): 517–28. Monetarist William Poole has written many articles that have political interest. One that includes some valuable commentary on recent history is "Burnsian Monetary Policy: Eight Years of Progress," *Journal of Finance* 34 (May 1979): 473–84. Another excellent analysis of the same period is by former top Federal Reserve staffer James L. Pierce, "The Political Economy of Arthur Burns," *Journal of Finance* 34 (May 1979): 485–96.

Anyone interested in the politics of the Federal Reserve will, of course, be interested in considering its internal operations. Three articles with an explicitly political slant were published many years ago but continue to have considerable contemporary relevance. These are Michael D. Reagan, "The Political Structure of the Federal Reserve System," *American Political Science Review* 55 (March 1961): 64–76; C. R. Whittlesey, "Power and Influence in the Federal Reserve System," *Economica* 30 (February 1963): 33–44; and Sanford F. Borins, "The Political Economy of the Fed," *Public Policy* 20 (Spring 1972): 175–98. An essential insider account of Federal Reserve policy making from the mid-1960s to the early 1970s is by former board member Sherman Maisel, *Managing the Dollar* (New York: Norton, 1973). A useful account of Federal Reserve operating procedures in the 1970s is William Poole, "The Making of Monetary Policy: Description and Analysis," *Economic Inquiry* 13 (June 1975): 253–65. Recently, board member Henry Wallich has assumed the role of explaining the System to economists. He is the author of many articles, but a particularly interesting example is, "Policy Research, Policy Advice and Policymaking," in Lombra and Witte, eds., *Political Economy of International and Domestic Monetary Relations.* This should be read together with Raymond Lombra and Michael Moran, "Policy Advice and Policymaking at the Federal Reserve," in *Monetary Institutions and the Policy Process,* Karl Brunner and Allen H. Meltzer, eds., vol. 13, Carnegie-Rochester Conference Series on Public Policy (Amsterdam: North-Holland, 1980). Also of considerable interest are: Gerald Epstein, "Domestic Stagflation and Monetary Policy: The Federal Reserve and the Hidden Election," in *The Hidden Election: Politics and Economics in the 1980 Presidential Campaign*, Thomas Ferguson and Joel Rogers, eds., (New York: Random House, 1981), and Robert Shapiro, "Politics and the Federal Reserve," *Public Interest*, No. 66, (Winter 1982):119–39.

Index